Writing for the Mass Media

Second Edition

James Glen Stovall
University of Alabama

PRENTICE HALL, Englewood Cliffs, NJ 07632

Library of Congress Cataloging-in-Publication Data

```
Stovall, James Glen.
  Writing for the media.

  Includes index.
  1. Mass media--Authorship.  I. Title.
P96.A86S8  1990        808'.066302        89-8801
  Isbn 0-13-970898-7
```

Editorial/production supervision: Debbie Young
Cover design: Diane Saxe
Manufacturing buyer: Carol Bystrom

**This book is dedicated to
MARTHA ELIZABETH STOVALL
1914-1982
who loved books and taught others to do the same.**

© 1990 by Prentice-Hall, Inc.
A Division of Simon & Schuster
Englewood Cliffs, New Jersey 07632

Printed in the United States of America

10 9 8 7 6 5 4 3 2 1

ISBN 0-13-970898-7

Prentice-Hall International (UK) Limited, *London*
Prentice-Hall of Australia Pty. Limited, *Sydney*
Prentice-Hall of Canada Inc., *Toronto*
Prentice-Hall Hispanoamericana, S.A., *Mexico*
Prentice-Hall of India Private Limited, *New Delhi*
Prentice-Hall of Japan, Inc., *Tokyo*
Simon & Schuster Asia Pte. Ltd., *Singapore*
Editora Prentice-Hall do Brasil, Ltda., *Rio de Janeiro*

Contents

Preface to the Second Edition

Writing is one thing; writing about writing is another.

Like most people, I cannot remember the first word or the first sentence that I wrote. (I am reasonably sure they were not momentous.) I can remember always being encouraged to write, however, by parents and teachers who knew the importance of writing.

I have always enjoyed and admired good writing, and I continue to be in awe of it. How Mark Twain could have created such a wonderful and timeless story as *The Adventures of Tom Sawyer*, how Henry David Thoreau could distill his thoughts into the crisp and biting prose of *Walden*, or how Red Smith could have turned out high-quality material for his sports column day after day—all of that is continually amazing to me. I frankly admit, I don't know how they did it.

And yet, here I am writing about writing. Why should I be doing this? At least three reasons occur to me immediately.

I am fascinated by the process of writing. I write about it so I can understand it better. For me, it is a process of self-education. I hope that some of the insights I have discovered will rub off on those who read this book.

I am convinced that while great writing might be a gift to a chosen few, good writing is well within the reach of the rest of us. There are things we can do to improve our writing.

I care about the language and the way it is used. Those of us fortunate enough to have English as a native language have been given a mighty tool with which to work. It is powerful and dynamic. An underlying purpose of this book is to encourage the intelligent and respectful use of this tool.

In the preface to the first edition of this book, I wrote that my approach to writing was a simple and straightforward one. To write well, one must first of all write. My outlook has not changed, and this edition offers plently of opportunities for students to write.

During the years since the first edition came out, however, I have been impressed by at least two phenomena that have affected writing for the mass media. The first phenomenon the proliferation of word processors. They have become the standard tool for writers, replacing the electric typewriter (which replaced the manual typewriter, which replaced the fountain pen, and so on). We are affected by our tools, and our products are different because of them. Consequently, in this second edition, I pay more attention to the process of writing with a word processor, and where appropriate, I have tried to gear writing instruction to that instrument.

The second phenomenon is the increasing use of graphic material to supplement and enhance the written word. Our age seems to have taken to heart the adage about the single picture and the thousand words. Again, where appropriate, I have tried to take this phenomenon into account in instructing students about writing. (This book itself, with all of its graphic material, is a good example of what is happening in this regard.)

Beyond this, those familiar with the first edition will note few changes in the basic structure and approach of this book. The structure has not changed because this is how students need to understand the writing process and how it relates to the modern mass media industry. The approach of the book has not changed because I still believe that writing can be taught and that efficient instruction and a lot of practice can go a long way in improving writing.

Many of the people who contributed to the first edition have been equally generous with their time and thoughts for the second. In addition, I would like to thank my colleagues at the University of Alabama, particularly **DeeDee Riffe, Charles Self,** and **Marian Huttenstine,** who have used this book and have given me many helpful suggestions; **Ed Mullins,** dean of the College of Communication, and **Jay Black,** chairman of the Department of Journalism; and the staff of the Communication Research and Service Center, especially **Cheryl Parker** and **Cecilia Hammond.**

Steve Dalphin, my editor at Prentice Hall, and **Debbie Young,** the production manager for this book, are two people most responsible for getting this edition into print.

I also need to thank **Nancy Andreola** for her excellent copy editing and **Glenn Himebaugh** (Middle Tennessee State University), **Steve Pasternack** (New Mexico State University), and **Joe Misiewicz** (Bradley University) for their helpful comments and suggestions.

My wife, **Sally,** remains my chief critic and proofreader and always a source of encouragement. My son, **Jefferson,** as I write this, is in the second grade and discovering the joys and frustrations of writing. Our cat, **Spooner,** kept my lap warm while I did much of this revision.

This book, like the first edition, is dedicated to my mother, **Martha Elizabeth Stovall,** who was my first editor.

James Glen Stovall
May, 1989

James Glen Stovall teaches journalism at the University of Alabama where he has been a faculty member since 1978. He received his Ph.D. from the University of Tennessee and is a former reporter and editor for several newspapers. He also has more than five years of public relations experience.

Preface to the First Edition

Of all those arts in which the wise excel,
Nature's chief masterpiece is writing well.

John Sheffield, Duke of Buckingham
1682

An irony of this era of "new technology" is that one of the oldest skills - the ability to write - is still one of the most important. More than ever, society needs people who write clearly, precisely, concisely, and logically. Writing is more than a knowledge of the rules of grammar, spelling, punctuation, and usage, and it is more that the consistent application of these rules. Writing well demonstrates the ability to think clearly. Good writing is more than a skill; it is an art.

Writing well is also hard work. Word processors have helped ease the pain of writing some, especially the pain of rewriting, but for a first draft, it doesn't matter if a writer is using a quill or an IBM Personal Computer. Writing is difficult because of the way the mind works. William Strunk and E. B. White, in *The Elements of Style*, described it this way: "Writing is, for most, laborious and slow. The mind travels faster than the pen; consequently, writing becomes a question of learning to make occasional wing shots, bringing down the bird of thought as it flashes by."

Writing is basic to any area of the mass media. Few things are printed or broadcast without being written down first. In addition, students hoping to enter media fields must be familiar with the forms of writing required by other fields. Newspaper reporters need to know what it takes to write a broadcast advertisement; advertising copy writers must be able to produce a news release; and public relations practitioners have to write letters, company reports, in-house advertisements, speeches and much more.

That's the reason this book was written. Communication and mass media programs in colleges and universities are recognizing that students cannot be run along narrow skills tracks. These programs must broaden students' skills education just as liberal arts requirements have been broadened. Students, too, must recognize that despite the narrowness of their interest, they must know a lot about the other parts of the mass media to survive and be successful. But programs and students have broadened their skills interests while textbooks have not. Most still take a narrow approach to news writing, advertising copy writing or writing for broadcast. This book seeks to cross those boundaries.

Writing for the Mass Media is written for the beginning student. An in-depth treatment of news reporting skills or advertising copy writing techniques will not be found here. The purpose of the book is simple: to introduce students to the major forms of writing for the mass media.

This simplicity of purpose is reflected in a simplicity of approach and structure. After introductory chapters on good writing, basic skills and style, each of the four major areas of the mass media — writing for print, broadcast, advertising and public relations — is dealt with in single chapters. The structure of the book also reflects my philosophy in teaching writing. That philosophy is that writers need a little instruction and a lot of practice. Consequently, chapter texts remain short while exercises are plentiful. The major "rule" of writing in this book is found in the title of Chapter 1, "Sit Down and Write." I hope this book helps readers to do just that.

This book was produced with the help of a great many people, and I am very appreciative of the support of my friends and colleagues. I would particularly like to thank the following people: **William H. Melson,** former dean, and **Ed Mullins,** present dean of the School of Communication at the University of Alabama; **Charles Self,** chairman of the Department of Journalism, and other members of the department faculty including **Frank Deaver,** who compiled the grammar and diagnostic tests at the end of the book, and **Marian Huttenstine; Jackie Solomon,** who helped in various stages of the production of this book, including producing many of the illustrations and writing text and exercise material; **Stanley Porter, Elizabeth Southwick, Lee Williams, Marie Parsons, Cindy Womble, Donna Barrett-Murdie, Tom Herrmann, Gina Stappas, Karen Green, Roosevelt Mosely III, Tim McDarby, Camille Elebash, Susan Motes, Bill Oates, Barbara Creswell,** and many others who contributed in various ways. A number of people at Prentice-Hall helped with this book, especially **Virginia McCarthy,** the production editor, and **Steve Dalphin,** my editor, whose directness, understanding and sympathy were impressive.

The students who took Mass Communication 102 while this book was being developed deserve a word of thanks. They served as my first and toughest critics as this book was being class-tested for a year and a half.

I would also like to thank my wife, **Sally,** and son, **Jefferson,** for their help and support in the writing of this book.

James Glen Stovall
Tuscaloosa, Alabama

1

Sit Down and Write

How do you write well?

That question defies an easy, quick, simple answer. Yet all of us—at one time or another—have had to consider it. We had begun that consideration at least by the time we were in the second grade when our teachers made us begin writing paragraphs. By the fourth grade, we were learning the rules of grammar and punctuation wondering what in the world these had to do with good writing. Outside the classroom, we were writing in our diaries or writing letters to friends and relatives.

At some point, we learned that whatever else writing is—fun, exciting, rewarding—it isn't easy. Writing is hard work; it can sometimes be very frustrating. As Red Smith, the late sports writer for the *New York Times*, once put it, "There's nothing to writing. All you do is sit down at a typewriter and open a vein."

Smith's point is not just that writing is hard but that it requires that we give of ourselves. Writing demands total commitment, even if it is just for a few minutes. We can think of nothing else, and we can do nothing else, when we are writing. The first step to good writing is recognizing this essential point.

But the question still remains. How do you gather together the words that will convey the information, ideas, or feelings you want to give to the reader? How do you write well?

What is good writing?

Good writing, especially good writing for the mass media, is clear, concise, simple, and to-the-point. It transmits information, ideas, and feelings to the reader clearly but without overstatement. It is writing that outlines pictures of ideas which the reader can fill in with his or her own imagination.

1

Good writing is efficient. It uses only the minimum number of words to make its point. It doesn't waste the reader's time.

Good writing is precise. A well-written piece uses words for their exact meaning; it doesn't throw words around carelessly or without cause.

Good writing is clear. It leaves no doubt or confusion in the reader's mind about its meaning.

Finally, good writing is modest. It doesn't draw attention to itself. Good writing does not try to show off the intelligence (or lack of intelligence) of the writer. It lets the content speak for itself, and it allows readers to receive messages directly. Despite what they say, few people enjoy reading. Rarely will you find anyone who delights in running his or her eyes across a page full of letters. People who like to read enjoy the ideas and information they get from reading. Writing, then, should not get in the way of what people need and want to read.

So, how do you do it? How do you write well?

You would not have to look very far to find many lists of techniques and pieces of advice about how to write well. There are numerous articles, books, pamphlets, and manuals listing some of the accepted conventions of good writing. Before discussing these conventions, however, we should look at four of the more basic prerequisites for good writing which these lists often ignore.

Know the tools of the trade. Good writers must know and understand the tools with which they work, just as a good carpenter knows his tools. For writers, a knowledge of the rules of grammar and spelling is mandatory. (Not all writers have to be great spellers, but they should know the rules, and they should always work with a dictionary close at hand.) Writers must know words and how to use them precisely; although they do not have to use every word they know, having a variety available gives the writer extra tools to use if needed. (Most of us have a vocabulary of about 5,000 to 6,000 words; one scholar estimated that Shakespeare knew about 30,000 words.)

Writers must not only know the language, but they must understand it and be genuinely interested in it. The written word is a powerful instrument with which the lives of many people can be affected. Writers who do not understand this fact do not know what they are dealing with and will not be able to use the language effectively. Writers should also be caretakers of the language, unwilling to see English misused and abused.

Know your subject. You must have a clear idea of what you are wiring about. If you do not understand thoroughly what you are writing about, your readers will not understand what you have written. Beginning writers frequently have trouble with this most basic requirement of good writing. They sometimes believe that they can "write" their way through a subject, that just getting the words down is enough. Even experienced media professionals sometimes fail to understand their topics. For example, some journalists try to write about events without properly researching the background or checking with enough sources. Some advertising copywriters try to compose ads without understanding the product or the audience to whom the ad is directed. In both cases, the writing misses the mark. It is often confusing and inefficient.

If you are writing about something you do not understand, stop writing and find out what you need to know. Ask questions of people who do know or do your own research. Or just think the subject through more thoroughly. Writing without understanding or without having your subject firmly in your own mind is like writing with a broken pencil. A reader isn't going to understand a subject if a writer does not.

Write it down. This may be the most basic point of all: you cannot be a writer unless you put words on paper (or on a computer screen). People can think, talk and agonize all night about what they would like to write. They can read and discuss; they can do research and even make notes. But no one is a writer until he or she begins to put ideas into words and sentences and paragraphs. At some point, the writer must sit down and write.

Writing is very hard work for most people, and few have the tenacity to stick with it. Anthony Trollope, a nineteenth-century English novelist, would begin writing at 5:30 a.m. He would write for two and a half hours, producing at least 250 words every 15 minutes. For Trollope, writing was hard work. It demanded his time and discipline. He responded to those demands with a strict routine.

Writing is physically difficult because it demands maintaining a sta-

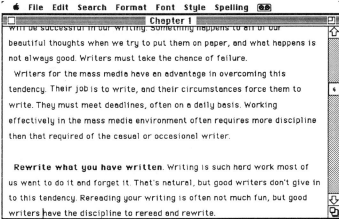

Figure 1-1
The top picture was the author's computer screen for the final draft of this chapter. This section appears on the next page. Even at this stage, the manuscript could be improved with some editing. Compare the top picture to the lower one, which shows the manuscript after one final editing.

tionary position and concentrating a long time. Writing is mentally difficult because of the effort it takes to know a subject well enough and to think clearly enough to put it down on paper. (That's one of the reasons we're using the telephone more and writing letters less.)

In addition, writing involves some risk. We can never be certain that we will be successful in our writing. Something happens to all of our beautiful thoughts when we try to put them on paper, and what happens is not always good. Writers must take the chance of failure.

Writers for the mass media have an advantage in overcoming this tendency. Their job is to write, and their circumstances force them to write. They must meet deadlines, often on a daily basis. Working effectively in the mass media environment often requires more discipline than that required of the casual or occasional writer.

Rewrite what you have written. Writing is such hard work that most of us want to do it and forget it. That's natural, but good writers don't give in to this tendency. Rereading your writing is often not much fun, but good writers have the discipline to reread and rewrite.

Rewriting requires that a writer reread critically. Writers cannot go through this process patting themselves on the back for all the fine words they have produced. Writers must be constantly asking if the writing can be made clearer, more precise, and more readable. And writers must not be afraid to say "This isn't what I wanted to say," or even "This isn't very good."

Again, writers for the mass media have some advantage in this regard. Often, their working circumstances dictate that someone else read what they have written and make judgments about it. Having another person read what you have written and then give you an honest evaluation of it usually makes for better writing. But writers for the mass media are also at a disadvantage because their deadline pressures often prevent thorough rereading and rewriting, which is required to achieve good writing.

Techniques for good writing

The following are some suggestions for improving your writing. Many of them are useful at the rewriting stage of your work, but you should try to keep them in mind as your words are going down on paper for the first time. Not all of these suggestions fit every piece of writing you will do, so they need not be considered a strict set of rules. They do constitute a good set of habits for a writer to develop, however.

Write simply. This is a thought you'll see repeatedly in this book. The key to clarity is simplicity. A clear, simple writing style is not the exclusive possession of a few gifted writers. It can be achieved by students who are just beginning a writing career if some of the following suggestions are kept in mind.

Use simple words. "It is a general truth," Henry Fowler wrote in *Modern English Usage*, "that short words are not only handier to use but more powerful in effect; extra syllables reduce, not increase, vigour." Fowler was talking about the modern tendency to use **facilitate** instead of **ease**, **numerous** instead of **many**, **utilize** instead of **use**, etc. Many people try to use the big word or the complicated word, thinking it will impress the reader. It doesn't; it has the opposite effect. Benjamin Franklin once wrote, "To write clearly, not only the most expressive, but the plainest words should be chosen."

Use simple sentences. Not every sentence you write should be in the simple sentence format (subject-predicate or subject-verb-object), but the simple sentence is a good tool for cleaning up muddy writing. For example, take the following sentence (which appeared in a large daily newspaper): "She was shot through the right lung after confronting a woman married to her ex-husband inside the Food World Store on Bankhead Highway shortly before 1 p.m." The confusion could be lessened by breaking this one sentence into three simple sentences: "She was in the Food World Store on Bankhead Highway shortly before 1 p.m. She confronted a woman married to her ex-husband. She was shot through the right lung."

Don't use one word more than necessary. Almost every writer, at least on first drafts, uses too many words. Even the best writers need to be edited. Go back a couple of paragraphs and look at the Fowler quote; it has at least two unnecessary words. Writers should use the minimum number of words necessary to express their ideas and information.

Simple, straightforward prose is mandatory for writing for the mass media. It has no substitute, and its absence will not be excused by readers or listeners.

A first cousin to simplicity is brevity. Writers should never use one more word than is necessary in their writing. They should be on the lookout for words, phrases, and sentences that do not add substantially to the content of what they are writing. They should also guard against those fancy phrases which draw attention to the writing and the writer—and take away from the content.

Eliminate jargon, cliché, and "bureaucratese." Jargon is the technical language that is used in specialized fields or among a small group of people. Scientists, sportswriters, and even students have their own jargon. Good writers, especially those for the mass media, should use words and phrases commonly understood by most people. It makes no sense to cut people off from receiving your ideas by using language that they cannot understand.

Clichés are overused words and phrases. They are phrases that have ceased to be meaningful and have become trite and tiresome. For example, "dire straits," "he's got his act together," and "vast wasteland" have been used so much that they have lost their original luster. All of us have our favorite clichés; the trick is not to use them.

Bureaucratese is a general name for a serious misuse of the language. In order to make themselves or what they write sound more important than it is, many people try to lather their writing with unnecessary and imprecise phrasing. A speechwriter once handed President Franklin Roosevelt a draft of a speech with the following sentence: "We are endeavoring to construct a more inclusive society." Roosevelt changed it to say: "We are going to make a country in which no one is left out." Roosevelt's simple words carry far more weight than those of his speechwriter.

Once the football coach of a major state university was on a recruiting trip and heard over the radio that he had been fired. The next day, the athletic director at the school issued the following statement: "I regret the premature publication of the decision before appropriate notification could be made to all parties involved." The athletic director would not have sounded like such a fool if he had simply said, "I'm sorry we didn't get to tell him before the story got out."

Use familiar words rather than unfamiliar words or foreign phrases. William F. Buckley, the conservative newspaper columnist, is a very well educated man (we might have said **erudite,** but not if we're following this rule). In each of his columns, he tries to include at least one or two words that will send his reader scurrying to a dictionary. Readers expect this of Buckley and seem to accept it. Buckley is the exception, however. There are times when a writer must use a word that is not known by all of a mass audience, but those times are rare in mass communication. Writers should not try to educate the masses by introducing them to new words. Such writing slows the reader down; it makes the reader think about the writing rather than the content; and it drives the reader away before very long.

Foreign phrases often have the same effect. They add little to the content and are often irritating to the reader. At times they may even be insulting, particularly when the writer does not bother to translate them.

Vary sentence type and length. There are four kinds of sentence structures: simple, complex, compound and compound-complex. Using only one kind of sentence is boring. A good variety of types and lengths of sentences gives pace to writing. It allows the reader's mind to "breathe," to take in ideas and information in small doses.

Such variation also helps the writer. Writers often get so involved in what they are writing that they have trouble expressing their ideas clearly. They try to pack too much into one sentence or one paragraph. Breaking down complex and compound sentences into simple sentences, and then putting these sentences back into a variety of forms, often promotes clarity in writing.

One thing writers should not overuse is the inverted sentence. A good example of this kind of sentence is the previous sentence—and this sentence. The inverted sentence is not a good idea in writing for the mass media. Writers want to get ideas and information to readers quickly and efficiently.

Remember that nouns and verbs are the strongest words in the language. Sentences should be built around nouns and verbs; adjectives and adverbs, when they are used, should support the nouns and verbs. Relying on adjectives and adverbs, particularly in writing for the mass media, is a mistake. In addition, remember to use active verbs when possible. They enliven writing.

Verbs are the most important words that a writer will use. A good verb denotes actions; a better verb denotes action and description. While adjectives and adverbs *modify* (that is, they limit), verbs *expand* the writing. They get the reader involved in the writing as no other part of speech does.

A good writers pays close attention to the verbs that he or she uses.

Transitions tie together what you have written. Unity in writing is a very important concept. Readers should be able to read through a piece of writing without stops or surprises. Introducing a new idea or piece of information without adequately tying it to other parts of a story is one way to stop a reader cold.

Writing for the mass media

Good writing is good writing. The good English theme has much in common with the good news story or the good letter to Mom or the informative label on a bottle of aspirin. All of these pieces of writing have different purposes and different audiences, and they express different ideas. But good writing is good writing.

Writing for the mass media differs from other forms of writing in several aspects:

Subject matter. Writers for the mass media must take on a wide variety of subjects, including news stories, feature stories, advertisements, letters, editorials, and so on.

Purpose. Writing for the mass media has two major purposes: to inform and to persuade.

Audience. Mass media writing is often directed to a wide audience, and this fact dictates not only the subject matter but the way in which something is written.

Circumstances of the writing. Writing for the mass media often takes place in the presence of others who are doing the same thing. The writing is frequently done under deadline pressure, and many times several people will have a hand in writing and editing a particular item for the mass media.

A few final thoughts

Here are a few final thoughts we should keep in mind as we begin the quest toward good writing:

With the proper study and practice, we can become better writers. Writing is not simply an inherent talent that some people have and some don't. There are steps that all of us can take to improve our writing, and in this book we'll try to examine some of those and put them into practice.

Writing is a process. That is, rules, techniques, and suggestions are put forth in this book for writing must be mixed in with the individual's style, thoughts and methods, and with the subject and form of the writing. They all should work together to produce writing that is good. The suggestions made in this book about achieving good writing are meant to help this process work.

Writing requires discipline. Most people give up writing as soon as they can because it is such hard work. It is physically, mentally, and emotionally demanding. The person who commits to writing must marshal all of his or her resources for the task.

Writing is building. Good writing doesn't happen all at once. It is formed, word by word, sentence by sentence, thought by thought. The writing process is often slow, tedious, and frustrating. But the product of this process—good writing—is well worth the effort.

Points for consideration and discussion

1. The author makes several strong points about what is and is not good writing. Did you find anything surprising or unusual about them? Do you agree with what he says about good writing?

2. Many teachers and philosophers believe the following: "Writing is thinking." How do you react to this statement?

3. Look up a passage from a book that you have read recently. What characteristics of good writing discussed in this chapter are exemplified in that passage? What characteristics of good writing are *not* present in that passage?

4. In the passage that you selected, make a list of the verbs. How many of them are linking verbs ("to be" verbs, such as is, was, were, etc.)? How many of them are active verbs? How many are passive?

5. The author says, "Good writing is good writing," no matter what form it's in. What does he mean by that? Do you agree?

Further reading

Rudolf Flesch, *The Art of Readable Writing*. New York: Collier Books, 1949.

H. W. Fowler, *A Dictionary of Modern English Usage*, (second edition, revised by Sir Ernest Gowers) Oxford: Oxford University Press, 1983.

H. L. Mencken, *The American Language*, New York: Alfred Knopf, 1936.

H. L. Mencken, *The American Language, Supplement I*, New York: Alfred Knopf, 1941.

Edwin Newman, *Strictly Speaking*, Indianapolis-New York: Bobbs-Merrill, 1974.

William Safire, *On Language*, New York: Avon Books, 1981.

William Zinsser, *On Writing Well*, 2nd. ed., New York: Harper & Row, 1980.

EXERCISES

The following section contains a variety of beginning writing exercises. You should follow your instructor's directions in completing them.

Letter to Mom

Write a letter to your mother, father or some other close relative. While you may want to tell the person to whom you are writing other things, the main part of your letter should be about this course. You will want to include some information about the professor for the course, what the course is about, the procedures for the class, the grading and attendance policies and anything else you think is important. You will also want to give the name of your lab instructor. The letter should be at least 250 words long.

Describe your neighbor

Desribe the person sitting nearest to you. Don't be general in your description by saying things like "She's a pretty girl." Instead, be specific; give the reader a lot of details about the person's physical appearance, including hair and eye color, height, shape of the face, the kind of clothes the person is wearing, and so on. Write at least 200 words.

An incident

Write about something that happened to you in the last week. It could be something dramatic, such as being in an automobile accident or meeting a famous person, or something common such as eating a meal or taking a ride on a bus. You should include some dialogue (quoting someone directly) in the description of this incident. Write 250 words.

Action

Decribe someone or a group of people doing something. It could be something like a couple of carpenters building a part of a house or your roommate trying to type a paper. Be sure to focus on the physical activity and on how people are doing it. don't try to describe how the people feel or what they may think about what they are doing. Simply write about what you can see and hear. Write 350 words.

Instructions

Tell step-by-step how to do something. For example, tell how to change the oil in a car, use a tape recorder or build a fire. Use simple terms and simple sentences so that anyone who can read could understand it. The following is an example of such a set of directions.

In order to drive a nail into a piece of wood, follow the steps below:
1. Be sure the wood is on a solid surface.
2. Check the nail you are using to make sure it is straight; if it is bent, discard it.
3. Hold the pointed end of the nail against the wood with the thumb and the first finger.

The activity which you describe should have at least seven steps.

Building

Describe the building in which this class is being held. Don't go outside and look at it but describe it from what you remember. Write at least 150 words.

Rewriting

Rewrite the letter on the following page using simpler language. Make sure that you include all of the information contained in the original letter.

Dear Stockholder:

In accordance with company policies and the federal law, this letter is to inform you of the general annual meeting of the stockholders of this company which will be held on the 30th day of March of this year. The place of the meeting will be in the ballroom of the Waldorf Hotel, which is located at 323 Lexington Avenue, in New York. The beginning time of the meeting will be at nine o'clock in the morning on the 30th of March.

The agenda for this meeting includes a number of items and actions of great import to the company and its stockholders. The election of officers for the company's board of directors will take place beginning at approximately half past ten o'clock. This election follows the annual reports on the company's activities and financial position which will be presented by the president of the company and the chairman of the board of directors. Other items on the agenda include discussions of the company's operations in the foreign arena and the possibilities for investments in new areas of technology. Time will also be appropriated for discussions of general concerns of stockholders and for the answering of questions from stockholders directed to the company's officers. It is the sincere wish of the company's board of directors and officers that you will be able to attend this most important and hopefully informative meeting. The input of the company's stockholders is an important part of this company's operation and planning for the future.

Sincerely,
The Company President

2

Basic Tools of Writing

Writing is impossible in any form unless you know the tools of writing and how to use them. By tools, we mean all the things a writer can use to present information and ideas—rules of grammar and punctuation, precise meanings for words, and proper spelling. The writer who knows these tools has the confidence to write with authority. That writer can take on the forms of writing demanded by the mass media.

English is a basic tool of the writer. Like any other worker, the writer must know the tools of the trade thoroughly—their possibilities as well as their limitations. Knowing when and under what circumstances these tools can be properly used is vital. Above all, a worker must know how to use the tools to get the job done. The writer needs to think of language as a tool, as a means of getting a job done. The writer who cannot coherently use the English language is like a carpenter who cannot saw a straight line. The products of such a writer or carpenter will not inspire confidence; nor will they be items people want to purchase.

Unlike the carpenter's hammer or saw, however, the English language is an extremely complex tool. It has many nuances and subtleties. People spend years mastering English. There are many rules for its usage and many arguments about the propriety of some of these rules.

One thing making English so complex is its dynamic nature. English is the closest thing the world has to an international language. It is spoken and understood in nearly every part of the globe. But no central control or authority governs its use. Consequently, the language is always changing. New words and expressions come into use as others fade. Old words take on new meanings. English is mixed with other languages. Spelling rules shift with differing usage. Mankind is discovering new phenomena needing description in the language. All this makes English a difficult but exciting tool.

Using the language effectively requires knowing the basic rules and conventions. Writers should know thoroughly the eight basic parts of speech (nouns, verbs, adjectives, adverbs, pronouns, conjunctions, interjections, and prepositions), and the basic unit of the English usage (the sentence) and its two parts (subject and predicate). They should not only have an eye for the language, but they should also have an ear for it. Writers should know when things that are technically correct sound wrong. Beyond that, they should be able to recognize—and hear—the confusing phrase, the unclear sentence, and the absence of transition. They must be able to spot the confusion and illogic that are the harbingers of misinformation, inaccuracy, and a failure to communicate. Like the carpenter, the writer should use the language to saw a straight line to the reader.

That straight line to the reader is one of the chief goals of the writer. The writer who does not use English correctly will annoy the reader and call the publication's credibility into question. A misspelled word will not destroy a publication, and an agreement error will not inspire calls for a repeal of the First Amendment, but too many such mistakes will convince the reader that a publication is not worth his or her time and money.

Grammar and punctuation

Sentences. A sentence is a group of words, with a subject and a verb, which expresses a complete thought. "John ran to the store" is a complete sentence; it has a subject, "John," and a verb, "ran," and it expresses a complete thought. "After the rain stopped" is not a complete sentence; it does have a subject and a verb, but it does not express a complete thought. A phrase like "after the rain stopped" is called a dependent clause; it contains a subject and a verb but cannot stand alone. "John ran to the store" is an independent clause.

Structurally, there are four kinds of sentences: simple, complex, compound, and compound-complex. A simple sentence is one that has an independent clause and no dependent clauses, such as

John ran to the store.

A complex sentence is one which has an independent clause and a dependent clause.

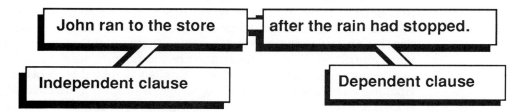

This is a complex sentence because it contains one of each kind of clause. A compound sentence is a sentence that contains two independent clauses, and these clauses should be separated by a comma and a coordinating conjunction.

The sentence above is a compound sentence because it contains two independent clauses; they are separated by a comma and the coordinating conjunction "but." Another common coordinating conjunction is "and." Sometimes a semicolon substitutes for the conjunction.

A compound-complex sentence is a sentence that contains two independent clauses and a dependent clause. The independent clauses should be separated by a comma and a coordinating conjunction, such as in the following sentence:

Here's a tip for recognizing the four different kinds of sentences. Look for the comma and coordinating conjunction. If a sentence doesn't have these two elements together, it's either a simple or a complex sentence. Then you need to look for a dependent clause. If there is one, it's a complex sentence; if not, it's a simple sentence. If the sentence does have a comma and coordinating conjunction together, it's either a compound or a compound-complex sentence. Again you need to look for the dependent clause. If it's there, the sentence is compound-complex; if it isn't, it's a compound sentence.

There are four types of sentences: declarative, interrogative, imperative and exclamatory. A declarative sentence is one which makes a statement. This is the most common type of sentence. An interrogative sentence is one which asks a question, and it is usually ended by a question mark (?). An imperative sentence is a command; it is usually ended by a period, but it may also end with an exclamation mark (!). An exclamatory sentence expresses some strong emotion (excitement, joy, fear, etc.) and usually ends with an exclamation mark.

Sentence fragments. Earlier we referred to sentences as groups of words with subjects and verbs which express a complete thought. Sometimes someone will write a group of words which does not express a complete thought. That is a sentence fragment. While there are some situations in writing where a sentence fragment may be appropriate, generally we should write in complete sentences.

Parts of speech. English contains eight parts of speech: nouns, pronouns, adjectives, adverbs, verbs, conjunctions, prepositions, and interjections. You should be able to recognize any of those in any sentence.

Nouns are the names of objects or concepts.

Pronouns are substitutes for nouns, and they are among the most confusing parts of speech. There are two ways of looking at pronouns. One way is to decide what "person" they refer to; they may be first-, second-, or third-person pronouns. Another way of looking at pronouns is at a pronoun's case: subjective, objective or possessive. Subjective case means that the pronoun can be used as the subject of a sentence; objective case means that it can be used as the object of a verb or a preposition; possessive case means that the pronoun is used as a modifier for a noun and indicates possession. Below is a chart containing cases and persons of pronouns.

Adjectives modify nouns; that is, they give some description to the noun or define it in some way.

Adverbs modify verbs, but they may also modify adjectives or other adverbs. Many adverbs end in **-ly**.

Verbs express action or state of being. We usually refer to verbs as being in a particular tense—or the time of the action. There are three basic tenses: past, present, and future. You should be able to recognize the tense of any verb in any sentence.

Conjunctions connect words, phrases, and clauses together. The most commonly used conjunctions are **and, but, so, or,** and **nor.**

Personal Pronouns

Singular	Subjective	Possessive	Objective
First person	**I**	**my, mine**	**me**
Second person	**you**	**your, yours**	**you**
Third person	**he, she, it**	**his, her, hers, its**	**him, her, it**
Plural			
First person	**we**	**our, ours**	**us**
Second person	**you**	**you, yours**	**you**
Third person	**they**	**their, theirs**	**them**

Relative Pronouns

Singular	**who**	**whose**	**whom**
Plural	**who**	**whose**	**whom**

Prepositions are words which go with nouns or pronouns to modify other nouns, pronouns or verbs. Some common prepositions are **in, at, from, to, on,** and **with.**

Interjections are words that express strong emotion ("wow!"), or they may be words inserted in sentences for style purposes (**however, nevertheless**). When they are inserted into sentences, they should be set off by commas.

Punctuation. Commas (,), semicolons (;), periods (.), and colons (:) are among the most common forms of punctuation.

The comma is a mere blip on a page of type. No other punctuation mark, however, gives students more problems, raises so many questions among writers and causes so much controversy among grammarians. Consequently, we need to give some added attention to the comma.

The comma is an extremely useful tool, and that's part of its problem. It is so useful that its uses are hard to prescribe.

For example, *Harbrace College Handbook* says that a comma should be used to separate items in a series, such as "red, white, and blue," including a comma before the conjunction (in this case, before "and"). Newspaper editors are afraid of using too many commas, so they have set up some rules against their use. Thus, the *Associated Press (AP) Stylebook* advises writers: "Use commas to separate elements in a series, but do not put a comma before the conjunction in a simple series." Using this rule, the example becomes "red, white and blue."*

James J. Kilpatrick, the newspaper columnist and commentator on grammar and usage, has advocated abolishing most rules for using commas, saying that there are too many exceptions for each of the rules to make them useful. A comma, he says, should simply be used whenever a pause is needed. That may be an adequate philosophy for the experienced writer, but for the student just learning the rules, the relevant questions are "When should I use a comma?" and "When is it wrong to use a comma?"

Webster's Seventh Collegiate Dictionary, in its grammar section, gives three general instances for using commas:

Commas used to set off items. These are commas used to set off parenthetical or independent words (*Inside, the building was dark and lonely. Nevertheless, the boys entered.*); appositions and modifiers (*The man, who was nearly seven feet tall, was arrested. His reaction, silent and calm, was a surprise.*); and transitional words (*On the other hand, the brothers held differing views.*).

Commas used to separate items. These commas separate introductory clauses or phrases from other parts of the sentence (*After driving all night, they were exhausted.*); items in a series (*The flag is red, white and blue*—if we use *AP* style); and parts of a compound sentence (*The sky is blue, and the grass is green.*).

Commas used arbitrarily. Some instances in writing simply demand commas, such as large figures (*28,000*), dates, addresses, and inverted names (*Smith, John. C.*).

Students trying to learn when to use commas should remember what the *AP Stylebook* has to say about punctuation in general: "Think of it (punctuation) as a courtesy to your readers, designed to help them understand a story." The comma that helps the reader is correctly placed.

Semicolons are used to separate independent clauses in the same sentence (see above) and to separate long items in a series (Attending the dinner were John Smith, mayor of Tuscaloosa; Mary Johnson, president of the League of Women Voters; Joe Jones, vice-president of Jones Steel, Inc.; and Rhonda Jackson, head of the Committee for Better Government).

Colons are often used to link the latter part of a sentence to some previous part. For example: "The flag contains the following colors: red, white and blue."

The period is most often used to end sentences, but it has other uses, such as ending abbreviations (Mr.). The question mark is used to end interrogative sentences, and the exclamation point ends sentences and expressions of excitement.

Agreement. Agreement refers to singular or plural references.

A singular subject takes a singular verb; plural subjects take plural verbs. In the sentence "The clock strikes on the hour," the subject is "clock." A singular noun, "clock," takes the singular verb, "strikes." However, if the sentence were "The clocks strike on the hour," the plural subject, "clocks," would take the plural verb, "strike." All that is fairly simple, but what about a sentence like this: "The consent of both sets of parents are needed for a juvenile marriage." The subject and verb in this sentence are not in agreement. "Consent" is the subject, not "sets" or "parents." Consequently, the verb should be "is," not "are."

Agreement is also a problem when you are using pronouns to refer to nouns. These nouns are called antecedents, and pronouns should always agree with their antecedents. In the sentence "The boys believed they could win," the antecedent "boys" agrees in number with the pronoun "they." Often, however, the following mistake is made: "The team believed they could win." The antecedent "team" is a singular noun, and its pronoun should also be singular. The sentence should read, "The team believed it could win."

Additional grammar problems

Besides those grammar problems we touched on in the previous sections, there are a few other problems which recur, particularly for beginning students. Some of them are discussed below.

Dangling participles. A participial phrase at the beginning of a sentence should modify the sentence's subject and should be separated from it by a comma. One would not write, "After driving from Georgia to Texas, Tom's car finally gave out." The car didn't drive to Texas; it was driven. We must assume from this sentence that it was Tom who did the driving.

The apostrophe. The proper use of the apostrophe probably gives more users of English more problems than any other form of punctuation. The apostrophe can be used in a number of ways. First, we use apostrophes to form possessives, as in "Mary's hat" and "Tom's book." If a word ends in "s" or the plural of the noun is formed by adding "s," the apostrophe generally goes after the final "s," and no other letter is needed. For example, the possessive of the word "hostess" is "hostess'." The plural possessive of the word "team" is "teams'." The plural possessive of "child" is "children's."

Even professionals have problems when the word **it** and an apostrophe come together. Is it **its, it's,** or **its'**? Here are some rules worth memorizing. **Its** (without the apostrophe) is the possessive of the pronoun **it,** as in *its final score.* **It's** (with the apostrophe) is a contraction meaning **it is,** as in *it's hard to tell.* **Its'** makes no sense because **it** has no plural form.

Appositive phrases and commas. Appositive phrases follow a noun and rename it. Such phrases are set off by commas in almost all cases. For example, in the sentence "Billy Braun, Tech's newest football star, was admitted to a local hospital yesterday," the phrase "Tech's newest football star" is the appositive to "Billy Braun." It is important to remember to put a second comma at the end of the appositive. This is easy to overlook if the appositive is extremely long. For example, the sentence "Job Thompson, the newly named Will Marcum State Junior College president who succeeded Byron Wilson has accepted the presidency of the Association of Junior College Administrators," needs a comma after "Wilson."

Comma splices and run-on sentences. When two independent clauses are connected, they must be connected by two things: a comma and a conjunction. When two clauses are connected only by a comma, that is called a *comma splice* or a *run-on sentence.* For example, "The team won its final game, now they are the champs" is a comma splice or run-on sentence. The reader needs a conjunction to help separate the two sentences. Just as incorrect is the compound sentence with no comma before the conjunction: "The team won its final game and now they are the champs."

Commas between subject and verbs. Commas should be used to separate phrases and other elements in a sentence, but they should not be used solely to separate a subject from its verb. Obviously, you wouldn't write, "The boy, sat on the bench," but neither would you write, "The moment the train comes in, is when we will see her" or "Having no money, is a difficult thing."

Spelling

We are living in an age of spelling rules. It wasn't always so. Centuries ago, when English was evolving as a written language, there were practically no rules of spelling. Writers spelled the way they thought words sounded, and that accounted for some wildly differing ways in which some words were spelled. As certain spellings were used more and more, they became generally accepted, although not universally so. By the eighteenth century, when the fathers of our modern dictionaries began their work, they not only had to decide among diverse spellings for words, but they also had to contend with generally accepted spellings that might not be the best or most efficient.

Since that time, movements to simplify the spelling of certain words have sprung up. These movements have targeted words that end in a silent "e," such as **give, live, have,** and **bake,** and other such silent combinations, such as "-ought" (for example, "thought" should become "thot," and "through" should become "thru").

Despite the efforts of many people during the last two centuries, spelling changes have occurred very slowly. People learn to spell most of the words they use before they are 10 years old, and they are not comfortable in changing what they have learned. It is not up to those in the mass media to lead the fight for most simplified spellings. (Several years ago a number of newspaper editors ran into some trouble on this very point. Thinking that the spelling of a number of words was clumsy and confusing , these editors arbitrarily changed the way these words were spelled in their newspapers. "Through" became "thru,' "thorough" became "thoro," and "employee" turned into "employe." Reader acceptance of these changes was less than complete, and many editors had to beat a hasty retreat.) Rather, people in the mass media should make sure that what they write conforms with the generally accepted rules of spelling and that the spellings they use do not distract or surprise the reader.

Spelling correctly involves three thought processes: applying phonics, memorizing some words, and knowing the rules that usually apply to most words. Writers should know how to do all three. Phonics can be learned, either in early years or later. One must memorize those words that are not spelled phonetically or do not follow spelling rules. However, most words can be spelled correctly without memorization because either rules or phonetics apply to the majority of English words. Some of the rules, with known exceptions, are explained in the following paragraphs.

1. With words of one syllable or words accented on the last syllable that end in a single consonant preceded by a single vowel, the final consonant is doubled before adding "ed" or a syllable beginning with a vowel—for example, **plan, planned; prefer, preferred; wit, witty; hot, hottest; swim, swimming; stop, stopped; bag, baggage; beg, beggar.**

There are a few exceptions. One illustrates the impact of accent. **Refer** becomes **reference,** without doubling the **r,** but the accent also changes away from the final syllable when the suffix is added.

There are other exceptions: words ending in **k, v, w, x,** and **y**; benefit, benefited; chagrin, chagrined (even though stress stays on the final syllable of the new word).

2. A final **e** is usually dropped on addition of a syllable beginning with a vowel: **come, coming; guide, guidance; cure, curable; judge, judging; plume, plumage; force, forcible; use, usage.** There are exceptions: **sale, saleable; mile, mileage; peace, peaceable; dye, dyeing.**

3. A final **e** is usually retained on addition of a syllable beginning with a consonant: **use, useless; late, lately; hate, hateful; move, movement; safe, safety; white, whiteness; pale, paleness; shame, shameful.** The case of **nine, ninety, nineteen,** but **ninth** is an exception. Other exceptions are **judge, judgment** and **argue, argument.**

4. Words ending in a double **e** retain both **e**'s before an added syllable: **free, freely, see, seeing, agree, agreement, agreeable.**

5. Words ending in a double consonant retain both consonants when one or more syllables are added: **ebb, ebbing; enroll; enrollment; full, fullness; dull, dullness; skill, skillful; odd, oddly; will, willful; stiff, stiffness.**

6. Compounds of **all, well,** and **full** drop one l: **always, almost welfare, welcome; fulfill and skillful.** (This is really a listing of exceptions to rule 5.) Exceptions include **fullness** and occasions when a word is hyphenated (as with **full-fledged**).

7. **I** before **e,** except after **c,** or when sounded like **a,** as in **neighbor** or **weigh: receive, deceive, relieve, believe.**

8. A final **y** preceded by a consonant is usually changed to **i** with the addition of an ending not beginning with **i: army, armies, spy, spies, and busy, business.** Some exceptions are **shy, shyness, pity, piteous** (but not **pitiful**). The **ay** endings are usually exceptions; for example—**play, played.**

9. This is really not a rule but just some information about a few tricky words, which must be described as exceedingly difficult. These must be memorized: **exceed, proceed,** and **succeed** all end with **-ceed,** but **supersede** ends with **-sede.** All others with this sound end in **-cede.** These include **precede, intercede, secede, concede, accede,** and **recede.**

Rule 9 tells you how to become a very good speller. Memorized the tricky words and the spelling "demons," and if you know both your rules and phonics, you can spell most of the rest.

You will also need to know some of the basic rules for forming plurals. Here are a few:

1. Most plurals for nouns are formed by simply adding **s** to the root word.

2. Nouns ending with **s, z, x, ch** or **sh** usually require an **es** ending to form the plural.

3. When a word ends with a consonant and then a **y,** the **y** is changed to **i** and an **es** is added (example: **army, armies**).

4. When a word ends in a vowel and a **y,** you can simply add an **s** for the plural (example: **bay, bays**).

5. Compound words without hyphens simply take an **s** on the end (**cupful, cupfuls**), but compound words with a hyphen take the **s** on the significant word (**son-in-law, sons-in-law**).

6. The *AP Stylebook* advises that '**s** should be used only in forming the plural of single letters (**A's, B's**) but not figures (**1920s, 727s**). Never use '**s** to form the plural of a word that is fully spelled out.

Word usage

Words are the basic building blocks of the language. The careful writer attempts to build a large vocabulary with a knowledge of the precise meanings and the generally accepted usages of words.

Using words correctly is a constant concern of the writer. Many people misuse the language, and the writer—particularly the writer for the mass audience—must guard against the common tendencies of this misuse. To help writers in this area, the Associated Press Managing Editors association put together the following list of 50 common writing errors.

1. Affect, effect. Generally, **affect** is the verb; **effect** is the noun: "The letter did not affect the outcome." "The letter had a significant effect." But **effect** is also a verb meaning "to bring about": "It is almost impossible to effect change."

2. Afterward, afterwards. Use **afterward.** The dictionary allows use of **afterwards** only as a second form.

3. All right. That's the way to spell it. The dictionary may list **alright** as a legitimate word, but it is not acceptable in standard usage, says Random House.

4. Allude, elude. You allude to (or mention) a book. You elude (or escape) a pursuer.

5. Annual. Don't use **first** with it. If it's the first time, it's not annual yet.

6. Averse, adverse. If you don't like something, you are averse (or opposed) to it. **Adverse** is an adjective: adverse (bad) weather, adverse conditions.

7. Block, bloc. A **bloc** is a coalition of persons or a group with the same purpose or goal. Don't call it a **block,** which has some forty dictionary definitions.

8. Compose, comprise. You compose things by putting them together. Once the parts are together, the object comprises or is comprised of the parts.

9. Couple of. You need the **of.** It's never "a couple tomatoes."

10. Demolish, destroy. They mean "to do away with completely." You can't partially demolish or destroy something; nor is there any need to say "totally destroyed."

11. Different from. Things and people are different from each other. Don't write that they are different than each other.

12. Drown. Don't say someone was drowned unless an assailant held the victim's head under water. Just say the victim drowned.

13. Due to, owing to, because of. We prefer the last. Wrong: The game was canceled due to rain. Stilted: Owing to rain, the game was canceled. Right: The game was canceled because of rain.

14. Ecology, environment. They are not synonymous. **Ecology** is the study of the relationship between organisms and their environment. Right: The laboratory is studying the ecology of man and the desert. Right: There is much interest in animal ecology these days. Wrong: Even so simple an undertaking as maintaining a lawn affects ecology. Right: Even so simple an undertaking as maintaining a lawn affects our environment.

15. Either. It means one or the other, not both. Wrong: There were lions on either side of the door. Right: There were lions on each side of the door.

16. Fliers, flyers. Flier is the preferred term for an aviator or a handbill.

17. Flout, flaunt. They aren't the same word; they mean completely different things, and they're very commonly confused. **Flout** means to mock, to scoff, or to show disdain for. **Flaunt** means to display ostentatiously.

18. Funeral service. A redundant expression. A funeral is a service.

19. Head up. People don't head up committees. They head them.

20. Hopefully. One of the most commonly misused words, in spite of what the dictionary may say. **Hopefully** should be used to describe the way the subject feels—for instance, "Hopefully, I shall present the plan to the president." This means that I will be hopeful when I do it, not that I hope I will do it. And it is something else again when you attribute hope to a nonperson. You may write, "Hopefully, the war will end soon." What you mean is that you hope the war will end soon, but this is not what you are writing. What you should write is, "I hope the war will end soon."

21. Imply and **infer.** The speaker **implies.** The hearer **infers.** You may also infer general principles from a sample.

22. In advance of, prior to. Use **before**; it sounds more natural.

23. It's, its. Its is the possessive, **It's** is the contraction of **it is.** Wrong: What is it's name? Right: What is its name? Its name is Fido. Right: It's the first time he's scored tonight. Right: It's my coat.

24. Lay, lie. Lay is the action word; **lie** is the state of being. Wrong: The body will lay in state until Wednesday. Right: The body will lie in state until Wednesday. Right: The prosecutor tried to lay the blame on him. However, the past tense of **lie** is **lay.** Right: The body lay in state from Tuesday until Wednesday. Wrong: The body laid in state from Tuesday until Wednesday. The past participle and the plain past tense of **lay** is **laid.** Right: He laid the pencil on the pad. Right: He had laid the pencil on the pad. Right: The hen laid an egg.

25. Leave, let. Leave alone means to depart from or cause to be in solitude. **Let alone** means to allow to be undisturbed. Wrong: The man had pulled a gun on her, but Mr. Jones intervened and talked him into leaving her alone. Right: The man had pulled a gun on her but Mr. Jones intervened and talked him into letting her alone. Right: When I entered the room, I saw that Jim and Mary were sleeping, so I decided to leave them alone.

26. Less, fewer. If you can separate items in the quantities being compared, use **fewer.** If not, use **less.** Wrong: The Rams are inferior to the Vikings because they have less good linemen. Right: The Rams are inferior to the Vikings because they have fewer good linemen. Right: The Rams are inferior to the Vikings because they have less experience.

27. Like, as. Don't use **like** for **as** or **as if.** In general, use like to compare nouns and pronouns; use as when comparing phrases and clauses that contain a verb. Wrong: Jim blocks the linebacker like he should. Right: Jim blocks the linebacker as he should. Right: Jim blocks like a pro.

28. Marshall, marshal. Generally, the first form is correct only when the word is a proper noun: John Marshall. The second form is the verb form: Marilyn will marshal her forces. And the second form is the one to use for a title: fire marshal Stan Anderson, field marshal Erwin Rommel.

29. Mean, average, median. Use **mean** as synonymous with **average.** Both words refer to the sum of all components divided by the number of components. **Median** is the number that has as many components above it as below it.

30. Nouns. There's a growing trend toward using them as verbs. Resist it. **Host, headquarters,** and **author,** for instance, are nouns, even though the dictionary may acknowledge that they can be used as verbs. If you do, you'll come up with a monstrosity like "Headquartered at his country home, John Doe hosted a party to celebrate the book he had authored."

31. Oral, verbal. Use **oral** when use of the mouth is central to the thought; the word emphasizes the idea of human utterance. **Verbal** may apply to spoken or written words; it connotes the process of reducing ideas to writing. Usually one speaks of an oral contract, not a verbal one, if it's not in writing.

32. Over, more than. They aren't interchangeable. **Over** is best used for spatial relationships: The plane flew over the city. **More than** is used best with figures: In the crowd were more than a thousand fans.

33. Parallel construction. Thoughts in series in the same sentence require parallel construction. Wrong: The union delivered demands for an increase of 10 percent in wages and to cut the work week to 30 hours. Right: The union delivered demands for an increase of 10 percent in wages and for a reduction in the work week to 30 hours.

34. Peddle, pedal. When selling something, you peddle it. When riding a bicycle or similar means of locomotion, you pedal it.

35. Pretense, pretext. They're different, but it's a tough distinction. A **pretext** is that which is put forward to conceal a truth. Right: He was discharged for tardiness, but this was only a pretext for general incompetence. A **pretense** is a "false show," a more overt act intended to conceal personal feelings. Right: My profuse compliments were all pretense.

36. Principle, principal. A guiding rule or basic truth is a principle. The first, dominant, or leading thing is **principal. Principle** is a noun; **principal** may be a noun or an adjective. Right: It's the principle of the thing. Right: Liberty and justice are two principles on which our nation is founded. Right: Hitting and fielding are the principal activities in baseball. Right: Robert Jamieson is the school principal.

37. Redundancies to avoid. Easter Sunday. Make it Easter. Incumbent Congressman. Owns his own home. Owns his home. The company will close down. The company will close. Johnson, Smith, and Jones were all convicted. Johnson, Smith, and Jones were convicted. Jewish Rabbi. Rabbi. 8 p.m. tonight. All you need is 8 p.m. today or 8 tonight. During the winter months. During the winter. Both Smith and Jones were denied pardons. Smith and Jones were denied pardons. I am currently tired. I am tired. Autopsy to determine the cause of death. Autopsy.

38. Refute. The word connotes success in argument and almost always implies an editorial judgment. Wrong: Father Bury refuted the arguments of the proabortion faction.

39. Reluctant, reticent. If he doesn't want to act, he is reluctant. If he doesn't want to speak, he is reticent.

40. Say, said. The most serviceable words in the journalist's language are the forms of the verb "to say." Let a person say something, rather than declare or admit or point out. And never let him grin, smile, frown, or giggle something.

41. Slang. Don't try to use "with-it" slang. Usually a term is on the way out by the time we get it in print. Wrong: The police cleared the demonstrators with a sunrise bust.

42. Spelling. It's basic. If reporters can't spell and copy editors can't spell, we're in trouble. Some ripe ones for the top of your list: It's **consensus**, not **concensus**. It's **restauranteur**, not **restaurnteur**. It's **dietitian**, not **dietician**.

43. Temperatures. They may get higher or lower, but they don't get warmer or cooler. Wrong: Temperatures are expected to warm up on Friday. Right: Temperatures are expected to rise on Friday.

44. That, which. That tends to restrict the reader's thought and direct it the way you want it to go; **which** is nonrestrictive, introducing a bit of subsidiary information. For instance: The lawnmower that is in the garage needs sharpening. (Meaning: We have more than one lawnmower. The one in the garage needs sharpening. It's in the garage.) The statue that graces our entry hall is on loan from the museum. (Meaning: Of all the statues around here, the one in the entry hall is on loan.) Note that **which** clauses take commas, signaling that they are not essential to the meaning of the sentence.

45. Under way, not **underway.** But don't say something got under way. Say it started, or began.

46. Unique. Something that is unique is the only one of its kind. It can't be very unique or quite unique or somewhat unique or rather unique. Don't use it unless you really mean **unique.**

47. Up. Don't use it as a verb. Wrong: The manager said he would up the price next week. Right: The manager said he would raise the price next week.

48. Who, whom. A tough one, but generally you're safe to use **whom** to refer to someone who has been the object of an action: A 19-year-old woman, to whom the room was rented, left the window open. **Who** is the word when the somebody has been the actor: A 19-year-old woman, who rented the room, left the window open.

49. Who's, whose. Though it incorporates an apostrophe, **who's** is not a possessive. It's a contraction of **who is. Whose** is possessive. Wrong: I don't know who's coat it is. Right: I don't know whose coat it is. Right: Find out who's there.

50. Would. Be careful about using **would** when constructing a conditional past tense. Wrong: If Soderhelm would not have had an injured foot, Thompson wouldn't have been in the lineup. Right: If Soderhelm had not had an injured foot, Thompson wouldn't have been in the lineup.

Conclusion

This chapter had concentrated on the rules of writing, and it's likey many beginning writing students find a lengthy discussion of these rules boring, if not oppressive.

Serious students of writing, however, will remember through all this discussion why we should be concerned about the rules: In writing for the mass media, we are trying to transmit information and ideas to an audience of readers and listeners. Will bad grammar, misspelling, sloppy punctuation and misuse of words help accomplish that goal? Will these mistakes tell the reader that the content of your communication is accurate and worthwhile—worthy of the audience's time and effort to understand it?

The answer, of course, is no. Good grammar, precise word usage, and correct spelling are a means to an end. That end is communicating with the reader or viewer.

Points for consideration and discussion

1. The author makes a strong case for knowing the rules of grammar, but some people do not think that this knowledge is very important. They believe that you can write well without knowing these rules. What do you think?

2. The text says that there are some times when a sentence fragment might be appropriate. When would that be?

3. What do you think are the most important rules for using a comma?

4. Explain the difference between **its, it's,** and **its'**.

5. Many of today's college students say they don't understand the rules of grammar because they didn't spend a lot of time with it in high school. What was your experience with grammar in high school?

6. Make a list of words that you think should be spelled differently.

7. Make a list of words that you often hear people misuing.

Further reading

R. Thomas Berner, *Language Skills for Journalists*, Boston: Houghton Mifflin, 1979.

John C. Hodges and Mary Whitten, *Harbrace College Handbook*, 7th ed., New York: Harcourt Brace Javananovich, 1972.

Lauren Kessler and Duncan McDonald, *When Words Collide*, 2nd ed., Belmont, CA: Wadsworth, 1988.

Floyd Watkins, William Dillingham, Edwin Martin, *Practical English Handbook*, Boston: Houghton Mifflin, 1970.

EXERCISES

The following section contains a variety of beginning writing exercises. You should follow your instructor's directions in completing them.

2-1 Writing Skills

The following sentences were taken from newspapers and television broadcasts. Correct the errors you find either by copy-editing or by rewriting the sentences. Underline your corrections. Some of the sentences are correct, and you should write <u>Correct</u> in the margin.

1. He is one of the greatest choreographers who has ever lived.

2. The general assumed what was then described as dictorial powers.

3. The couple has two children.

4. Inside the box was a man and a woman.

5. Absent from the meeting were the mayor and two councilmen.

6. Every fireman in the city, 250 in all were called out.

7. A total of 650 Eskimos was examined and tested.

8. Only two in four were urgent cases, a group that included cardiacs, asthmatics and those found unconscious.

9. The chairman stated that response to the committee's activities has convinced him that the money for renovation can be raised.

10. Business administration and journalism courses provide the student with good background for work in public relations.

11. Here comes the famous Kilgore College Rangerettes onto the field to perform at halftime.

12. Pacing the United States' show of strength were Arthur Ashe and Clarke Graebner.

13. The investigation revealed that none of the team members were involved in illegal endorsements of sports clothing.

14. "There's two knocked out cold on the floor!" the sportscaster shouted.

15. Every one of us have asked that question sometime in our lives.

2-2 Writing Skills

Correct the following sentences.

1. The assistance of three lawyers, one an expert, and two advertising men (was, were) necessary.

2. A list of the semester's reading assignments (have, has) been posted on the bulletin board.

3. Around us in every direction (was, were) miles of empty desert.

4. The chancellor, as well as the provost and the dean, (was, were) going to camp.

5. Five members of the class, including John (was, were) going to camp.

6. There (was, were) two newspapers in town, but there (was, were) only one editorial policy.

7. Airplanes (was, were) Randall's chief interest in life.

8. Randall's chief interest in life (was, were) airplanes.

9. Neither had finished (their, his) job.

10. Maybe some day each person will have (his or her, their) own helicopter for commuting to the city.

11. I have always maintained that a person should mind (his or her, their) own business.

12. After basic training, almost everyone is sent to different schools, ac cording to (his or her, their) ability.

13. Neither of the two nephews (live, lives) in Montana.

14. Neither had finished (their, his or her) job.

2-3 Writing Skills

Do whatever is necessary to correct the following sentences.

1. Their rival forces meanwhile prepared to meet Wednesday to patch up peace.

2. Pasadena California is the site of the Rose Bowl.

3. It was O. J. Simpson (who, whom) the coach praised so highly.

4. The tomb of the pharaoh had (laid, lain) buried in the desert for centuries.

5. I heard the train whistle at the crossing that was going to Denver.

6. She borrowed an egg from a neighbor that was rotten.

7. For a year we almost heard nothing from our former neighbors.

8. There was a canary in a cage that never sang.

9. We hope that you will notify us if you can attend the banquet on the en closed post card.

10. Come here Mary and help us.

11. I know she (swum, swims) the channel regularly in this weather.

12. The children looked forward to celebrating Christmas for several weeks.

13. After setting foot on the uninhabited island of Europe, off Africa, to di rect the filming of the sea turtles, a hurricane whirled across the Indian ocean and hit the island.

14. He ran swiftly the dog in front of him and plunged into the forest.

15. The casings had (tore, torn) (loose, lose) from their bearings.

2-4 Punctuation

Insert the correct punctuation in the following sentences.

1. In fact I hope to leave tomorrow

2. My friends we have no alternative

3. He said "the story has been told

4. Our failures not our successes will be remembered

5. Sandburg the biographer of Lincoln was awarded the Pulitzer Prize

6. My companions were James White M.D. and Rufus Black Ph.d.

7. William the Conqueror invaded England in 1066

8. My son James is sick

9. The work is on the whole very satisfactory

10. He was inducted into the army at Fort Oglethorpe Georgia on Sept 30, 1942

11. Please send all communications to 750 Third Ave New York New York 10017

12. Pearl Harbor Hawaii was bombed on December 7 1941

13. Manuscripts should be mailed to the Managing Editor 109 Parrington Hall University of Washington Seattle Washington

14. "We believe" he replied "that you are correct"

15. We believe however that you should go.

2-5 Punctuation

In the following sentences, insert the correct punctuation.

1. I subscribe to the *New Yorker Harper's Magazine* and the *Reporter*

2. Seven legislators from the southern part of the state changed their votes and with their help the bill was passed.

3. Do you like your steak rare medium or well done?

4. A tape recorder gives very accurate reproduction and it has the great advantage that it can be used at home as well as at the studio.

5. The gun went off and everyone jumped

6. The new cars are certainly more powerful but it is doubtful that they are any safer

7. Light entered the room through cracks in the walls through holes in the roof and through one small window.

8. Hundreds of church bells ringing loudly after years of silence announced the end of the war

9. The book was lying where I left it

10. The advisor who is never in his office makes registration difficult

11. Some years ago I lived in a section of town where almost everyone was a Republican

12. Hearne was still disclaiming with great eloquence but no one in the crowd was listening

13. I bought a large bath towel

14. We were sitting before the fire in the big room at Twins Farms and Lew is had rudely retired behind the newspaper

15. The ranchmen rode with their families into the little town and encouraged their sons to demonstrate their skill with broken horses

2-6 Clauses

In the following sentences, underline the independent clause and circle the subordinate (dependent) clause.

1. They agreed to open negotiations when both sides ceased fire.

2. If he had known, he would never have said that.

3. Since the current was swift, he could not swim to shore.

4. The horse came up to the first jump, when he stumbled and threw Jean off.

5. This is called the cryptozoite stage, after which the plasmodia break out of the liver cells and float about in the blood stream.

6. An especially big wave rolled in, when I finally managed to get my line unsnagged.

7. While walking past the building, the night watchman noticed the door was unlocked.

8. Harkey's injured knee has failed to heal completely; therefore, he may see little action against Notre Dame on Saturday.

9. The Ace Manufacturing Company, where I used to work, went bank rupt.

10. This last semester, if it has done nothing else, has given me confidence in myself.

Write five correct sentences containing independent and subordinate clauses.

1.

2.

3.

4.

5.

2-7 Word Choice

In the following sentences, fill in the blank with one of the words that appears in parentheses.

1. _____are good reasons why _____about to
   sell_____house.(there, their, they're)

2. _____not_____late_____give the cat milk.(its, it's, to, too)

3. If _____going home, take_____books with you. (your, you're)

4. Do you know_____the_____is pleasant_____?(whether, weather, there, their, they're)

5. They_____known for a long time that you
   would_____gone if you had heard_____the game
   in time. (have, of, 've)

6. Where_____are many opinions, most people feel justifed in holding on
   to_____own; and while there are several scientific explanations for
   stubborness,_____be few changes unless we can convince men that
   they ought to be more open-minded. (there, their, they're, there'll)

7. My_____objection to the _____of that school is
   that he is a man of no_____(principal, principle)

8. Not until_____will you be able to tell whether you have
   more_____ you need. (than, then)

9. If_____strap is_____, you may_____your books. (lose, loose, you're, your)

10. Not even in the_____would I_____the table before eat
    ing_____ (desert, dessert)

11. "_____going to punch_____nose?" (whose, who's)

12. We_____the ruling without protest, although we_____all
    those over 45. (except, accept)

13. His speech_____the audience greatly. (affected, effected)

14. _____50,000 people attend the opening game of the World Se
    ries. (Over, More than)

15. He was always one to do things_____.(different, differently)

2-8 Pronouns and Verbs

In the following sentences, underline the correct pronoun or verb.

1. He is the player (who, whom) probably will play shortstop.

2. Is this the person (who, whom) you want?

3. Each of the three quarterbacks (is, are) a good runner.

4. Both Baylor and Arkansas (has, have) won six games and lost two.

5. Either of the two players (are, is) eligible.

6. Each of the members (was, were) in (his, their) seat(s) when the session began.

7. (Who, Whom), then, would the tax hurt?

8. Do you know to (who, whom) that notebook belongs?

9. (Who, Whom) is going with the reporter to get a picture of the crash?

10. He declared that everybody must play (his, their) part.

11. This story is between you and (I, me).

12. No matter how you look at it, it was (I, she, her) (who, whom) they opposed.

13. Bryan is the kind of man (whom, who) always thinks before he acts.

14. This is the only one of the typewriters that (is, are) working.

15. Everyone was on (their, his or her) best behavior.

2-9 Verbs

In the following sentences, underline the correct form of the verb.

1. What (lays, lies) in the future for Alaska?

2. He had been (lain, laid) on a stretcher.

3. "(Lay, Lie) down and be quiet for an hour," he ordered.

4. The 6 year-old boy was just (setting, sitting) there in the ruins, trying not to cry.

5. The Ohio State football team (sat, set) back and enjoyed the movie of its game with Michigan.

6. The men worked all night (raising, rising) a monument in spite of the (raising, rising) tide of the river.

7. After lunch she had (laid, lain) down for a nap.

8. The hard tackling by the Georgia Bulldogs had really (began, begun) to tell.

9. Suddenly a cloud of dust (rises, raises) in the west.

10. Had the tight end simply (fell, fallen) on the ball, he would have (catched, caught) it.

11. Spillane (led, lead) you to believe that the butler was the murderer.

12. Chris Gilbert had (proved, proven) to be the outstanding player.

13. He said that he could (loose, lose) his fortune, but he had (chose, chosen) to gamble all he had.

14. The Smiths (use, used) to live in San Francisco.

15. If Martin hadn't (drown, drowned), he surely would have been (hanged, hung).

2-10 Brevity

Edit all unnecessary words from the expressions below.

a bald-headed man

a pregnant Cuban woman

returned back home

skirted around obstacles

wearing a happy smile on her face

set a new record

a near approximation

throughout the entire day

cannot possibly be

assembled crowd of people

his other alternative

was engaged in studying

red- colored cloth

in the year 1962

at the hour of noon

2-11 Brevity

Edit all unnecessary words from the expressions below.

wore a white goatee on his chin

throughout the length and width of the entire nation

was positively identified

appeared to be ill

a dead body was found

in the city of Los Angeles

cost the sum of $10

broke an existing rule

for the month of May

for a short space of time

an old pioneer

the present incumbent

will draw to a close

at the corner of 6th and Elm streets

for the purpose of shocking

3

Style and the Stylebook

s you enter the world of writing for the mass media, you will hear much about "style." By style, we are not talking about a particular writer's style, such as Ernest Hemingway's style or William Faulker's style, but about two things of more immediate concern to the writer: the conventions or assumptions underlying the writing and the generally accepted rules of writing and usage for a particular medium. We will discuss both of those in this chapter.

The ABC's of media writing are accuracy, brevity and clarity. The most important of these is accuracy.

Accuracy

The chief goal of any writer for the mass media is accuracy. A writer will spend much of his or her efforts in "getting it right." That is, the writer will make every reasonable attempt to ensure that everything in the writing is factually correct and that the language and style the writer uses correctly present that information.

Accuracy is important to the writer for a number of reasons. First, our society puts much stock in truth and honesty, and most people in our society have come to expect that the mass media will take reasonable steps to be accurate in the information they present. There is a great tendency for mass audiences to believe what they see and read in the mass media, and this tendency translates into a responsibility that those who work in the mass media must fulfill.

A very practical reason for an emphasis on accuracy is that people will not watch or subscribe to media they believe to be inaccurate. A newspaper, television station, advertising agency, or public relations department that does not tell the truth will not be trusted by the people it is trying to serve and ultimately will not be effective.

The most compelling reason for a strong emphasis on accuracy, however, comes not from the audience but from the person who works in the mass media. Few people, if any, want to be false in what they do or want their life's work to be looked upon as worthless. Consequently, they feel a moral need to do the best they can; in the mass media professions, that means trying to produce accurate and honest information.

How can a writer for the mass media be accurate? What are the steps he or she can take to be sure that the information presented in the writing is correct? We'll discuss some of the practical things that can be done in the next two chapters as we talk about gathering information and writing news. We can begin our thinking about accuracy here by making the following observations.

Writers for the mass media should have an open mind. They should be receptive to new ideas and to various points of view. They should be willing to listen to those with whom they may disagree as well as agree. They will not put everything they read and hear in their writing, but the more they know, the better judgments they can make about the accuracy of what they write.

Following closely on this characteristic is that writers for the mass media should read widely. Reading, even in the age of video, is still the best way for a person to prepare himself or herself as a writer.

Writers for the mass media should pay attention to the details of what and how they write. In the previous chapter we discussed the importance of using the language correctly. That discussion will continue in this chapter as we talk more about style. Individually, many of the points made in each of these chapters are small ones, but as a whole, they are important for the writer's effort to achieve accuracy. Accuracy may be thought of as a large building made up of many small bricks. The writer is the bricklayer and must pay attention to each of the bricks as they are put down.

Clarity

Clarity must be one of the chief goals of a writer for the mass media. Facts that are unclear are of little use to the reader. The English language is extremely versatile, but that versatility can lead to confusion when the language is in the hands of amateurs. Writers must be experts in the language and in the proper and clear structuring of a story. Writers must be on constant guard against writing or story structures that could be confusing to the reader.

The pursuit of clarity is a state of mind for the writer. Everything the writer does must promote the clarity of the copy. After a piece of copy is written, a writer must look at it with a fresh mind—one that is unencumbered with too much knowledge of the subject. The writer must, like the reader, approach a story as one who was not there and did not see it happen and who has not talked with anyone about it. This approach is doubly difficult for the writer who has followed one of the first rules of good writing—knowing the subject thoroughly. Editing for clarity demands a rare degree of mental discipline on the part of the writer.

The opposite of clarity is confusion. Confusion can infiltrate a story in many ways, and it is the writer's responsibility to eliminate this confusion. The chief source of confusion is often the writer who does not understand what he or she is writing about. Writers who do not understand their subjects are likely to write a story that other people cannot understand.

Clear writing is an art, but it is also a skill. Expressing thoughts, ideas, and facts in a clear way is one of the most difficult jobs a writer has—even though the product may read as if the clarity were easily accomplished. The mind moves much faster than we can write or even type; thoughts can be easily jumbled and so can writing. The key to clear writing is understanding the subject. When a writer can express thoughts about a subject in clear terms, then that understanding has been achieved.

The following are some tips for helping writers and editors achieve clarity in their writing:

Keep it simple. Many people believe that they can demonstrate their intelligence by using complex terms (like **terminology**). Their language, they feel, will show others that they have mastered a difficult subject or that they speak or write with authority. Consequently, they use big words and complex sentences to express the simplest ideas.

The problem with this attitude is that people forget their original purpose for writing—to communicate ideas. Any writing that draws attention to itself, and thus draws attention away from the content, is ineffective. Writing, especially for the mass media, should be as simple and straightforward as possible. Reporters and editors should use simple terms and sentence structures. They should avoid piling adjectives and phrases on top of one another. They should do this, not in order to talk down to their readers, but to transmit ideas and facts as efficiently as possible.

Avoid all kinds of jargon—even your own. Jargon is specialized language which almost all groups in society develop. Students, baseball managers, doctors, and gardeners use words that have special meaning for them and no one else. Journalists are not doing their jobs if they simply record jargon, however accurately, and give it back to the reader. Today's journalists must be translators. They must understand the jargon of different groups they cover but must be intelligent enough not to use it in their stores. Writers, too, must keep a watch out for the jargon that can slip into stories. Phrases like "viable alternative," "optimum care," and "personnel costs" must be made to mean something by journalists. They cannot simply thrust them on the reader and believe that they have done their job adequately.

Be specific. Journalists must set the stage of the story for their readers. They must make sure that their readers understand what is going on, when it is happening, where it is happening, and how it is taking place. Reporters and editors cannot assume that readers know very much about the stories they write and edit. They cannot get by with telling readers that it was a "large crowd" or a "long line" or a "beautiful girl." Stories are built on facts—little facts and big facts. Sometimes it is the little facts that will make the difference in whether or not a reader understands a story.

Readers who have not seen what reporters have seen won't know what reporters are talking about. One aspect of this problem occurs with the use of "the," especially by less experienced reporters. For example, a lead paragraph may begin in the following way, "City council tonight approved funds for purchasing the new computer system for the finance department." A reader is likely to ask, "What new computer system?" While covering the story, the reporter kept hearing everyone talk about "the new computer system," so that's what appeared in the story. Writers particularly need to watch for this kind of assumption and to make sure that readers are not left behind by the assumptions a writer makes.

Check the time sequence. Most news stories will not be written in chronological order, but readers should have some idea of the narrative sequence of the events in a story. When the time sequence is not clear, readers may become confused and misunderstand the content of the story.

Transitions. Transitions, as we have mentioned before, are necessary for smooth, graceful, and clear writing. Each sentence in a story should logically follow the previous sentence or should relate to it in some way. New information in a story should be connected to information already introduced. Readers who suddenly come upon new information or a new subject in a story without the proper transition will be jolted and confused. The following first paragraphs of a story about the high costs of weddings will serve to illustrate the point about transitions:

```
     The nervous young man drops to one knee,
blushes and asks that all-important question.
     What about all the planning involved in a
wedding, from  reserving the church to choos-
ing the honeymoon site? June and July are the
traditional months for making the
big  decision, according to Milton Jefferson
of the Sparkling Jewelry Store.
     Jefferson said most engagements last from
seven to 16  months.
     A woman sometimes receives a ring that has
been passed  down through her fiancé's family
for generations, or maybe her boyfriend has
bought an estate ring.
```

The first paragraph assumes that the reader will know what "that all-important question" is. This assumption might be acceptable if the second paragraph followed the lead properly, but it doesn't. Instead, it plunges the reader into the subject of planning a wedding; the reader has no indication from the lead that this is coming next—and what happened to "that all-important question?"

In a similar manner, the second sentence of the second paragraph introduces yet another new subject to the reader, again without the proper transition. The reader is taken from a question about planning to the traditionally popular months for weddings, with no connection being made between them. In addition, the attribution forces the reader to make another transition. The reader must say, "The man is a jewelry store owner. Jewelry stores sell wedding rings. The jewelry store owner, then, is an authority about when weddings occur."

The third paragraph introduces yet another new subject—the length of engagements. Again, the reader has no transition—merely bombardment by one fact after another.

The fourth paragraph talks about how prospective brides attain their wedding rings. What has this information got to do with what has been said? The writer has left it to the reader to figure it all out. The writer has said, "My story is about weddings. Therefore, anything I put in my story about weddings is okay."

Good writers need to develop a mental discipline that prevents this kind of thing from happening. They must read their own copy with cold and glaring eyes, never assuming that a reader will take the time and effort to "figure out" what the writer has written.

Brevity

"Brevity is the soul of wit," according to Polonius, Shakespeare's ill-fated character in *Hamlet*. Polonius was, in reality, one of Shakespeare's most verbose personalities. Words came tumbling out of his mouth. He went on and on. He was not only verbose; he was boring. Polonius was one of those people you try to avoid at parties and hope you don't have to take a long car ride with. He talked too much.

Writers can do the same thing. They can use too many words, piling phrase upon phrase and letting the sentences run on far after their thoughts have run out. They put too many words in the way of what really needs to be said.

Writers need to recognize when they are being long-winded. They should remove the well-turned phrase that is unnecessary and eliminate that which has already been stated. The process can go too far, of course. Accuracy and clarity should never be sacrificed for brevity's sake, but brevity should be another major goal in the mind of the writer.

The following are some tips for achieving brevity:

Get to the point. What is the story about? What does the story need to tell the reader? A writer needs to be able to answer these questions in the simplest terms possible. Answering these questions is sometimes the hardest part of writing or editing, but once that is done, the writing or editing job can become much easier.

Watch for redundancies and repetitions. Redundancies show a lack of disciplined thinking. They slip into writing unnoticed, but their presence can make the most important stories seem silly. Repetition is also an indication that the editor was not concentrating on the story. Sometimes facts need to be repeated for clarity's sake, but this is not often the case.

Cut out the unnecessary words. There may be words in a story that simply add nothing to its meaning. These words are hard to pin down, but a sharp-eyed writer can spot them. They are words like **really, very,** and **actually**. They're simply phrase-makers, but they don't tell the reader very much.

Finally, when you have run out of things to write about, stop writing.

Journalistic conventions

A strong sense of professionalism has developed in journalism during the 300 years of its history in America. With this professionalism has come a powerful tradition of conventions in journalistic writing. Like rules of style, these conventions are known to trained journalists and used by them to communicate things about their stories to readers. Most readers do not think about what these conventions are when they read the newspaper, yet most regular readers of newspapers know these conventions and what they indicate about the judgments made by editors and reporters.

The conventions include both the basic structures of the stories and the individual ordering of facts and even words within sentences that regularly are used in certain types of stories.

Inverted pyramid. The inverted pyramid is the structure most commonly used for the modern American news story. For the writer, the inverted pyramid structure means two things: Facts should be presented in the order of their importance, with the most important facts coming at the beginning, and a story should be written so that if it needs to be cut, it may be cut from the bottom without loss of essential facts or coherence. The inverted pyramid is certainly not the only acceptable structure for the presentation of news, but its use is so widespread that if it is not used, the facts of a story must dictate the alternate form used by the writer.

Types of stories. The news values we will discuss in the next chapter make it incumbent upon editors to cover and give importance to certain types of stories. These kinds of stories are handled so often that a set of standard practices governing how they are written has been established. For instance, the disaster story must always tell early in the story if anyone was killed or injured. Another example of this routinization of stories is the obituary. Newspapers develop their own styles for handling obituaries, and some even dictate the form in which the standard obituary is written. For instance, the *New York Times* has a set two-sentence lead for an obituary: "John Smith, a Brooklyn real estate dealer, died at a local hospital yesterday after a short illness. He was 55 years old."

Other types of routine stories are those concerning government actions, the courts, crime, holidays, and weather.

Balance and fairness. One of the basic tenets of American journalism is fairness. Journalists should attempt to give all people involved in a news story a chance to tell their sides of it. If an accusation is made by a news source concerning another person, that person should be given a chance to answer in the same story. Journalists should not take sides in a controversy and should take care not to even appear to take sides.

Writing and editing a balanced story means more than just making sure a controversial situation or issue is covered fairly. In a larger sense, balance means that journalists should understand the relative importance of the events they cover and should not write stories that overplay or underplay that importance. Journalists are often charged with "blowing things out of proportion," and sometimes the charge is a valid one. They should make sure that they are not being used by news sources and being put in a position of creating news rather than letting it occur and then covering it.

The impersonal reporter. Closely associated with the concepts of balance and fairness is the concept of the impersonal reporter. Reporters should be invisible in their writing. Reporters should not only not report their own views and opinions, but they should avoid direct contact with the reader through the use of first-person (**I, we, me, our, my, us**) or second-person (**you, your**) pronouns outside of direct quotes.

Reporters and editors inherently state their opinions about the news in deciding what events they write about, how they write about them, and where they place those stories in the paper. No journalist can claim to be a completely unbiased and objective observer and deliverer of information. Yet stating opinions directly and plainly is generally not an acceptable practice. Even for reporters to include themselves with readers is not a good idea. For example, the following lead is not acceptable because of its use of a first-person pronoun: "The Chief Justice of the Supreme Court said yesterday our legal system is in serious trouble." There may be someone reading this story who makes no claim to the United States' legal system, and the reporter should write for that person as well as for all who do.

Reliance on official sources. Much of the information printed in a newspaper comes from what we might call "official" sources. These sources are those which are thought to have expertise on the subject being written about, not those who may merely have opinions about the subject. An example of this reliance might be found in a story about inflation. A journalist writing a story about inflation would probably use information from government reporters and the studies and opinions of respected economists and influential politicians. These would be the "official" sources, and they would have a large amount of credibility with the reader. An "unofficial" source might be a homemaker, who would certainly have an opinion about the effects, causes, and cures of inflation, but who would not have information that would be credible in the mass media.

Young journalists often make the mistake of relying on these unofficial sources rather than on official sources of information. They interview people who have opinions about news events, such as their roommates, rather than those who can provide information to support an opinion about a news event. Use of official sources means that when a source is quoted in a story, it should be readily apparent why that source was used. Joe Johnson, a college student from Beantown, is not going to have much credibility in a story about resistance to draft registration laws. However, Joe Johnson, the leader of the Draft Registration Resistance Movement, will have high credibility in the story.

Attribution and quotes. Journalists should make it clear to readers where information has been obtained. All but the most obvious and commonly known facts in a story should be attributed. Writers should make sure that the attributions are helpful to the reader's understanding of the story and that they do not get in the way of the flow of the story.

A number of journalistic conventions have grown up around the use of indirect and direct quotes. First, except in the rarest instances, all quotes must be attributed. The exception is the case where there is no doubt about the source of the quote. Even then, editors should be careful. Second, journalists disagree about whether a direct quote should be the exact words a person speaks or the exact meaning the quoted person intended. Most of the time, people's exact words will accurately express their meaning. Finally, direct quotes in news stories rarely include bad grammar, even if the person quoted used bad grammar. Quoting someone using English incorrectly can make that person appear unnecessarily foolish and can distract from the real meaning of the story. In a news story, a journalist usually cleans up bad grammar in a direct quote. (Feature story writers may choose not to follow this practice.)

These conventions are important to observe if journalists are to gain the respect of their readers and colleagues. Conventions should not be looked upon as arbitrary rules which must be followed at the expense of accuracy and clarity. Rather, they are a set of sound practices which are extremely useful to journalists in the process of deciding what to write and how to write it.

Journalistic style

English is an extremely diverse language; it gives the user many ways of saying the same thing. For instance, 8:00, eight o'clock, 8 A.M., eight a.m., and eight in the morning may all correctly refer to the same thing; a reference may be to the president, the U.S. president, the president of the United States, and so on. All of these references are technically correct, but which one should a journalist use? And does it really matter?

The answer to the first question is governed by journalistic style. Style is a special case of English correctness which a publication adopts. It does so in order to promote consistency among its writers and to reduce confusion among its readers. Once a style is adopted, a writer won't have to wonder about the way to refer to such things as time.

Journalistic style may be divided into two types of style: professional conventions and rules of usage. Professional conventions have evolved during years of journalistic endeavor and are now taught through professional training in universities and professional workshops. The rules of usage have been collected into stylebooks published by wire services, news, syndicates, universities, and individual print and broadcast news operations. Some of these stylebooks have had widespread acceptance and influence. Others have remained relatively local and result in unique style rules accepted by reporters and editors working for individual news organizations.

For example, a publication may follow the *Associated Press Stylebook* and *United Press International Stylebook* and say that **AM** and **PM** should be lower-case with periods: a.m. and p.m. The writer will know that a reference to the president of the United States is always simply "president," lower-cased, except when referring to a specific person, such as President Bush.

Likewise, the reader will not be confused by multiple references to the same item. Unconsciously, the reader will expect the style that the publication uses. Consequently, if the reader uses a college newspaper regularly and that paper always refers to its own institution as "the University," upper-case, the reader will know what that means.

Similarly, a reporter may follow the usual convention in newspaper writing and write the sequence of time, date, and place of a meeting despite the fact that it may seem more logical to report the date before reporting the time.

Having a logical, consistent style is like fine-tuning a color television. Before the tuning, the colors may be there and the picture may be reasonably visible. Eventually, however, the off-colors and the blurry images will play on the viewer's mind so that he or she will become dissatisfied and disinterested. That could cause the viewer to stop watching altogether. In the same way, consistent style fine-tunes a publication so that reading it is easier for a reader and offers few distractions from the content.

Beyond that, the question may still remain: Does style really matter? The answer is an emphatic "yes!" Many young writers think of consistent style as a repressive force hampering their creativity. It isn't. Style is not a rigid set of rules established to restrict the creative forces in the writer. Style imposes a discipline in writing that should run through all the activities of a journalist. It implies that the journalist is precise not only with writing but also with facts and with thought. Consistent style is the hallmark of a professional.

Editors are the governors of the style of a publication. It is their job to see that style rules are consistently and reasonably applied. If exceptions are allowed, they should be for specific and logical reasons and should not be at the whim of a writer. Editors and writers should remember that consistent style is one way of telling readers that everything in the publication is certified as accurate.

Stylebooks

Stylebooks are a fact of life for writers for the mass media. Any area of writing, from newspapers to advertising agencies to public relations firms, will require the use of some form of stylebook. Stylebooks deal primarily with three things, the first and foremost being **consistency.** The main reason for the existence of any stylebook is to promote consistency in writing. To do this, a stylebook establishes the **rules of writing** for a publication. These are often arbitrary rules, such as using "a.m." instead of "AM" to refer to morning times and spelling certain numbers out while using figures for others. These rules also eliminate inconsistencies in spelling, such as mandating that the Southeast Asia country be spelled **Vietnam** rather than **Viet-Nam**. Stylebooks also deal with **usage,** particularly when dictionaries assign a variety of meanings to a word. A good stylebook will say when a word should be properly and consistently used. Beyond that, a good stylebook helps a writer find the precise words he or she needs.

This chapter refers mostly to the *Associated Press Stylebook and Libel Manual* because that is the most commonly used reference for writers in the mass media. The first AP stylebook appeared in 1953, growing out of demands from newspaper editors who subscribed to the Associated Press wire service. Many of these editors wanted to make their local copy consistent with the copy they were receiving and running from the AP. Many of these same newspapers also subscribed to the nation's other major wire service, United Press International, and they wanted the wire services to use a consistent style. Consequently, AP and UPI got together and came up with a common stylebook in 1960. These first stylebooks were simply small handbooks that dealt mainly with the rules of writing. During the next decade, newspaper editors saw the need for a book that would also deal with usage, so in 1975 a committee of editors from AP and UPI again got together and put together a comprehensive stylebook that is in use today.

A number of other publications have produced comprehensive stylebooks. Two of the most influential are the *New York Times Manual of Style* and the *Los Angeles Times Stylebook*. Each contains many local references and has become the major style reference for writers on those publications. Most publications, however, have small stylebooks that deal with local style questions and preferences and rely on a larger reference, such as the *AP Stylebook and Libel Manual*, to answer broader questions. Any publication, even college newspapers and yearbooks, should have its own stylebook because there are always local questions a major reference will not answer. For instance, how should students be identified? One college newspaper stylebook says that students should be identified by class rank and major, as in "Mary Smith, a junior in journalism"; a stylebook for another student newspaper says that students should be identified by major and hometown, as in "Mary Smith, a journalism major from Midville." It doesn't take much imagination to come up with a number of style problems like this one that need to be answered by a local stylebook.

Students should be aware of two other major style references. One is *A Manual of Style* by the University of Chicago Press. This book is the chief reference for something known as the "Chicago style," and the Chicago style is used in most books. It contains a number of major differences from the *AP Stylebook*. For instance, Chicago style mandates that numbers one through one hundred be spelled out, while AP style says that numbers one through nine should be spelled out. Chicago style began as a single proofreader's sheet in 1891 and was first published for those not working with the University of Chicago Press in 1906. Today it is more than 500 pages long and deals extensively with footnotes, referencing, and many other style problems that arise when books are produced.

Another important style reference is the *Style Manual* of the U.S. Government Printing Office. This is the style guide for all government publications and is particularly good in dealing with governmental material and foreign languages.

Are stylebooks necessary? That question is argued, even among seasoned journalists. Most come down on the side of using stylebooks, but usually with reservations. Roy Copperud, author of *A Dictionary of Usage and Style*, criticizes those who use style rules arbitrarily or who enforce style rules that make no sense. "Meditation and prayer lead to the conviction that the best style is the one which governs least." Style rules should not inhibit creativity or initiative in writing. They should promote readability. Style, as the *United Press International Stylebook* points out, is the "intangible ingredient that distinguishes outstanding writing from mediocrity."

The Associated Press Stylebook

Several years ago, the two major U.S. wire services negotiated an agreement on the basic rules of style found in their two stylebooks. As a result, the AP and UPI now publish stylebooks that are in fundamental agreement on the basic rules of style. This has resulted in widespread adoption of these rules by newspapers around the United States. Since the Associated Press has published its stylebook in a form commonly available to students in universities around the country, we shall refer to that stylebook in this section of our discussion. Keep in mind that this style is now held in common with PI and is accepted by many newspapers nationwide.

Most publications base their style on that found in the *Associated Press Stylebook*. Here are some representative problem areas and some advice generally taken from the Associated Press Stylebook.

Capitalization. Unnecessary capitalization, like unnecessary punctuation, should be avoided because it slows reading and makes the sentence look uninviting. Some examples: Main Street, but Main and Market streets; Mayor John Smith, but John Smith, mayor of Jonesville; Steve Barber, executive director of the State Press Association. (Note lower-case title after name, but upper-case for State Press Association, a formal name and therefore a proper noun.)

Abbreviation. The trend is away from alphabet soup in body copy and in headlines, but some abbreviations help conserve space and help to simplify information. For example: West Main Street, but 20 W. Main St. The only titles for which abbreviations are called for (all before the name) are Dr., Gov., Lt. Gov., Mr., Mrs., Rep., the Rev., Sen., and most military ranks. Standing alone, all of these are spelled out and are lower cased. Check the stylebook for others.

Punctuation. Especially helpful are the sections of the stylebook dealing with the comma, hyphen, period, colon and semicolon, dash, ellipsis, restrictive and nonrestrictive elements, apostrophe, and quotation marks.

Numerals. Spell out whole numbers below 10, and use figures for 10 and above. This rule applies to numbers used in a series or individually. Don't begin sentences with numerals, as a rule, but if you must, spell them out.

Spelling. In journalism a word has but one spelling. Alternate spellings and variants are incorrect (because of the requirement of style consistency). Make it **adviser**, not **advisor**; **employee**, not **employe**; **totaled**, not **totalled**; **traveled**, not **travelled**; **kidnapped**, not **kidnaped**; **judgment**, not **judgement**; **television**, not **TV**, when used as a noun; **under way**, not **underway**; **percent**, not **per cent**; **afterward, toward,**

upward, forward (no's); **vs.**, not **versus** or **vs**; **vice president**, not **vice-president**. Check the stylebook or a dictionary for others.

Usage. Comprise means to contain, not to make up. "The region comprises five states," not "five states comprise the region" and not "the region is comprised of five states." **Affect** means to influence, not to carry out. **Effect** means a result when it's a noun and means to carry out when it's a verb. **Controller** and **comptroller** are both pronounced "controller" and mean virtually the same thing, though **comptroller** is generally the more accurate word for denoting government financial officers, and **controller** is better for denoting business financial officers. **Hopefully** does not mean it is hoped, we hope, maybe, or perhaps —it means in a hopeful manner: "Hopefully, editors will study the English language" is not acceptable usage of the word. Good editors use fad expressions because readers do, but they do not use them as crutches, and they should know when they are using them.

Ages. Use numerals always: a 2-month-old baby; he was 80; the youth, 18, and the girl, 6, were rescued.

Dates. Feb. 6 (current calendar year); in February 1978 (no comma); last February.

Dimensions. He is 5 feet 9 inches tall; the 5-foot 9-inch woman; 5-foot-9 woman; a 7-footer; the car left a skid mark 8 inches wide and 17 feet long; the rug is 10 by 12. The storm brought 1 1/2 inches of rain (spell out fractions less than one).

Conclusion

In this chapter, we have attempted to introduce you to the concept of "style" and what it means to those who work in the mass media. Conforming to the rules and conventions of the medium in which you are working is the mark of a true professional. Strict adherence to the details of style shows that you care about what you write.

Points for consideration and discussion

1. How has this chapter changed your thinking about the meaning of "style" and its use in writing for the mass media?

2. What are some of the reasons why there is such a strong emphasis on accuracy in writing for the mass media? How does adherence to a consistent style contribute to goal of accuracy for a journalist?

3. Find a piece of writing in which you think that writer used big words instead of simple ones. Rewrite it using the simpler language. Now compare the two pieces of writing. Which is better?

4. Some people say that a consistent style restricts creativitiy, while oth

ers say it enhances creativity. What are the arguments on both sides of this question.

5. The concept of objectivity is a controversial one in the field of journalism. Why do you think it causes so much controversy?

Further reading

The Associated Press Stylebook and Libel Manual. Rev. Ed., New York: The Associated Press, 1987.

Theodore Bernstein, *The Careful Writer, A Modern Guide to English Usage.* New York: Atheneum, 1973.

Theodore Bernstein, *Watch Your Language.* Manhasset, N.Y.: Channel Press, 1958.

Roy Copperud, *A Dictionary of Usage and Style.* New York: Hawthorne Books, 1964.

A Manual of Style. Chicago: University of Chicago Press, 1982.

The New York Times Manual of Style and Usage. Rev. Ed. by Lewis Jordon. Chicago: Quadrangle Books, 1976.

William Strunk and E.B. White. *The Elements of Style.* Rev. Ed. New York: Macmillan, 1972.

U.S. Government Printing Office Style Manual. Rev. Ed. Washington, D.C.: Government Printing Office, 1973.

EXERCISES

The following section contains a variety of style exercises. You should follow your instructor's directions in completing them.

3-1 Using the stylebook

Correct the following items so that they conform with AP style.

1. The defense department is about to propose a new missele system.

2. F.C.C., hitch-hiker, three dollars, 4 million

3. The three most important people in his life are his wife, son, and mother.

4. part-time, 10 year old child, 5 PM, 5300

5. The cardinals won the last game of the world series, 7 to 5.

6. spring (season), fall (season), south (point on compass), south (region)

7. November 15, the last day of Feb., Mar. 16

8. 13 people travelled to Austin, Tex. for the rally.

9. He had ten cents left in his pocket.

10. home-made, well-known, Italian-American, questionaire

3-2 Using the stylebook

Correct the following items so that they conform with AP style.

1. The U.S. is sometimes not the best market for U.S. products.

2. Circle the correct form:

   upward, upwards

   British (Labour, Labor) Party

   Riverside (Ave., Avenue)

   cupsful, cupfuls

   eying, eyeing

3. The Republican differed from the democrat many times during the debate.

4. Dr. John Smith and Dr. Mary Wilson preformed the operations.

5. Circle the correct form:

   donut, doughnut

   pants suit, pantsuit

   plow, plough

   U.S. Weather Bureau, National Weather Service

6. He said he was neither a Communist or a member of the Communist Party.

7. After her surgery, she had to wear a Pacemaker.

8. "What a hair-brained scheme!" she exclaimed.

9. preempt, speed-up (noun), 55 miles per hour, hookey

10. The underworld, or mafia, was responsible for the murder.

3-3 Using the stylebook

Correct the following items so that they conform with AP style.

1. He was charged with trafficing in drugs.

2. The Rev. Billy Graham said God was alive and His will would triumph.

3. pianoes, nation-wide, P.T.A., Viet-nam war

4. The flag, which Frances Scott Key saw, has been preserved.

5. life-like, outfielder, inter-racial, IOU's (plural)

6. The train will arrive at twelve noon on Tues.

7. The US Census Bureau defines the south as a seventeen-state region.

8. The judged ruled that because of his oral skills he had entered into a verbal contract.

9. She had an afternoon snack of some oreo cookies and cake.

10. harrass, accomodate, weird, likeable

6-4 Using the stylebook

Correct the following items so that they conform with AP style.

1. His solution turned out to be the most equal of the two.

2. Ga. Sec. of State George Smith testified at the Congressional hearing.

3. tis, the Gay 1890's, a South America country, 1492 A.D.

4. Write the plurals for the following words: Eskimo,_____;
   chili, _____; memorandum, _____; ski,
   _____

5. The ballif opened the court by saying, "Oyes, oyes, oyes!"

6. He spread out his palate and went to sleep.

7. carry-over (adj.), nitty-gritty, nit-picking, know-tow

8. What do the following abbreviations stand for?

   USIA _____

   GOP_____

   EST _____

   TVA _____

   Are any of these abbreviations acceptable for first reference? _____

9. The pan had a teflon surface.

10. He was graduated from a teacher's college in the north.

6-5 Using the stylebook

Correct the following items so that they conform with AP style.

1. Write the plurals for the following words: referendum,
   _____.; court martial, _____;
   1920, _____; dead end, _____.

2. Daylight savings time begins on the last Sun. in April.

3. He made the Dean's List after Dean Smith talked to him.

4. The game, that was scheduled for to-night, was rained out.

5. He said the car would go further on premium gas.

6. The movie which starred Sam Jones received an r rating.

7. He had run the gauntlet of criticism and abuse for his views.

8. The woman who the article referred to was a German Jewess.

9. judgement, naval orange, resistable, self-defense

10. He played semi-pro baseball for 3 years.

6-6 Using the stylebook

Correct the following story so that it conforms with AP style. The story contains other errors besides style errors that you will need to correct. Use the proper editing marks.

Baseball game

The Bay City Bluebirds rallied from a 3-run defict last night to defeat the Carmel Cardinals 6-3 and win the Western Tri-state division championship.

The bluebirds are now assured a place int eh Tri-state playoffs which begin next week. Their opponent will be determined tonight in a game between the Santa Ana Gnerals and the Redwood Knights.

The cardinals led the bluebirds for most of the game, and they hasa 3-0 lead in the eighth inniny.

In the bluebird hafl of the eighth, Tim Story, the first baseman, walked and stole second. Left fielder Biff Carbosi was walked intensionally, and both runner moved up a base on a wild pitch by cardinal started ronnie Miller. Miller was then relieved by Chuck Nelson.

Bluebird secondbaseman Carbo Garbey lined Nelson's first pitch into deep centefield, scoring both baserunners. Two pitches later, Garbey stole home to tie the game.

Nelson got the next 2 hitters out, but then Carey Clark, the bluebird catcher, homered to put the bluebirds ahead. The bluebirds added two more runs in the ninth to insure their victory.

3-7 Using the stylebook

Correct the following story so that it conform with AP style. The story contains other errors besides style errors that you will need to correct. Use the proper editing marks.

Survey

Over half of the nation's high school principles favor some sort of corporal punishment for students who are discipline problems, according to a survey conducted by the American Education Association (A.E.A.)

The survey found that 53% of the principals in the U.S. felt teachers and administrators should have the option of using corporal punishment on students who were discipline problems. 29% of the principals disagreed, saying teachers and administrators should not have this option.

AEA president Virginia Howell said the survey showed that administrators are concerned with discipline and ""want as many options avaiable as possible.

Classroom Discipline, she ssaid, is a continuing problem for many teahers and principals. "The disciplien problem gets in the way of effective teaching, and its not fair to the students who are there to learn." she said.

Miss Howell said the results of the survey indicated that many people are not becoming teachers today because they do'nt want to deal with "the disciplien problems their hearing about in the schools."

3-8 Using the stylebook

Correct the following story so that it conforms with AP style. Use the proper editing marks.

Guilty verdict

A jury found a Midville man guilty of Second-Degree Manslaughter after an hour's worth of deliberations on Tuesday.

Johnny Gene Garber was convicted at the end of a 3-day trial which featured his mother testifying against him. He was charged in the death of a thirty-nine year old brickmason, Gardner Jackson, of Number Twelve, Ninth Street in Jonesville.

Mr. Garber stood sliently as the jury read the verdict. The Presiding Judge, Jonas T. McMillan, set a sentencing hearing for next Monday at eight o'clock in the morning.

Garber was charged with being druck while driving down highway 69 last March. His car served out of control and ran head on into a car driven by Mr. Jackson, who had been attending services at the Midville Baptist church.

During the trial, the Prosecution Attory, Able Sasson, called Garber's mother, Mrs. Minnie Lee Garber, to testify that her son had been drinking heavily at there home that evening before the accident occured.

Garber could recieve a sentence of two to five years in prison for the crime he committed.

3-9 Using the stylebook

Correct the following story so that it conforms with AP style. The story contains other errors besides style errors that you will need to correct. Use the proper editing marks.

City council

The city council passed an ordinance last night requireing people convicted of their second drunk charge to serve a minimum of thirty days in jail and to have their driver's license suspended for six months.

The ordinance was passed by a vote of five to three.

Councilman Clarissa Atwell sponsored the change in the law which wil take effect on December 31st of this year.

"I think this new law will save the lives of a lot of people, Miss Atwell said.

The council chamber was filled to overflowing with people interested in the law. Many of the people there were members of Mothers Against Drunk Driving (M.A.D.D.)

One Councilamn who voted against law, Les Honeycutt, said he felt the laws against drunk driving were strong enough and that they needed to be inforced for rigidly. His comments received hoots and jeers from the crowd, and at one point the council president, Harley Sanders, trhreatened to have some of the audience removed and evicted.

3-10 Using the stylebook

Correct the following story so that it conforms with AP style. Use the proper editing marks.

Power failure

Power was cut off to nearly a 3rd of the residents of Midville, last night, after a violent storm ripped through the city around six o'clock.

Police chief Robert Dye said that power was restored to most homes within about two hours, but "a substantial number of people," had to go without power for most of the night.

Chief Dye said that many of the city's traffic lights were knocked out by the storm, and traffick problems developed on several of the more busy streets.

Chief dye says that everything should be back to normal today.

A Power company official said that more than 1500 homes were without electricity for some part of the night. They said that crews worked throughout the entire night to get people's power turned on.

The storm dumped over 2 inches of rain on the city in about 30 minutes. The power failure was due to lighting hitting one of the power companys substations in the Western part of the city.

4

The News Story

News is one of the elements that holds a society of diverse and scattered people together. The fact that a group of individuals share the same information—and that the information is current—allows the group to operate as a community. If we were a society of hermits, or if we dealt with only the small group of people we have physical contact with, news might not matter so much. Our business and interests extend far beyond the group of acquaintances we have, however, and one of the ways we establish relationships with those beyond our acquaintance is to understand that we share the same current information.

This centrality of news makes the news story a fundamental form of writing for the mass media. The news story is one of the basic ways in which we share information through the mass media. Those who would use the mass media for any purpose should first understand and master the news story format. This is the first step in mastering all forms of writing for the mass media.

Writing for the mass media is one of the most important jobs in our society. People who do this job are the keepers of records and the recorders of events, and they have a tremendous impact on the shape and direction of the community. These people tell us about ourselves. They establish a bond between the individual members of the society and the community and nation as a whole. The people who choose this profession must be honest, talented, and dedicated. The job is too important and too difficult for people of lesser qualities.

In this chapter we will discuss the news story as it is most commonly defined and understood by the industries of the mass media. Our focus here will be on what goes into making the news story. Here we should think of news and information in a broad way. News is not only something that appears in a newspaper or on television; it is also information that appears in a company's newsletter or employee magazine. Advertising is also a form of news in that it deals with delivering information about a product or service (although the form of writing advertising copy is different from the news story, as we shall see in Chapter 7).

The writer for the mass media has two jobs. The first is gathering information; the second is putting that information into the form appropriate for the medium in which he or she is working. This chapter will concentrate on that first job because an understanding of the defining and gathering of news is essential to the writing process. In the following chapters, we will discuss the most common forms of writing for the mass media.

News: the front line

Learning what a news story is and how to write it is the starting point for anyone who is interested in working for the mass media. The content of the mass media is centered around the dissemination of news and information. That makes knowledge of newswriting important in its own right, but there are other reasons for understanding the way a news story is written. The news story is a basic form of writing for the mass media. It demands simple, straightforward prose, clear thinking, and complete understanding of the subject on the part of the writer as well as conciseness and precision in the use of the language. All forms of writing for the mass media demand these same things. That's why we start with news. Knowing how to write news will help you with your basic writing skills and will help you to become a better advertising copywriter, television production person, or public relations consultant.

News in our society is built on some traditional **news values** which beginning students need to understand. These news values are the basis on which journalists decide whether or not an event is news. There are millions of "events" which occur in our society every day. Only those few events which editors select and which have at least one of the following criteria can be classified as news.

Impact. Events that affect people's lives are classified as news. The event itself might involve only a few people, but the consequences may be wide-ranging. For example, if Congress passes a bill to raise taxes or if a researcher discovers a cure for a form of cancer, both actions will affect larger numbers of people. They have impact, and they would be considered news.

Timeliness. Timeliness is a value common to almost all news stories. It refers to the recency of an event. Without the element of timeliness, most events cannot be considered news. For example, a trial that occurred last year is not news; a trial that is going on right now may be news. How much time has to elapse before an event can no longer be considered news? No one answer to that question applies to every case. Most events that are more than a day to a day and a half old are not thought to be news. (Look in today's newspaper and see if you can find a news story about an event that occurred two days ago.)

Prominence. Prominent people, sometimes even when they are doing trivial things, make news. The president of the United States is a prime example. Whenever he takes a trip—even for purely personal and private reasons—his movements are covered in great detail by the news media. The president is a prominent and important person. Anything he does is likely to have an impact on the country, and people are very interested in his actions. The president is not the only example of a prominent person who often makes news. Movie stars, famous politicians, advocates of social causes—all of these people make news simply because they are very well known.

Proximity. Events that occur close to home are more likely to be news than the same events that occur elsewhere. For example, a car wreck killing two people that happens on a road in our home county is more likely to be reported in the local news media than the same kind of wreck which occurs 1,000 miles away. We are interested in the things that happen around us. If we know a place where something goes on, we are more likely to picture that event and have a feeling for it and for the people involved.

Conflict. When people disagree, when they fight, when they have arguments—that's news, particularly if one of the other news values, such as prominence, is involved. Conflict is one of the journalist's favorite news values because it generally ensures that there is an interesting story to write. One of the reasons that trial stories are so popular with newspaper readers and television watchers is that the central drama involves conflict—two competing forces, each vying to defeat the other.

The bizarre or unusual. A rare event is sometimes considered news. There is an adage in journalism that goes something like this: "When a dog bites a man, that's not news; when a man bites a dog, now that's news." These events, though they may have relatively little importance or involve obscure people, are interesting to readers and enliven a publication. For example, it's not news when someone's driver's license is revoked (unless that someone is a prominent person); it is news, however, when a state department of transportation revokes the license of a person called "the worst driver in the state" because he had 22 accidents in the last two years.

Currency. Issues that have current interest often have news value, and events surrounding those issues can sometimes be considered news. For example, a panel discussion of doctors may be held in your community. Normally, such a discussion might not provoke much interest from journalists. If the discussion topic were "The Morality of Abortion," the news value of the event would change, and there would likely be a number of newspaper, radio, and television journalists covering it. Issues that have the value of currency come and go, but there are always several such issues being discussed by the public.

A news writer must make decisions about the events he or she covers based on these news values. They should be used in deciding the kind of information needed for a story and in helping the writer structure the story so that the most important and interesting information gets to the reader in the most efficient manner.

Gathering the news: 5 Ws and 1 H

A journalist gathering information or writing a story tries to answer six basic questions for the reader:

Who. Who are the important people related to the story? Is everyone included so that the story can be accurately and adequately told? Is everyone properly identified?

What. What is the major action or event of the story? What are the actions or events of lesser importance? A journalist ought to be able to state the major action of the story in one sentence, and this should be the theme of the story.

When. When did the event occur? Readers of news stories should have a clear idea of when the story takes place. The when element is rarely the best way to begin a story because it is not often the most important piece of information a journalist has to tell a reader, but it should come early in the story and should be clearly stated.

Where. Where did the event occur? Journalists cannot assume that readers will know or be able to figure out where an event takes place. The location or locations of the event or action should be clearly written.

Why and How. The reader deserves explanation about events. If a story is about something bizarre or unusual, the writer should offer some explanation, so that the questions the event raises in the reader's mind are answered. The writer also needs to set the events or actions in a story in the proper context. Reference should be made to previous events or actions if they help to explain things to the reader.

Sources of information

Now that we have discussed the most basic elements that go into defining news, one of the next logical questions is, Where does the information in a news story come from? A news reporter has three fundamental sources of information for a news story: people, records (any information that is written or stored so others may find it), and personal observation.

Most information in most news stories comes from **personal sources**—that is, people. A news reporter is likely to spend most of his or her nonwriting time talking to people either personally or over the telephone. In fact, many would argue that the more people the reporter talks to, the better the story is likely to be because of the variety of information and views the reporter can obtain.

Here are some examples of paragraphs from news stories in which the information comes from personal sources:

```
According to the theater owner, Martin Mill-
er, about 340 attended the first-night show-
ing of the controversial film.
```

> Although he attended the inauguration, the
> congressman said he disapproved of the amount
> of money spent on the event.

> "I'm against that proposal because it's un-
> fair to the middle class," the senator said.

The first two of the examples are indirect quotations (often referred to as "quotes"), or paraphrases; the third is a direct quotation. We'll discuss the handling of direct and indirect quotations in the next chapter.

When a reporter talks to a source, it's called interviewing. This is a skill that must be carefully cultivated if the reporter is to be effective. A reporter tries to determine what information the source has and would be willing to share. Then the reporter attempts to ask the kind of questions that would elicit this information.

To make this job easier, reporters will develop sources among the people whom they contact regularly; that is, the reporters will find people who have information and are willing to talk with the reporter about it. Reporters soon realize that many people can provide them with information and sometimes that information can come from surprising sources. For instance, most reporters who are assigned to a beat—a term in journalism meaning a place or topic a reporter must write regularly about— learn that secretaries, rather than their bosses, are the best sources of information. Secretaries often know what is happening before their bosses do. Consequently, many reporters get to know the secretaries on their beats very well. As reporters and sources deal with each other, they should develop a relationship of mutual understanding. Reporters find out whom they can trust among their sources, and sources realize that the information they give to reporters will be used wisely.

One general rule governs the relationships that reporters have with their sources—reporters should always identify themselves clearly to their sources. Sources should know before they talk to reporters that the information they give may be used in a news story. Sources should have the opportunity not to talk with news reporters if they do not want to.

he second major source of information for the news reporter is **observation.** Whenever possible, news reporters like to attend the events they are writing about. They like to see for themselves what happens, even though they rarely write from a first-person point of view. Here are some examples of news reports that have used observational sources:

> The state premier of the controversial
> film *The Last Temptation of Christ* was shown
> with little disruption Friday evening, de-
> spite a handful of demonstrators who picketed
> in front of the Capri Theater.
> The demonstrators picketed the film be-
> cause it depicts Christ having sexual hallu-
> cinations on the cross.

> San Francisco's Mike Cofer kicked a 14-
> yard field goal in the first period, and Cin-
> cinnati's Jim Breech had a 34-yarder in the
> second period to account for the second-

> lowest scoring first half in Super Bowl his-
> tory.

> The packed courtroom listened in a hushed
> silence as the defendant took the witness
> stand and began to tell her story.

In each of these cases, it is clear that the reporters attended the events they described. The thing that lets us know this is the lack of attribution in each of these paragraphs. Attribution in a news story means telling readers where information comes from. Attribution phrases are those such as "he said," "she said," and "according to officials." Most of the major information in a news story needs to have some attribution. (Attribution is another topic we'll discuss more in the next chapter.) If some information is not attributed to some source, it is likely that the reporter gained that information through personal observation.

The third major source of information available to news reporters is records, or **stored sources.** This type of information includes any books, reports, articles, press releases, documents, and computer information to which a reporter has access. Here are some examples of reporters using stored sources:

> Furillo, who died Sunday, played right
> field for the Brooklyn and Los Angeles Dodg-
> ers from 1946 through 1960. He won the NL
> batting title with a .344 average in 1953,
> when he missed the last few weeks of the sea-
> son because of a broken hand he sustained
> during a fight with manager Leo Durocher.

> A City Social Services Department report
> estimated that more than 10,000 people were
> "without permanent or temporary shelter" in
> the city last year.

> A statement issued by the new administra-
> tion said that foreign policy problems would
> be high on the president's agenda.

Stored sources are located in many places—government documents, company records, books, magazines, and so on. A news reporter should be familiar with the holdings of the local public library because that can be a major source of stored information.

In most cases, information that comes from stored sources—like that which comes from personal sources—should be attributed. In two of the foregoing examples, the attribution is clear. Occasionally, as in the first example, the information may either be common knowledge or be available in many references so that telling the reader the source is not that important.

The importance of accuracy

One of the underlying assumptions and goals of a news reporter is accuracy. The attempt to be accurate must govern all of the actions of the the writer, from the way he or she gathers information to the language that is use to convey that information. We have talked in previous chapters about the necessity to use the language accurately and about the attention that a writer must give to the format, style and usage in writing. These details are important because ultimately they help increase the accuracy of the writing that is produced.

This attention to the details of writing should be preceded by an attention to the details of reporting. Developing good habits in gathering information will pay off for the reporter in many ways. In this section, we will discuss some of the things a news reporter must pay particular attention to in gathering and writing information for the mass media.

Spell names correctly. One of the most important possessions a person has is his or her name. The misspelling of a name is more likely to offend someone than almost any other mistake. Consequently, news reporters should take special care to make sure they have the correct spelling for the names they use in their stories. They should never assume they can spell a name correctly. For instance, "John Smith" may really be

John Smithe
John Smythe
John Smyth
Jon Smith

The person whose name you are spelling is the best source for the correct spelling, and you should never be afraid or embarrassed to ask. In fact, asking specifically often demonstrates to the source that you are trying to be careful and might increase the confidence that source has in you.

Checking with the person may not always be possible, however. In that case, telephone directories and city directories are generally reliable sources for correctly spelled names. That's because the people who put these directories together are professionals and understand that they are creating a resource that will be checked by others. Police reports, printed programs and other such material are not reliable sources, and they should not be used for name checking.

Quote your sources correctly. While we will discuss using quoted material more fully in the next chapter, we can begin out thinking about it here. Many people who are used as sources in news reports complain about being "misquoted" or "quoted out of context." Often that is a way for the source to back away from what he or she has said after it has been printed or broadcast.

On the other hand, news reporters do make mistakes, and it is their responsibility—not that of the source—to make sure they have heard and understood what the source has said. The simplest solution to not understanding what the source has said is to ask. Make sure you know not only what words the source has used but the meaning that the source has given to them.

News stories use two kinds of quoted material—direct quotations and indirect quotations. Direct quotations are those words that the source has use to express an idea; those words should be surrounded by quotation marks.

> "I believe the tax reform proposal that the Congress is debating would wreck our economic recovery," the president said.

Indirect quotations, or paraphrases, express what the source said but use different words from those the source used.

> The president expressed his opposition to the tax reform propošal currently before Congress, saying it would hurt the nation's economic recovery.

A paraphrase may use some of the exact words of the source, and the writer may want to put those inside quotation marks.

> The president expressed his opposition to the tax reform proposal currently before Congress, saying it would "wreck our economic recovery."

Get information from more than one source if possible. As a general rule, news stories are better if more sources are used. That's because different people know various things about a situation, or they may have differing viewpoints about it. The more people a news reporter talks to about a story, and the more records that he or she checks, the more likely he or she will be to understand the story fully.

Make sure that the numbers in a story add up correctly. Numbers don't have to throw journalists, but they often do. For instance, consider this paragraph about a student election that appeared in a college newspaper:

> Officials said a total of 5,865 ballots were cast, representing a 34.2 percent turnout. Smith defeated Jones by receiving 3,077 votes to Jones' 2,385, a margin of 393 votes.

The reporter should have done two things with this story. He or she should have added up to the totals for the two candidates to make sure that total matched the total number of ballots cast. If the numbers did not match, the news reporter should have found out why. Second, the story says that "officials" said there was a 34.2 percent turnout. The reporter should have gotten the figures that these officials used and done his or her own calculations. It may be that the 34.2 figure is correct. The reporter should have made sure.

Conclusion

This chapter has given you some idea of what a news story is and of how a news reporter gathers information to put into a news story. Once the news-gathering process is finished, it's time for the news gatherer to become the news writer. We'll discuss that process in the next chapter.

Points for consideration and discussion

1. The author says that writing for the mass media is "one of the most important jobs in our society." Do you agree or disagree?

2. Look at three news stories in your local newspaper. What news values are present in each of them?

3. One of the criticisms of the news media that many people make is that journalists emphasize "bad news" rather than "good news." What do you think that people mean by that? Do you agree? Do the news values listed in this chapter mean that journalists are more likely to look for "bad news" than "good news?"

4. The author says that secretaries are often good sources of information. Can you think of other job categories that would make good sources for journalists?

5. Why is it important for a journalist to get information from more than one source?

Further reading

Fred Fedler, *Reporting for the Print Media*, 3rd Ed., New York: Harcourt Brace Jovanovich, 1984.

Julian Harriss, Kelly Leiter, and Stanley Johnson, *The Complete Reporter*, 4th Ed., New York: Macmillan, 1981.

Ralph S. Izard, Hugh M. Culbertson, and Donald A. Lambert, *Fundamentals of News Reporting*, 4th Ed., Dubuque: Kendall/Hunt, 1983.

Bruce D. Itule and Douglas A. Anderson, *News Writing and Reporting for Today's Media*, New York: Random House, 1987.

Ken Metzler, *Newsgathering*, Englewood Cliffs, NJ: Prentice-Hall, 1979.

EXERCISES

This chapter introduces the student to the news story. It talks about the elements of a news story and how a news story is put together. The exercises in this chapter consist of analyzing news stories in light of the various items we discussed in this chapter. Three complete news stories are presented here. Follow your instructor's direction in answering the following questions about them.

1. What are the news values that are present in each of the stories?

2. List the **who, what, when, where, why,** and **how** elements of each story.

3. Which of the three major types of sources of information are used in these stories?

4. List the sources specifically mentioned in each story. How do you think that the reporters were able to get this information?

5. Based on your limited knowledge about the events, analyze each of the stories for accuracy. Are there points in the story that might not be accurate? If you were the editor, what would you question? What would you want the reporter to double-check?

Story No. 1- Crash

LISBON, Portugal (AP) — An American charter jet filled with Italian tourists slammed into a fog-covered mountain in the Azores today and exploded, and all 144 people on board were feared dead, officials and news reports said.

Maria della Versesi, a spokeswoman at the Italian Embassy in Lisbon, said all 137 passengers were Italian and the seven crew members were American. She did not release any names. The aircraft belonged to the U.S. airline Independent Air Corp., based in Smyrna, Tenn.

The flight originated in Bergamo, Italy, and was to have proceeded to Puerto Plata in the Dominican Republic, and Montego Bay in Jamaica, after making a refueling stop in the Azores.

The Portuguese news agency LUSA quoted an official from the Azores Civil Protection Service as saying about 50 bodies had been recovered and it appeared all on board died. LUSA also quoted an unidentified member of a local flying club as saying all the passengers and crew had been killed.

Afonso Pimentel, a LUSA reporter based in the Azores, said the Boeing 707 was preparing to land at Santa Maria airport when it crashed into Pico Alto, a fog-covered, 1,794-foot-high mountain, and burst into flames. LUSA quoted the civil protection official, who was not identified, as saying the pilot asked the airport to clear a runway for an emergency landing.

The Civil Protection Service is a state body that provides rescue services and assistance in civilian emergencies. A.L. Pittman, president of Independent Air Corp., said in an interview in Smyrna that the 15-year-old company makes 400 to 500 charter flights a year, mostly in the Caribbean and Europe.

Pittman, who declined to identify the seven American crew members, said the 20-year-old jetliner that crashed had a relatively low number of flight hours and no history of trouble. Pittman said the airplane, one of two Boeing 707s owned by the company, had 12,500 cycles, or takeoffs and landings, and less than 50,000 hours in the air.

Jack Barker, spokesman for the Federal Aviation Administration in Atlanta, said those figures were not unusually high for such an airplane.

Story No. 2-3-pointer

ENTERPRISE, Ala. (AP) — Gwen Smith's favorite shot is the 3-pointer.

Last week, the 5-foot-10 senior guard at Coffee Springs High School in Geneva County hit 11 of the long-range shots to set a new national high school record.

Bruce Howard, record book editor for the National Federation of State High School Associations in Kansas City, Mo., said Wednesday the previous girls' record of 10 3-pointers in a game was held jointly by players in Louisiana and Florida.

Smith, who connected on 11 of 16 3-pointers in the 75-32 victory over G.W. Long last Friday night, said she spends a lot of time at practice working on her outside shooting.

"One thing that helps me is the 3-point drill," said Smith, who scored a career-high 52 points in the game. "In each practice, we shoot about 20 each, and my favorite shot is the 3-pointer."

"She had a good night," Coffee Springs Coach Trey Holladay told The Enterprise Ledger. "She plays well on defense and plays down low. But on offense she plays guard because she can handle the ball and shoot so well."

The old state record for 3-pointers was held by Katrina Davidson of Buckhorn, who hit nine last year in toe Class 5A playoffs.

Story No. 3 – Gooden

NEW YORK (AP) — Dwight Gooden became the highest-paid player in baseball this year and the highest-paid player in the history of the New York Mets when he agreed Wednesday to a three-year contract worth $6.7 million.

Gooden, who made $1.4 million in 1988 after losing in arbitration, will get a $500,000 signing bonus, $2.25 million this year, $1.7 million in 1990, and $2.25 million in 1991, a source familiar with the negotiation told The Associated Press.

Including a prorated share of the signing bonus, Gooden will receive $2,416,667 this season, topping the salary of Minnesota Twins third baseman Gary Gaetti, who will get $2.4 million. But Gaetti will get $500,000 in 1990, the season that may be disrupted by a player strike or an owners' lockout.

The highest salary ever paid by the Mets previously was to catcher Gary Carter, who made about $2.3 million last season, including deferred money.

Gooden can make an additional $290,000 each year in bonuses. He would get $100,000 for winning the Cy Young Award and $50,000 for finishing second through fifth. He would get $100,000 if named Most Valuable Player of the World Series and $50,000 if named MVP of the playoffs.

He also would get $25,000 if selected for the All-Star Game and $15,000 if he wins a Gold Glove. Gooden was 18-9 last season with a 3.19 earned-run average and 175 strikeouts in 248 1-3 innings. In the playoffs, he failed to win in both his starts, allowing a two-run ninth inning homer to Mike Scioscia in Game 4. The Mets went on to lose the game in 12 innings and lost to Los Angeles in seven games.

Gooden, the 1984 National League rookie of the year and the 1985 NL Cy Young Award winner, is 91-35 in five major league seasons. He would have been eligible for free agency after the 1989 season. He missed the first two months of the 1987 season after cocaine was detected in his urine. He spent April 1987 at a drug rehabilitation center in New York and another month training in the minor leagues.

He was 5-7 after he returned and last winter went to salary arbitration, where he requested $1.65 million and lost.

5

Writing for Print

The person who writes for the mass media always works at two jobs: gathering information and putting that information into an acceptable form—that is, writing. In the previous chapter we discussed the information that is necessary for a news story and some of the ways that a news reporter gathers that information. Having the proper information—all the relevant facts of a story, the people involved, the times and dates, quotes, etc.—is vital to the writing process, but it is only the beginning. There comes a time when the information gathering must cease and the writing must begin.

The ability to write well requires that the writer have a thorough knowledge and understanding of the news event. In addition, the writer must understand the basic structure of the news story and the conventions or customs of news writing in order to complete the process.

In this chapter we will examine the structures and conventions of writing that are acceptable for the most basic of all writing for the mass media—the news story. The focus of this chapter is writing a story as if it would appear on the pages of a newspaper. Students of the mass media need to learn this form even if they never plan to work for a newspaper or to be reporters. Mastering the news story is the first step on the road to mastering all writing for the mass media.

The inverted pyramid

Once a writer has gathered the information necessary to begin a story, he or she must decide on the structure of the story. The goal of a proper structure is to get information to the reader quickly and to allow the reader to move through the story easily. The reader must be able to see the relationships between the various pieces of information that the reporter has gathered.

The most common structure for writing news stories is called the inverted pyramid. The daily newspaper contains many stories. Most stories must be written so that readers can get the most information in the least time. The inverted pyramid structure concentrates the most interesting and important information at the top of the story so that readers can get the information they need or want for a story and then can go on to another story if they choose to. Headlines and leads should be written to describe what the story contains as succinctly and as interestingly as possible.

The lead, or first paragraph, is the focal point of the basic news story. It is a simple statement of the point of the entire story. It should be written as simply as possible and should contain as many of the five Ws as can be easily understood. We'll discuss lead paragraphs more fully in the next section of this chapter.

The body of the inverted pyramid story adds detail to information

Figure 5-1
This depiction of the inverted pyramid structure for news stories shows how the important information in the story comes at the beginning, and information of lesser importance comes later.

The Inverted Pyramid

Nursing graduates at the State University turned in their worst-ever performance on the February national licensing exam, with only 58 percent passing.

In the inverted pyramid structure, the first paragraph tells the most important information in the story.

It was the second time in the last three exams that about 40 percent of the University's nursing graduates failed the test. In February 1988, 62 percent passed, while 83 percent in July.

The statewide passing rate for first-time candidates from the eight state schools who took the exam is 79 percent, according to Stan Linder, executive director of the State Board of Nursing.

The second and third paragraphs follow up on the information by expanding on the lead and adding information that is of lesser importance to the story.

The exam to become a registered nurse "measuressafe, competent nursing" at the entry level, Pearl Bones, dean of the University's College of Nursing, said.

The percentage of University students who failed the test was nearly four times the national average.

As the story continues, more information is added, but it is of lesser importance and serves to support the information at the top of the story.

that has been introduced in the lead and the first two or three paragraphs. The body should provide more information, supporting evidence, context, and illumination in the form of more details, direct and indirect quotes, and other description.

The major concept of the inverted pyramid structure is to put the most important and latest information toward the top of the story. As the story continues, the writer should be using information of less importance. There are two reasons for writing a story this way. One is what we have already talked about: Putting the most important information at the top allows a reader to decide quickly whether or not to stick with the story.

It also organizes the information in such a way that the reader can be efficient. Not every reader will read all of every story in a newspaper. In fact, one of the strengths of a newspaper is that it offers a wide variety of information that will appeal to many people. The inverted pyramid structure for news stories allows the readers to get as much of the most important information in that story as quickly as possible; it also allows the readers to stop reading and go on to something else when they have satisfied themselves with that story.

This process would not be possible if all stories were written chronologically. Very often, what happens at or near the end of the story is the most important or interesting thing to the reader. Readers are not accustomed to wading through a lot of less important or interesting information to get to these parts. Consider a story that begins with the following paragraphs:

> The City Council opened its meeting last night with a prayer from the Rev. Jonathan Fowler, pastor of the Canterbury Episcopal Church.
>
> The minutes of the previous meeting were read and accepted without changes.
>
> Mayor H.L. Johnson then called for a report from the city budget director, Hiram Lewis, who said that property tax collections were running behind what had been expected when the budget was adopted last year.
>
> "If property tax collections continue at this rate, the city will be facing a major deficit," he said.
>
> When Councilmember Fred Greenburg asked what that meant, Lewis replied that the city would have to borrow money or cut back on some of its services.
>
> Johnson then proposed that the council raise the property tax rate by 5 percent for most property owners. The new rates would go into effect next year and would last for only one year, he said. This increase would allow the city to continue operating without any cutbacks in service.
>
> Council member Marge Allen objected to the increase, saying the citizens of her dis-

```
trict already had too many taxes to pay. She
also said that an increase in the property
tax would discourage industries from locating
in the city. . . .
```

Think about the reader of that story who is a property owner in the city. Most likely, that person is asking, "Are my taxes going up?" The reader should not have to wait for six or more paragraphs to find out the answer to that question. Instead, the answer should come immediately in the first paragraph:

```
The City Council voted against raising
property taxes 5 percent last night, despite
warning from officials that the city faces a
cutback in services unless it gets more mon-
ey.
```

Another reason for the inverted pyramid structure is a technical one. When stories are prepared for printing, they are set in type and laid out on a page. An editor must decide how to fit stories together on a page. Sometimes stories will be longer than the space allotted for them. If this is the case, an editor will try to cut a story from the bottom, knowing that if the story is written properly, none of the essential facts will be lost.

The inverted pyramid structure is the most commonly used structure in print journalism. It is a structure which the beginning student must master before proceeding very far in the profession. It demands that the writer make judgments about the importance of the information that he or she has gathered—judgments based on the news values discussed earlier in this chapter.

The inverted pyramid structure, though it is the most common, is not the only type of story structure that can be used in news writing. There are several others, which we will discuss in the next few paragraphs. These structures are not rigid. If one style alone won't do, a writer should search for combinations of styles which will best fit the information and ideas he or she is trying to organize.

The lead paragraph

The most important part of the news story is the first, or lead (pronounced LEED), paragraph. The first job of the lead is to tell the reader the most important information in the story. Beyond that, however, the lead should be written so that the reader will be interested in going further into the story. Let's go back to the example of the city council story in the previous section. A lead on that story might simply say:

```
The City Council voted against raising
property taxes last night.
```

That is certainly the most important information in this story, but it does little to invite the reader to continue reading. A lead should do more, as the following one does:

```
     The City Council voted against raising
property taxes 5 percent last night, despite
warning from officials that the city faces a
cutback in services unless it gets more mon-
ey.
```

This one tells the reader, "There was a debate about this matter, and it has some consequences that you might be interested in."

An otherwise good story will not be read by many people if the lead is dull or confusing. The lead is the first part of the story a reader will come in contact with after the headline, and if the lead does not hold the reader's interest and attention, little else will.

In a news story written in the inverted pyramid style, the lead should contain the most important and the latest information that the reporter has. A writer must make a judgment on what to put in a lead based on the news values discussed earlier in this chapter. The writer has the duty to get information to the reader quickly, but that information must be transmitted in an accurate and interesting way. Accuracy, speed, and entertainment are finely balanced in a good lead paragraph.

Leads on news stories generally contain at least four of the five Ws and H that were discussed earlier in this chapter. Those four elements are who, what, where and when. A lead paragraph may emphasize any one of these elements, depending on the facts that are available to the reporter, but usually all four of these questions are answered in the lead. Sometimes the lead will contain or emphasize the way and the how of a story, but stories like this are unusual.

Lead paragraphs should say neither too much nor too little. One of the mistakes that beginning news writers often make is that of trying to put too much in a lead. A led should not be overcrowded with information; rather, it should tell enough to answer the reader's major questions about a story and to do so in an interesting way. If a lead tries to tell the reader too much, it can quickly become boring or confusing.

Leads can come in a wide variety of forms and styles. While journalistic conventions restrict what writers can do in some ways, there is still plenty of room for creativity. The following types of leads and examples demonstrate some of the ways writers can approach a story.

The "straight news" lead is a just-the-facts approach. It delivers information quickly and concisely to the reader, and does not try to dress up the information. For instance:

```
     Two people were killed and four were in-
jured today when a truck collided with a pas-
senger car on Interstate 59 near the Cotton-
dale exit.
```

This straight news approach is the most common type of news lead, and lends itself to most of the stories a reporter will have to cover. Because of this, a couple of technical rules have been developed for this kind of story. Such leads should be one sentence long, and they should contain about 30 words (a maximum of 33 words). It is particularly important for the beginning writer to master this one-sentence, 30-word approach because of the discipline of thinking that it requires. A writer must learn that words cannot be wasted, particularly at the beginning of the story.

The "summary" lead is one in which there may be more than one major fact to be covered. Again, the one-sentence, 30-word approach should be used even though such an approach may require even more effort on the part of the writer. For example:

```
A tanker-trailer truck carrying dangerous
chemicals crashed on Interstate 59 today,
killing one person, injuring four others, and
forcing the evacuation of several hundred
people from their homes.
```

Again, the emphasis in this kind of lead is on getting information accurately and quickly to the reader. Writers using summary leads need to take care that they do not crowd their leads with too much information

Rewriting Leads

As we stated in the text, the lead paragraph is the most important part of a news story. It should present the reader with the most important information in the story. It should be long enough to give the reader a good idea about what is in the story, but it should be short enough to let the reader get through them quickly. In other words, a lead is not easy to write. Quite often, it takes more than one try to write a good lead. Below on the left are some lead paragraphs as they appeared in print. The writers and editors who produced them did not have the time or make the effort to rewrite them. On the right are rewritten versions that are considerable improvements over the first efforts.

A new law that gives prosecutors additional power to halt the distribution of movies they believe are obscene prompted videotape rental stores in Decatur to pull nearly 2,000 adult films off their shelves.

Rewrite
Owners of videotape rental stores in Decatur have pulled nearly 2,000 tapes off the shelves because of a new law that gives prosecutors more powers to halt the sales of obscene materials.

Several steps are being taken to prevent a repeat of the error that caused an ambulance answering a heart attack call to be sent to the wrong street last week, the Emergency 911 board of directors was told Tuesday.

Rewrite
Emergency 911 is taking several steps to make sure that ambulances are sent to the correct addresses, according to testimony before the E-911 board.

Civilian unemployment, rising at the fastest clip in more than three years, jumped to 5.3 percent last month, the government said Friday in a report that was taken as the strongest evidence yet of an economic slowdown.

Rewrite
Unemployment is up to 5.3 percent, the steepest rise in three years, according to a government report, and many economists believe that is the strongest sign yet of an economic slowdown.

and that they do not generalize too much. A balance should be achieved between including enough detail to make the story interesting and enough general material to avoid confusing the reader.

Up to this point, we have been dealing with **straight** leads for the most part. Straight leads give the who, what, when, where, and why elements of the story to the reader in a straightforward, no-frills fashion. Other types of leads exist, however, and the good news writer should be aware of when they can be used most effectively.

The **blind** lead is a lead in which none of the people in the story are named. The two previous examples are blind leads. This kind of lead is common when the people in the story are not well known. In the last lead about the accident, we assume that none of the people involved in the accident are well known. If one of the people hurt was the mayor of the city, we would not want to write a blind lead. We would want to mention his name in the lead.

The **direct address** lead is one in which the writer speaks directly to the reader. The main characteristic of this lead is the word **you,** present or implied.

```
     If gardening is your hobby, you'll need
to know about Tom Smith.

     If you're a property owner in the city, the
City Council is about to take at least $50
more from you each year.
```

The direct address lead is a good way of getting the reader's attention, but it should be used sparingly. It is also important to follow up a direct address lead quickly in the second and third paragraphs with information about the lead. By implication, the direct address lead promises the reader some immediate information.

The **question** lead attempts to draw the reader into the story by asking a question.

```
     Do you really want to know how hot dogs are
made?

     Why doesn't the president tell Congress
how he stands on the pay increase issue?
```

The question lead has some of the same advantages and disadvantages as the direct address lead. It is a good way of getting the attention of the reader. On the other hand, it can easily be overused. It, too, promises to give the reader some immediate information, and the writer should make good on that promise.

The direct address and the question lead also imply that the story has some compelling information for the reader. That's why writers should be careful to use them only when that is the case. Otherwise, the reader will likely be disappointed.

The **direct quote** lead uses a direct quotation to introduce the story and to gain the reader's attention. The direct quote, of course, should be something that one of the participants in the story said, and it should be compelling and informative enough to serve as the lead.

```
        "Read my lips. No new taxes."
        That's what presidential candidate George
    Bush promised today as he hit the campaign
    trail in . . .
```

Any of these leads can be used when a writer feels that the facts of a story warrant their use. Writers should be careful, however, not to use one of these leads simply for the sake of using something different and not to use them when a story does not lend itself to their use.

Developing the story

The inverted pyramid requires that writers make judgments not only about what should be at the beginning of the story but also about the relative importance of all of the information they present in the story. In other words, writers must then decide what the most important information is for the lead, but they must also decide what the second and third most important pieces of information are. Developing the story in a logical and coherent way requires much skill and practice.

If the lead paragraph is the most important part of the news story, the second paragraph is the second most important part of the story. In some ways, it is almost as important as the lead but for different reasons.

A lead paragraph cannot contain all of the information in a news story. If it is written well, it will inform the reader, but it will also raise certain questions in the reader's mind about the story. Chief among the roles of the second (and succeeding) paragraphs is to answer these questions. The writer does this by providing additional information about the story. The writer must decide what information is most important and what will help the reader to understand the story.

One method that writers use to make these judgments is to put themselves in the place of the reader and ask, "If I were a reader of this story, what would I want to know next?" For instance, a lead might say

```
        Authorities are searching for a state
    prison inmate who escaped from a work crew at
    the Kidder Correctional Facility yesterday.
```

That lead gives us some information about the story, but it also raises a number of questions, such as:
Who was the inmate?
Why was he in prison?
How long had he been there and how long was his sentence?
How did he escape?
Where is the search for him taking place?
Is the inmate dangerous?
What does he look like?
How have the prison officials explained his escape?

These are just a few of the questions that could be asked about this story. The writer must answer these questions in a logical and coherent manner that will result in a unified and interesting story. The order in which these questions are answered will depend on the specific information that the writer has to work with.

The writer will probably want to give the name of the inmate quickly and the circumstances of the escape. Beyond that, the type of information the writer has will dictate the order in which the questions are answered. For instance, the second paragraph might go something like this:

> Billy Wayne Hodge, 22, who was convicted two years ago for armed robbery, walked away from his work crew yesterday afternoon at about 3 p.m., according to prison officials. The crew was picking up trash along Highway 69 about four miles from the prison at the time of the escape.

This paragraph answers some of the questions but leaves others unanswered. Even though a second paragraph can be longer than the lead, it still cannot answer all of the questions a lead can raise. Now the writer will have to decide what questions he or she will answer in the third paragraph. Again, those decisions will be based on the kind of information the writer has. The writer might want to say something about the search for the prisoner. For instance:

> Sheriff Will Harper said last night that he thought the prisoner was still in the thick woods in the area of the escape. He said deputies would patrol the area tonight and a full-scale search would begin early today.

Or the writer may expand on the circumstances of the escape:

> "It appears that one of our guards wasn't watching the prisoners as closely as he should have been," Sam Mayer, the prison warden, said. "There were 15 men in the work crew and only two guards."

Either choice might be correct, depending on the circumstances of the story and the writer's preference. Still, the writer has not answered all of the questions raised by the lead, but the story is becoming more complete.

The following is another example of the way in which a story can be developed:

An automobile accident occurs on a busy street in your city. Three cars are involved. The driver of one of the cars is arrested for drinking and driving. One person is killed and another is seriously injured. The accident occurred during the afternoon rush and tied up traffic for more than an hour.

A reporter covering that accident would get all of the information listed above plus other details. Of all of these facts, however, which one would you say is the most important? Which one would rank as the second most important fact? the third?

Death and personal injury are usually considered the most important facts in a story such as this one. The fact that one person was killed and another seriously injured would be the most important thing that the reporter would have to tell the readers.

The reporter would then have to decide what the second most important fact was. It could be that the arrest of one of the drivers would be second in the mind of the reporter, especially since drinking and driving is in the news a lot these days. Or it might be that the reporter would think that traffic being tied up for so long on a busy street was the second most important fact; a lot of people (and possibly many readers) would have been affected by the traffic jam. A reporter would have to decide about this, and about the other information he or she would gather.

If the fact that one person was killed and another seriously injured is the most important fact, the reporter will want to use that fact to start the lead. But what else will be in the lead? Think about the "what," "when," and "where" or the story. If we put all those things together in one sentence, it might come out like this:

> One person was killed and another seri-
> ously injured in a three-car accident Tuesday
> afternoon during rush hour on Chester Street.

What do you think? Is this the best lead that could be written for a story like this one, or can you think of a better approach to this story? (One of the most noticeable problems about the way it is written is that it uses the passive voice—something we try to avoid in writing for the mass media.)

This paragraph above is a serviceable lead, but there may be more that can be done with it. Adding a few more details, such as more identification of the person who was killed, might make it more interesting for the reader. Then we might have the following lead:

> A Centerville man is dead and another
> person seriously injured after a rush hour
> collision on Chester Street on Tuesday after-
> noon.

Or if we wanted to take a different tack and try to work in the fact that one of the drivers was arrested, the lead might read like this:

> One person is dead and another seriously
> injured after a three-car accident on Chester
> Street on Tuesday, and police later arrested
> one of the drivers involved in the collision.

As you can tell from this one example, there are many approaches to even the simplest story. Note some things about each of these examples, however. All of them begin with the most important information—the fact that one person was killed and another injured. All of these are one sentence long and contain 30 words or less. And all use simple, straightforward language to give the reader information. The writer does not try to bowl the reader over with fancy words or phrasing but rather tries to keep the language as simple as possible.

Now for the second and third paragraphs of the story. The reporter would want to give the name and identification of the accident victims and would want to relate a few more details about the events surrounding the accident. A second or third paragraph for this story might read this way:

```
George Smith, 2629 Silver St., was killed
when the car he was driving crashed into a
```

Figure 5-2 Transitions

While each new sentence in a news story should introduce some new information, the story should follow a logical sequence so that the reader is not surprised or shocked. One of the best transitional devices is the use of reference, words that refer to things mentioned previously in the story. Some of the referents in this story are marked and tied together with diagonal lines. Another good transitional device is the use of words that refer to the time sequence of the story. Some of those words are boxed in the story below. Finally, in the sixth paragraph, the word "however" ties that paragraph to the information in the previous two paragraphs.

> A Brownsville woman received a 20-year prison sentence yesterday for her part in a robbery of the Trust National Bank last year.
>
> Anne Yeager, who had lived with her mother on Mine Road before the robbery, wept softly as Circuit Court Judge John Bolus read the verdict to a packed courtroom. The 20-year prison sentence means that she could be eligible for parole in seven years.
>
> Yeager's attorney, Harriette Solomon, said after the court recessed that she was planning to file an appeal.
>
> "I think that we will be able to demonstrate that Miss Yeager was an innocent victim and did not receive a fair trial," Solomon said.
>
> She said the appeal will be filed sometime next week.
>
> District Attorney Ed Sims said, however, that he thought the trial had been a fair one and that Yeager had received the sentence she deserved.
>
> Yeager was convicted last week of first degree robbery for driving the get-away car for her boyfriend, Reggie Holder, after he robbed the bank of almost $29,000 last Dec. 29. Holder was convicted last month of first-degree robbery and also received a 20-year sentence.
>
> Yeager testified during her trial that she drove the car for Holder but that she thought she was simply taking him to the bank to make a deposit and pay some bills.

```
telephone pole after being hit by another
car. His wife, Sylvia Smith, was also injured
in the accident and is in serious condition
in General Hospital, according to hospital
officials.
     Police said they arrested Sam Johnson, 30
Pine Ave., and charged him with driving under
the influence of alcohol in connection with
the accident. Sgt. Roland Langley, the offi-
cer who investigated the accident, said the
car Johnson was driving swerved across the
road and hit the Smith vehicle, driving it
into a telephone pole. A third car was also
hit, but no one in that car was injured.
```

At this point, the writer might want to make the story even more interesting by adding some direct quotations from the news sources.

```
     "A number of witnesses said they saw John-
son's vehicle swerving all over the road, and
it appears that he was going pretty fast,
too," Langley said. The police measured 60-
foot skid marks made by the Johnson vehicle,
Langley added.
     A spokesman for the City Jail said Johnson
was being held pending other charges that
might be lodged against him. A bail hearing
for Johnson was set for today.
```

So far, the story has concentrated on the accident. Now, however, the writer might return to the victims and give more details about them.

```
     Hospital officials said Smith suffered
head injuries, and he died shortly after he
arrived at the hospital. Mrs. Smith also suf-
fered injuries to her head and neck and has
three broken ribs and a broken arm.
     The third car in the accident was driven
by Lester Matson, 406 Altus Drive. Matson
said Johnson's car smashed into his after it
had hit the Smith's car. "There was simply
nothing I could do to get out of the way," he
said. "I saw this car up ahead, swerving all
around the road, but there were cars all
around me, and I couldn't go anywhere." Mat-
son was not hurt, but he said his car was
damaged in the accident.
```

The two examples in this section should give you some idea as to how a news story is developed. That development is based on a series of decisions that the writer must make about the information he or she has. Even with simple stories, these decisions are rarely simple ones. They require that the writer understand the news story structure as well as the facts of a particular story.

In putting together a story, the writer seeks to unify the writing through transitions. We discussed transitions in Chapter 3. (You may want to review that section as you study this one.) Transitions are a way of tying the information together and tipping the reader off as to what may come next. Readers should not be surprised by a brand new subject in the middle of a news story.

If news stories were written chronologically, writers could use chronological transitions, such as "then," "after that," "meanwhile," "next," etc. News stories do not often follow such chronological patterns, however, so the transitions must be more subtle. In news stories, transitions most often come through repeated references to people, things or events in the story. In the figure on page 105, we have taken a news story and graphically demonstrated some of the transitions that are contained within it and how they tie a story together.

How should a news story end? A writer should stop writing when all of the logical questions have been answered and when all of the interesting information has been presented in the story. A writer should not be concerned with concluding or summarizing a story, particularly when he or she is beginning to learn how to write news. Instead, the writer should make sure that the reader can understand and be satisfied with what is written.

Attribution

One of the most important elements in a good news story is proper attribution. Attribution simply means telling readers where the information in a story comes from. As we discussed in Chapter 4, reporters have three major sources of information: personal, stored and observational. The personal sources of information are the people a reporter talks to; they constitute the most common source of information for reporters. One estimate says that about 80 percent of what is printed in a newspaper comes from personal sources. These people may be quoted directly, or a reporter may paraphrase their quotes—that is, put their ideas into a different set of words but still give them credit for saying them. In either case, a reporter must attempt to quote personal sources accurately. Stored sources are those which are written down somewhere. They may include government reports, formal statements and speeches, press releases, articles, books, papers, etc. These sources, too, must be quoted accurately. The third source a reporter has is observational—that which the reporter observes. For this type of information, direct attribution, such as "I saw" or "I heard," is not desirable. A simple description of the event is sufficient, but the information should be written in such a way that the reader will realize that the reporter is the source of the information.

Why is attribution important? The most obvious reason is credibility. Readers are more likely to believe that the publication is trying to be accurate in its reporting if they know clearly the source of the information. News reports in which the information is properly attributed reflect the professionalism of the publication and its reporters.

A second reason for attributing information in a story is to allow the reader to assess the information by assessing its source. Some sources are more credible than others. By telling the reader where information comes from, the news reporter is letting the reader make up his or her mind as to whether the information can be believed.

Beginning news writers sometimes have trouble with attribution be-

Verbs of Attribution

Said is a word that connotes only the fact that words were spoken or written. It says nothing about the way the words were spoken, the circumstances of the utterance, or the attitude of the speaker. The word is a modest one, never calling attention to itself. It can be used repeatedly without disruption to the writing.

Consequently, there are few real substitutes for **said.** There are words you can use in its place, however, when it is proper for you to do so.

Explain means that more facts are being added to make something more understandable. It can be a neutral synonym for **said,** but it must be used in the right context. It is incorrect to write: The presidency is the nation's most important office," he said. "George Bush is our current president," he explained.

Point out means to call attention to a matter of fact. A speaker can point out that grass is green, but a journalist should not write: The majority leader pointed out that the president was tough in standing up to the communists. That statement is opinion, not fact.

State should be used for formal speeches or announcements such as the State of the Union address in January. It is incorrect to write: Smith stated that the party would begin at 8 p.m.

Declare, like **state**, implies formality.

Add indicates more facts or comment about the same subject or an afterthought, a comment less important than what has been said before. It is incorrect to write: She said she was unable to finish her paper. "My typewriter was broken," she added.

Revealed and **disclosed** are suitable only when referring to something that previously was unknown or concealed.

Relate means to pass along facts. It implies an absence of opinion on the part of the speaker.

Exclaim means to cry out in surprise or sudden emotion. It can easily be overused, so writers should be careful. It is usually written with an exclamation point. It is incorrect to use it in the following way: "The meeting will be at 3 p.m.," she exclaimed.

Assert implies formality, but it also implies an intensity on the part of the speaker.

cause it can occasionally be awkward to work into a sentence. In most cases, however, the attribution can be included in a natural or unobtrusive way. Look at these examples:

```
        The mayor said the city is facing a bud-
    get crisis.

        According to the police report, the car
    skidded 50 feet before stopping.

        The grand jury's report will be announced
    tomorrow, the prosecutor said.
```

Most of the major facts in a news story should be attributed to some source (unless they come from an eyewitness account by the reporter), but writers can attribute too much as well as too little.

Writers can go overboard in attributing facts in their stories. Information that is common knowledge to most readers usually does not have to be attributed. For instance, in the sentence, "A heavy cloud of smog hung over the city today, National Weather Service officials said," the attribution is unnecessary and even silly. As in many other aspects of writing, a balance should be struck. Too much attribution will get in the way of a story; too little attribution will harm the credibility of the story and confuse the reader. The good writer wants neither of these things to happen.

Many writers, particularly beginning journalists, complain that the word **said** is used too much in news stories. It is a colorless word which does not add much to the life of the copy. With this thought in mind, many writers begin the tortuous search for adequate substitutes for **said.** Surely, they think, the English language can come up with at least a few good words to use in its place.

While English does have many words that can describe the way words are spoken, there is no word that does the job the way **said** does it. **Said** is a neutral word. It simply connotes that words have been spoken; it doesn't say anything about the way in which they were spoken. Consequently, it is the kind of word that journalists ought to be using. Another point in the word's favor is that **said** is fairly unobtrusive in a news story. Even if used repeatedly, it does not jump out at the reader and get in the way of the information that is being transmitted.

Trying to find substitutes for the **said** is a dangerous game for the beginning journalist. While there are many words that might be used in its place, writers should remember that they must use words for their exact meaning, not simply for variety's sake. Too often writers misuse these substitutes and create erroneous impressions about what was said. Another danger in the search for substitutes for **said** is that most substitutes are not neutral. If used, they make a statement about how the journalist feels about what was said. For instance, a person accused of a crime may "say" that he is innocent, or he may "claim" that he is innocent. That second verb carries a more negative or doubtful connotation, one which the journalist should not be implying.

Direct and indirect quotations

A news writer must understand the relationship between direct and indirect quotations in a news story. Because most information for most news stories comes from personal sources—that is, people that a reporter talks to—that information appears in a news story in two forms: direct and indirect quotes. (**Quotes** is often used in journalism as the shortened form of **quotations**.) A direct quote is the actual words that a person has spoken, and they are set off in a sentence by quotation marks ("). An indirect quote, or paraphrase, relates what a speaker has said but does not use the actual words that a speaker uses. Indirect quotes do not have quotation marks setting them off from the rest of a sentence.

What do we mean when we say "understanding the relationship between direct and indirect quotations in a news story"? A good news story often has a mixture of direct and indirect quotes, and a news writer must have a good sense of when to use a direct or an indirect quote. In the following paragraphs, we'll give you some guidelines.

Most news stories will use more indirect quotes than direct quotes, so let's look at them first. An indirect quote may contain one or a few of the same words that a speaker has used, but unless it has exactly what a speaker has said, it is still an indirect quote. You should never put quotation marks around that something that a person has not said.

What you strive to do with indirect quotes is to maintain the meaning of what the speaker has said but to use fewer words than the speaker has used. If you are a competent writer, you will quickly learn that most people use more words than necessary to say what they have to say. As a good writer, you can probably paraphrase what people say more efficiently than they can themselves. And as a news writer, you will find that you can get more information into your story if you use indirect quotes.

If that is the case, why worry about using direct quotes at all? Why not just use indirect quotes all of the time?

Direct quotes can be used by the skillful writer to bring a story to life, to show that the people in the story are real, and to enhance the story's readability. Occasionally, people will same something in a memorable or colorful way, and that should be preserved by the writer. Think about some of the famous direct quotes in American history:

"Give me liberty or give me death." (Patrick Henry)
"What did the president know and when did he know it?" (Howard Baker)
"We have nothing to fear but fear itself." (Franklin Roosevelt)
"Four score and seven years ago . . ." (Abraham Lincoln)

Another reason for using a direct quote is that some quotes simply cannot be paraphrased. They are too vivid and colorful and they capture a feeling better than a writer could. For instance, a little old lady showed up for a city council meeting to protest something the council was about to do. She listened to the debate for a while and become more and more incensed about what she heard. When she was finally given the chance to speak, she said, "Anyone who would do this would steal the dimes off a dead man's eyes." Can you imagine trying to paraphrase a quotation like that?

If you are going to use direct quotes in your stories—and you should—you should follow some basic rules.

Use the exact words of the speaker. Anything that is within quotation marks should be something the speaker actually said. The words should be the speaker's, not the writer's.

Use direct quotes sparingly. Good writers will let people speak, but

News story critique

Below is a news story written in a typical inverted pyramid structure. This story demonstrates a number of points that have been made about newswriting in this chapter. We have pointed out some of them on the right. See if you can find others.

The FBI has begun questioning two of its most wanted fugitives about the unsolved death of a Memphis woman in the Great Smoky Mountains National Park.

An FBI spokesman, however, was careful not to declare Howard Williams, 44, or his wife, Sarah, 36, suspects in the deal of Gladys Roslyn. Roslyn's skeletal remains were found by hikers in the park more than two years ago.

"At this point, they are being regard as material witnesses, and that's about all that we can say about the case," Larry Tims, assistant special agent in charge of the local FBI office, said Tuesday.

Clark Summerford, a lawyer for the couple, confirmed that the FBI is seeking information from them about the woman's death, but he, too, emphasized that the FBI was not about to charge them with any additional crimes.

"As far as I know, the FBI has no evidence directly linking the Williams with this woman's death," Summerford said.

The Williams were captured last week after more than a decade on the run. They were spotted by a local truck driver who said he had seen them on "America's Most Wanted," a television show that features stories about fugitives from justice. They Williams escaped from a Massachusetts jail more than 10 years ago after they had been convicted of armed robbery of a bank in Salem, Mass.

The lead summarizes the story and gives the latest and most important information to the reader.

Note that FBI is not spelled out, even on first reference. Acording the the *AP Stylebook,* FBI is so well known that it does not need to be spelled out on first reference.

The second paragraph builds on the lead paragraph with additional information. By the end of the second paragraph, the reader has most of the major information of this story.

Note the use of the direct quotes in the third and fifth paragraph. They reinforce information that has been presented previously. The direct quotes also add life to the story; they let the readers know that this story is about real people.

The last paragraph gives the reader some background information on this story. We can assume that the information has already been published, but this paragraph informs the readers who haven't heard about this incident and reminds those who have.

they won't let them ramble on. Most news writers avoid putting one direct quote after another in a story. You should never pile one direct quote onto another in paragraph after paragraph of a story. The writer who does that is not a writer but a stenographer.

Use direct quotes to supplement and clarify the information presented in the indirect quotes. In a news story, a direct quote is rarely used to present new or important information to the reader. It is most commonly used to follow up information that has already been put in the story.

Knowing how to deal with direct and indirect quotes is one of the most important skills that a newswriter can acquire. It takes some practice to paraphrase accurately and to select the direct quotes that should be used in a story. The key to both is to listen—listen carefully so that you understand what the speaker is saying and so that you remember the exact words that the speaker has used.

The correct sequence for a direct quote and its attribution is DIRECT QUOTE, SPEAKER, VERB. This sequence is generally used in news stories because it follows the inverted pyramid philosophy of putting the most important information first. Usually, what has been said is the most important element a journalist has; who said it, assuming that person has already been identified in the story, is the second most important element; the fact that it was said is the third most important element.

One of the common faults among many writers is the inverted attribution—putting the verb ahead of the subject.

"I do not choose to run," said the president.

There is no good reason for writing this way, and it violates one of the basic structures of English sentence: Subjects come before verbs. Remember, one of the major goals of the journalist is to make the *writing* of a story unobtrusive and the *content* of the story dominant. Sticking with basic English forms is one of the ways the journalist can do this.

One additional note: Use the past tense of verbs in news stories unless the action is continuing at the time of publication or unless it will happen in the future. Writing

"I do not choose to run," the president says.

is inaccurate unless the president goes around continually saying it. Chances are that it was said only once. It happened in the past, and that's the way it should be written. Although you would probably be able to find many examples of the use of the present tense in many publications, it is inaccurate when it is referring to things that have happened and to action that has been completed.

Characteristics of newswriting

Writing a news story is a challenging assignment, even for the most experienced of journalists. Learning to write a news story is easier if you learn some of the basic characteristics of newswriting. These characteristics are common to almost all news stories, and they should be put into practice with every news story that you attempt.

News stories use short sentences and short paragraphs. Remember that the newswriter is trying to get information to the reader as quickly as possible. That is accomplished more easily if the writer uses short sentences. They are easier for the reader to digest.

Unlike other forms of expository writing, the news story does not require that a writer fully develop paragraphs. Paragraph length usually should be kept to three sentences or less and to less than 100 words. Again, the goal is getting information to readers, not fully developing an idea. Another reason for short paragraphs is that the width of a column of type in a newspaper is so narrow that a long paragraph is difficult and daunting for the reader.

News stories are written in the third person. A writer should not intrude into a story by using first person pronouns (unless they are part of a direct quotation from one of the story's sources). Even if a writer witnesses an event, he or she should not tell the story from the point of view of the first person.

WRONG
From where I was sitting, it looked like the umpire made the wrong call.

RIGHT
The manager protested the call by the umpire.

WRONG
The principal said enrollment at our school has gone down.

RIGHT
The principal said enrollment at Central High has gone down.

By the same token, news stories rarely directly address the reader by using the second-person pronoun **you**. Occasionally, lead paragraphs are questions directed at the reader, but this device can be overused quickly, and it is best avoided when you are beginning to learn newswriting.

Personal opinions—or what journalists call "editorializing"—should be kept out of news stories. News reporters should report only what they see and hear. How they feel about that information is not relevant to the news story. They should present the information and let the readers make up their own minds about it.

Another word about accuracy

The chief goal of a journalist is accuracy. We have already discussed that goal in earlier chapters of this book, but we need to emphasize on the point again as we begin learning about the journalistic writing process. The journalist works to get correct information and to present it correctly. Much of the working time of the journalist is spent making certain that all of the information he or she has is correct. In the previous chapter, we discussed some of the ways the journalist does this.

Here, however, we should say a word about the attitude that a journalist has in beginning his or her work. Achieving accuracy is not just a matter of techniques of reporting and writing but a state of mind that the journalist should foster. A journalist should never be satisfied with false information or with information about which he or she has doubts. The journalist should make whatever effort it takes to alleviate those doubts and to clear up any discrepancies.

This attitude should extend not only to the major information that a journalist has but to the smallest bits of a story. Making sure that dates and identifications are correct, that numbers in a story add up properly, that locations are correct—all of these things are part of a journalist's job. Journalists should take special care with the names of people to make sure they are spelled correctly.

Journalists strive for accuracy because they realize that their readers and viewers trust them and expect their reports to be accurate. If those reports are not accurate, journalists will lose that trust and eventually lose their readers.

Feature styles

Dividing feature stories from news stories is misleading. The two actually have a great deal in common. The difference really is in emphasis. The styles commonly used for feature stories assume that the reader has a little more time. They still require focus, a central point. The reader still must be able to summarize the point of the story. But the writing may require that the reader go further in order to fully understand the point that the news story will make. Of course, that means the writer must sustain interest for a longer period of time.

Feature writing is a way for both readers and writers to get away from the facts-only approach that most news stories take to events and people. Feature stories generally contain more detail and description. They go beyond most news stories by trying to discover the interesting or important side of an event which may not be covered by the seven basic news values.

Feature stories are also a way of humanizing the news, of breathing life into a publication. Most features center around people and their activities and interests. A good way for a feature writer to approach the job is to believe that every person he or she meets is worth at least one good feature story.

Feature stories not only vary in content but also vary in structure. The following is a brief discussion of some of the structures a feature writer may use. Unlike the news story, feature stories have no single structure that is used most of the time. Feature writers are freer to adapt whatever structure is suitable to the story they are trying to tell.

Anecdotal features. This style usually begins with an anecdote of some kind and usually will follow with a statement of facts to support the point of the anecdote. Quotes, anecdotes, and facts then weave in and out of one another throughout the story—sustaining the reader's interest, but feeding him or her facts. The trick is to keep the quotes and the anecdotes relevant to the point of focus and to keep the story interesting without making it trite.

Suspended interest features. This style is often used for producing some special effect. Usually it is used for a short story with a punch line. But sometimes it is drawn out into a much longer story. In either case, the style requires the writer to lead readers through a series of ambiguous paragraphs while at the same time keeping them puzzled and interested in solving the puzzle. At the end, the story is resolved in an unexpected way.

The question and answer. This is a simple style used for a specific effect. An explanatory paragraph usually starts the story. Then the interviewer's questions are followed by the interviewee's answers word for word. To use this style, articulate principles or participants in the interview usually are required. Sometimes, however, it is used to make clear how inarticulate an interviewee is about a topic about which he or she is thought to be articulate. In any case, it is effective for showing the reader an unfiltered view of the interviewee's use of language. But it can sometimes obliterate the importance of what an interviewee is saying by calling attention to his or her poor language habits (or yours).

Characteristics of feature writing

To the reader, the feature story seems to exhibit a more relaxed style of writing than a news story. It may be easier to read than a news story, and because of its content it may be more entertaining. Feature writers, however, work just as hard and are just as disciplined as news writers. They may work under a slightly different set of rules than news writers, but the goals of a feature writer are essentially the same ones that a news writer has: to tell a story accurately and to write well.

The main thing that sets feature stories apart from news stories is the greater amount of detail and description features contain. This difference is the backbone of a good feature story. While the news story writer wishes to transmit a basic set of facts to the reader as quickly as possible, the feature writer tries to enhance those facts with details and description so that the reader will be able to see a more complete picture of an event or a person. For instance, while the news writer might refer to "a desk" in a news story, the feature writer will want to go beyond that simple reference by telling the reader something more—"a mahogany desk" or "a dark mahogany desk."

The three major kinds of descriptions that should be contained in a feature story are description of *actions*, description of *people*, and description of *places*. All of these are important to a good feature story, but the description that makes for the strongest writing is generally the description of action. Telling about events, telling what has happened, telling what people are doing—these things make compelling reading. Descriptions of this type help readers to see a story, not just read about it. In addition, feature writers should make sure that readers see the people in their stories, just as the writers themselves have seen the people. Feature writers also need to describe adequately the places where the stories occur. Readers need an idea of the surroundings of a story to draw a complete picture of the story in their minds.

A couple of tips will help writers attain more vivid descriptions in their stories. One is the reliance on nouns and verbs. In Chapter 1 we made the point that nouns and verbs are the most potent words in the language. That point should be reemphasized here. Beginning writers sometimes feel that they should use as many adjectives and adverbs as

Feature Articles

Below are the beginnings of three feature articles. Take a close look at each of them. Any feature story can be approached and written in a variety of ways. Note the approach of each. What are the attention-getting devices? What are the sources of information in each article? Do you have any changes that you would suggest for any of these articles?

She spends most of her day in her six by ten-foot cell, reading her Bible, writing a letter occasionally and walking back and forth a little. She rarely speaks to other inmates at the Miranda State Women's Prison even when she has the chance. She prefers to keep to herself.

"All my life I've been around other people. I never had any privacy," she says. "That's the one good thing about being in this place all alone."

"This place" for Wendy Hoffman is Death Row, an isolated corner of the third floor of one of Miranda's cellblocks. She's "all alone" because she is currently the only woman in the state living under a death sentence.

Hoffman has been there for six months now, ever since the end of her celebrated trial in Molene. There she was convicted of shooting a 13-year- old Chrissy Staten on the orders of her husband. The trial generated a barrage of international publicity for everyone involved, including Dax Hoffman who is also living under a death sentence at the Norton Jones State Prison, about 100 miles away.

Hoffman is glad the trial is over and that the reporters and TV cameras are gone. She reluctantly consented to an interview with this reporter last week.

"I don't want any more publicity," she said.. . .

Norma Sasser is determined that next Wednesday will be like any other day has been for the last 45 years. She'll walk into her first grade classroom at Rockwood Elementary, give her students their final report cards and wish them a happy summer.

The problem is that however much "Miss Norma" follows her routine, it won't be the same. It will be her last day of teaching kids to read, write, count and be still.

She knows that, and even though she dreads the last day, she's looking forward to what comes after that: lots of travel, time to read and gardening, she says.

The day might be more normal if all she had to do was meet with this year's students. But soon after they've received their grades, a day-long celebration will begin at the school all in her honor. More than 1,000 of her former students will be there, some of whom will travel from distant parts of the country.

"That's the part I dread, not leaving the classroom for the last time," she said. "I'm just afraid that a lot of people have gone to a lot of trouble to be here."

Among them will be U.S. Senator Harley Akens who "learned the basics" from Miss Norma more than 35 years ago. ...

Every morning, Sam Price would stop in at the Koffee Klub restaurant, meet some friends, have breakfast and then see what another day of retirement had in store for him. That was about two years ago. Then one morning he came in and his friends told him that the Koffee Klub was about to go out of business. Eilene Baker, the owner, was getting too old to manage the place, and none of her children cared anything about running it.

That's when Sam Price decided to become a restaurateur.

"I thought I had quit work for good," he said at 5:30 a.m. one day recently. He was about to break some eggs while overseeing some bacon on a hot grill. He was dressed in a chef's apron and also wore a large grin. "I just couldn't let this place go out of business. It meant too much to me and some of the other boys, so we talked about it, scraped up the cash and bought it."

Price, Randall Parrish, George Meek and Eddie Morgan, all retirees from the Cottontone Plant, put together about $19,000 to buy the business. "Eilene didn't want much - she just wanted to get out from under the business," Price said. "One of her terms was that she could get a free meal anytime she came in here."...

possible to enhance their writing, and in doing so, they tend to use a lot of dull and overused nouns and verbs. That approach is a mistake if a writer is trying to produce lively, descriptive writing. A second tip for writers is to remember the five senses. Often writers simply describe the way things look, and they forget about the way things sound, feel, taste, or smell. Remember, the five senses and incorporating them into a story will help make a description come alive for a reader.

Feature stories often contain more quotes and even dialogue than news stories. Newswriters, as we saw earlier in this chapter, use direct quotes for enhancement and illumination of the facts they are trying to present. Feature writers do the same thing, but they go beyond this by using quotes to say something about the people who are in their stories. Quoted material is generally used much more freely in feature stories, although, as in news stories, dumping a load of quotes on a reader without a break often puts too heavy a burden on the reader. Dialogue and dialect are other devices a feature writer may use if the story calls for them.

One of the charms of feature writing for many writers is that they can put more of themselves into a story. Unlike news stories, in which writers stay out of sight as much as they can, feature writers are somewhat freer to inject themselves and their opinions into a story. While feature writers have a little more latitude in this regard, they must use this latitude wisely and make sure that a feature story doesn't become a story about themselves rather than about the subject they are trying to cover.

Parts of a feature story

Feature stories generally have three parts: a lead, a body, and an ending. Each should be given special attention by the feature writer.

Like the news story, the lead of a feature story is its most important part. Feature writers are not bound by the one sentence, 30-word lead paragraph structure that newswriters must often follow. A lead in a feature story may be several sentences or paragraphs long. From the beginning sentence, however, the feature writer must gain the reader's attention and give the reader some information of substance—or at least promise some information of substance. A newswriter can depend on the story's subject to compel the reader's interest. A feature writer must sell the reader on the subject in the first few words or sentences.

A good lead uses the first words or sentences of a story to build interest in the story's subject, but the reader must soon discover some benefit for reading the story. That's why the writer should build a lead toward some initial point that the story is to make, something that will hook the reader for the rest of the story.

The end of a lead should be a sentence or paragraph that gives the reader this payoff and sets the stage for the rest of the story. It should also put the story in some context for the reader and find some way of telling the reader why the rest of the story should be read. Writers on the subject of feature writing have given various names to this sentence or paragraph—the *fat* paragraph, the *snapper*, the *why* paragraph. Whatever it's called, it should be in the story fairly soon, and it should make the reader stick with the story.

The body of the feature story is the middle of the story which expands and details the subjects introduced in the lead. The body should answer every question raised in the lead, and it should fulfill every expectation raised within the reader. Like products bought in a store, features often promise more than they deliver. They often tell the reader in the lead that the information they contain will be of interest or help to the reader, and they turn out to be neither interesting nor helpful. The body should contain the substance of the article, and it should be what the reader has been led to expect.

The ending of the story also deserves the feature writer's attention. Newswriters generally don't have to worry about the ending of their stories since they are written in the inverted pyramid structure. Feature writers should not expect their stories to be cut from the bottom, however, and they need to take care as to how a story ends. The ending of a story may be used to put the story in some perspective, to answer any lingering questions that a reader may have, or to make a final point about the story's subject. The major point about an ending is that a writer should not allow a story to go on too long. Like any other writer, the feature writer should stop writing when there is nothing of substance left to say.

A final word of advice

In this chapter we have talked a lot about writing stories for print, and we have tried to make the points in this chapter with a few examples. Reading about good writing is only the first step to learning about good writing. Reading good writing is the next step. If you are interested in learning to write well, in any form, you should read as much as possible—newspapers, magazines, books, and anything else you can get you hands on.

The next step is writing itself. The first chapter of this book tells you to "sit down and write." That's the only way to do it. That's the only way to become a good writer.

Points for consideration and discussion

1. Why is the inverted pyramid structure such a common one for news stories? What are its advantages and disadvantages?

2. Some critics argue that the inverted pyramid news story structure should be abandoned by newspapers. They say that television and radio deliver news much faster than newspapers; therefore, newspapers should not be concerned so much with getting information to readers quickly as with getting more complete and accurate information. What do you think?

3. In chapter 3 we discussed journalistic style and the conventions of journalism. How does what you learned in that chapter fit in with the principles presented in this chapter?

4. The authors says you shouldn't go out of your way to find substitutes for the verb "said." Do you think that is good advice?

5. The text says that a direct quote "should be the exact words of the speaker." Can you think of any circumstances where this would not be true?

6. Journalists often go to great lengths to keep their opinions out of the stories they write. Some people argue that this impossible to do, however. What do you think?

Further reading

Everette E. Dennis and Arnold H. Ismach, *Reporting Processes and Practices: Newswriting for Today's Readers*, Belmont, CA: Wadsworth, 1981.

Don Fry (editor), *Best Newspaper Writing 1987*, St. Petersburg, FL: The Poynter Institute, 1987.

Melvin Mencher, *Basic Newswriting*, Dubuque: William C. Brown, 1983.

William Metz, *Newswriting from Lead to "30,"* Englewood Cliffs, NJ: Prentice-Hall, 1977.

M. L. Stein, *Getting and Writing the News*, New York: Longman, 1985.

Hiley Ward, *Professional Newswriting*, New York: Harcourt Brace Jovanovich, 1985.

EXERCISES

A NOTE TO THE STUDENTS: The following section contains a variety of exercises for news and feature writing. You should follow your instructor's directions in completing them. Some of the exercises are written in sentence fragments while others are written in complete sentences, often in narrative form. If you are assigned to write news stories from the exercises in this section, you should use the **information** but not the exact wording contained in the exercises (except for the direct quotes). Many of the exercises are badly written on purpose. It will be your job to rewrite the information you have so that it is better written than the exercise material.

Writing leads

Write a lead paragraph from each set of facts.

Wreck

Two trucks collided on I-59 last night

Caused a traffic jam because the road was blocked both ways for about 45 minutes

Fuel from both trucks spilled onto the highway and caused a big oil slick

One truck was refrigerated and most of the contents thawed, causing a loss of an estimated $10,000 worth of goods.

Accident happened on a part of I-59 undergoing repairs, so it was two lanes at that point; the trucks met head on.

Honor society

Alpha Alph, university honor society, to hold inductions next Friday

5 sophomores, 20 juniors, 10 seniors will be named

names will be kept secret until ceremony

ceremony will be at 10 AM at Student Center

Faculty death

Education prof Elizabeth Billson, dead at age 58

had taught here for 36 years

estimated to have taught 10,000 future teachers during her years

awarded University's "Outstanding Professor" award last year

had suffered from cancer for 10 years

Baseball star

Junior baseball star drafted by St. Louis Cardinals

Willie Ames says he won't turn pro this year but will stay in school

Ames says Mom advised him to stay in school: "She was never able to finish high school. It's important to her for me to get my education. I can play baseball later."

Ames was reportedly offered a signing bonus of $15,000 by the Cardinals

New Course

Political science department announces new course, "Communism and Socialism," to begin next semester

Open to juniors and seniors who have had the freshman level beginning political science course

taught by Jerald Wiseman, Associate Professor

Wiseman: "These two political theories have been major forces in helping develop our 20th Century political world."

Poll

Local polling firm, City Research Associates

poll of more than 500 city residents completed last week

showed 65 percent of citizens "satisfied" or "very satisfied" with the quality of life in the city; showed 75 percent of those with school-age children "satisfied" or "very satisfied" with city school system

poll sponsored by Chamber of Commerce

Computer donation

Mike McCracken, president of Computer Corporation of America, headquartered in the city, made this announcement this morning

his company donating 10 computers to local high school; donation worth more than $30,000

Schools Supt. Harvey Butterworth says computers will be used to teach word processing and business programs

computers should be in use by the fall term

Drinking bill

State legislature just finished marathon debate; 30 straight hours in the senate and then 30 hours in the house

bill would raise drinking age in state from 19 to 21

bill passed by house, 55-40 early today; passed by senate, 18-12, yesterday

bill sponsored by local legislator, Representative Tom Hartley

Water alert

Brownsville, twenty miles south of your city

last week placed on a "water alert" by state health commission because of "parasitic contamination"

alert lifted by commission

Jones Lamson, head of commission, says testing by commission shows the danger has passed residents had been boiling their water since the alert began

Theft investigation

Police chief Clayton Wheat, at press conference this morning

talks about department's continuing investigation into auto theft ring

says ring responsible for 200 to 300 auto thefts in city last year

says investigation has been expanded into surrounding counties

says most cars were disassembled and sold for parts

Industry returning

Local group of investors, lead by First Trust Bank president Joe E. Jamison

announcement made this morning

buying abandoned Lochs Papermill plant

investor to team up with Textron Corp. to start a machine tool plant refurbishing

the plant will take about a year

when machine tool plant is opened it will employ about 200 people

Football game

School's football team defeats arch-rival, 2-0

final game of the season

only score, saftety, comes with 5 seconds left on the clock

breaks 3-game losing streak

arch-rival unbeaten this season until this game

Leads and Second Paragraphs

Write a lead and second paragraph for each of the following sets of information.

Curriculum changes

University president announces changes in requirements for graduation

students entering next fall must take one math, computer science, and foreign language course

President: "We feel that these new course requirements will allow us to turn out better educated persons."

recent study showed only 15 percent of students took a foreign language course and only 20 percent took a math course while at the University

Arrest

Cathy Bensen, 22-year-old senior, arrested for driving under the influence of alcohol for third time in six months last night

daughter of locally prominent attorney Jim Bensen, 211 Green Grove Drive mother, Sharon Bensen, lives in Canada

Cathy was this year's Homecoming Queen; has been cheerleader; straight-A student; going to Vanderbuilt University for graduate studies in biology

Protest

Group of citizens angry because University biology class is teaching evolution

Group led by Wilbur Straking, pastor of the Ever-Faithful Church of the Living Water

Staking: "I plan to lead a group of 25 dedicated Christians to the state capital next Monday to speak with legislators about this problem. We believe the teaching of evolution is against the principles of this Christian country, and we want to put a stop to it."

Class they're objecting to is taught by Laura Cliff, associate professor of bioloy; she wouldn't comment on the group's charges

Neither would University president

Law suit

Suit files in Circuit Court today; for $100,000

Against Amburn's Produce Market

By Ellie Maston, 313 Journey Road

Charges market with negligence; suit says green beans left on floor of market; she walked through them and slipped and broke her hip

Suit says she "suffered permanent bodily and mental injuries, incurred medical expenses and lost income."

Accident happened April 1 this year

Agreement announced

Clyde Parris, president of Ambrose Steel Company, and Charles Pointer, president of United Steelworkers Local 923, make joint announcement

Company and union have reached collective bargaining agreement

Strike set for midnight tonight has been called off

Strike would have stopped production at

Ambrose and put 457 steelworkers off the job

Terms of agreement will be read tonight to a meeting of the union, Pointer says

Parris says contract includes "substantial wage agreement" but won't say how much; that will be announced tonight

Union will vote on contract next week

Pointer says contract "the best we can get out of the company"

Malpractice suit

Two doctors being sued for malpractice; Barney Olive and Stephen Rogers, both of whom practice at Riverside Hospital

William Hamilton, lawyer for plaintiff, Bertie McNicholls, 623 Leanto Road

Hamilton, beginning final arguments in case, has heart attack

Quick work of Olive and Rogers save his life

Hamilton, 73, now recovering at Riverside Hospital

Trial to resume next week

Alumni festival

University Alumni Association planning spring festival for April

games, contests will be held on football field

barbeque lunch and exhibition baseball game

all proceeds to go to school library, plus alumni hoping to raise more money through pledges

date depends on whether or not baseball team makes it to playoffs this year

alumni president Bobby Don Willis: "This kind of activity is one of the positive things we can do to make this university a better educational institution

Writing news stories

Write news stories from the following sets of information.

Vandalism

Two students at your school have been

caught smashing windows in the new gymnasium

Identified as Bobby Ray Williams, 20, a sophomore, and George Hatfield, 22, a senior

Students are both rom Snadeville; Williams majoring in Business; Hatfield majoring in Biology

Janitor, Eddie Vinson, caught them throwing bricks at the first floor windows at approximately 6:45 a.m. this morning

15 windows valued at $55 each were smashed

Two ran from Vinson after throwing bricks at him

He knew them both and reported incident to campus police

Police arrested them later in the morning

Said they did not deny their guilt

Punishment will be decided by Student Court in one week; Williams and Hatfield are suspended until the hearing

No charges will be filed with police, Oswald said

The new gym, a $1 million facility, was to have been dedicated today. Postponed until repaired

Williams is a stright-A student who plans to attend a summer honors program at a nearby university this summer. Hatfield has lettered in football and basketball for two years

Harvey Oswald, chief of campus security: "I just can't understand how they could do such a thing. They weren't drunk or on drugs, they are good students who have contributed to the school, they've never been in trouble before. It's a real mystery to me. I have no idea what the Student Court will recommend in this case."

Vinson: "They were acting crazy, laughing and hollering. I heard one of them — I think it was George — say 'to hell with this school.'"

Hatfield refused to comment on incident; Williams only said, "We won't be fooled again."

Disruption

A fact-finding commission has been investigating a campus disturbance for three weeks since a campus incident. It issues a statement from which the following material has been excerpted by the college news office and distributed to the local press:

The disorders on May 7 in from of Laughton Library were the result of self-appointed guardians of student life deciding what their fellow students could hear and read. We have no sympathy with this act or its perpetrators regardless of their motives.

Nevertheless, we do recommend no action but the publicity that they have already received and that this report may achieve.

These six students who tore down banners, heckled speakers, and destroyed pamphlets of the Unifying Church on the afternoon of May 7 denied the young men and women of the Church their Constitutional rights of expression and assembly.

We realize that the Church did not have college permission to use the campus, but students are not the enforcement arm of the administration.

Our commission of seven students, three administrators, and four faculty members voted as follows on the matter:

Condemnation without further sactions: Students — 5.2 in favor; Faculty — 3-1 in favor; Administration — 3-0 in favor.

We thank President ruth Pitts Renaldi for giving us full access to college files and records.

You check the clips at the newspaper and find out that the Unifying Church is a unit of a large proselytizing organization that has enlisted many young people in its Christian Crusade. There were four young men and three young women singing hymns and handing out pamphlets when the incident occurred. A group known as Youth Against Fascism and War had been picketing the Church members when suddenly several students casued a commotion. Campus guards took six students into custody and a study committee was appointed to examine the matter.

You call student members of the committee and learn Albert Towden and Steve Rabin cast the negative votes. they tell you:

Towden: "I wanted some kind of suspension. These students were rowdies. They are nothing more than fascists who would impose on us a way of life in which their ideas would be the only acceptable ones. I don't like people who in the guise of democracy would tear it down."

Rabin: "I was the student lawyer for the six students before the student judicial panel that recommended this study committee. Speaking on behalf of the six, I feel that they should not have been condemned.

"No democracy can thrive when it gives freedom to those who would brainwash innocents on behalf of a fascisitc ideology. We know the Unifying Church wants cadres of young people to propagandize the public to follow a charismatic leader. Foreign and U.S. Business interests are financing this. We will continue to oppose the Church here and elsewhere."

Development

About six months ago the Roberts Development Company announced that it wanted to build an apartment complex on Park Lane, a residential area of the local community. The complex would be, a spokesman said at the time, about 120 units and would be built on a farm owned by P.T. Rodney, who had agreed to see it for that purpose. The complex would cover about 15 acres. In order to get permission to build the complex, the company had to apply to the City Council for a rezoning of the area from "R-1," which allows only single-family residences, to "R-2," which would allow the apartment complex to be built.

Immediately after the announcement, the Park Lane Residents Association said it opposed the complex and would ask the City Council not to grant the rezoning request. The association's president is George Houghton. The association was joined in its opposition by the City Neighborhood Preservation Association. Both groups appeared before the council to fight the rezoning. The council voted 7-0 not to rezone the property, but Roberts Development said it would try to work out a compromise with both groups and resubmit the rezoning application.

Today, six months after this happened, you (a reporter for the local newspaper) receive a call from the president of the City Neighborhood Preservation Association, whose name is John Hedrick, saying his group is no longer opposed to the rezoning. Hedrick says, "We've had several meetings with Roberts Development people, and they have given us assurances about what will happen to the property. We're satisfied that the neighborhood will retain its character, so we will be backing them up when they go to the City Commission tomorrow to ask for another rezoning of the property." Hedrick said the reason for the turaround by his group is that Roberts had redesigned much of their original plans so that the apartment complex would be more architecturally compatible with the neighborhood.

The city commission meeting is tomorrow morning, and you have to do a story on this situation for this afternoon's paper.

Olin Millsaps, president of Roberts Development Company, tells you, "We're very pleased with the preservation association's support. I think we have a shot at turning this thing around at the meeting tomorrow."

Gardner Lacy, who is president of the Park Lane Residents Association, says, however, that his group is still opposed to the petition. "I don't think the development people have changed their plans that much. What they are trying to do would still disrupt the neighborhood. The way the streets are now, they just can't hold the traffic an apartment complex like that would generate. Frankly, and I don't have any evidence to back this up, I think the neighborhood preservation people sold out to the development company. I wouldn't be surprised if Roberts made a big contribution to their treasury."

The president of the city council, Harvey Latton, says he can't predict how the vote will go. After numerous calls, you reach the other six council members, and none of them will tell you how he or she will vote on the issue. They all say they will wait until tomorrow before making up their minds.

Alcoholism

The Department of Health and Human Services (HHS) issued a 121-page report today. Congress recently passed a law which required the department to issue a report on alcoholism each year, and this was the first such report. The report was prepared by a committee of 11 within HHS.

The report said losses caused by alcoholism are high. It said alcohol causes 28,000 trafic deaths a year, and the deaths cost the nation a total of $15 billion. Nearly 9 million persons suffer from alcoholism or lesser drinking problems, and they constitute 10 percent of the work force within the United States.

The report also contained some statistics about the use of alcohol. It said that in the last year, the average American drinker drank the equivalent of 44 fifths of whiskey. The report concluded that alcohol is the "major drug problem in this country." It said HHS will spend $200,000 next year to pay for advertisements to warn the public about the dangers of excessive drinking. The liquor industry has endorsed the campaign. The advertisements will be used on radio and television and in newspapers and magazines. But an official added, "We will not tell people not to drink. That is a personal decision. What we are saying is that citizens have a responsibility not to destroy themselves or society."

The 121-page report suggests that the problems of alcoholism is not adequately understood by most Americans, who seem more concerned about other drugs, such as marijuana and heroin, even though those drugs do not cause as many problems as alcohol. To prove that point the report pointed out that New York City has an estimated 600,000 alcoholics but only 125,000 heroin users. Yet the city spends 40 times more to fight narcotics addiction than it does to fight alcoholism. The report explained that most persons do not know much about alcoholism and do not consider alcohol a serious problem. People also are reluctant to admit that they have a drinking problem or are alcoholics.

Alcoholism is a particularly serious problem among certain groups. For example, the report said that on some Indian reservations alcoholism has reached epidemic proportions. On some reservations 10 percent of the residents are alcoholics, twice the national average, and the rate of alcoholism rises to as much as 25 percent on some reservations.

Shooting

Write a 250-word story using the following information. The story is for the first edition of this afternoon's newspaper.

On your regular telephone rounds of the area police and sheriff departments, you talk with sheriff Carmen Townsend of Sevier County. He says: "Yeah, we had a pretty bad incident here last night. A Mrs. Bertie Clancy was shot and killed by her husband. At least, I think she was killed. The hospital didn't expect her to live long. They lived on Caney Creek Road near Pigeon Forge. She was sixty-eight years old. The way I understand it, they had this kid — Randy — and he's the kind of kid who ain't all there, you know what I mean. Anyway, he and his old man, a fellow named Darris Clancy, got into an argument. Randy was all the time coming around, asking for money. He was drawing some disability money from the government, about $300 a month, but that was never enough. He was always hitting his folks up for some more, and as I understand it, they usually gave it to him. Well, they got into this argument, and the old man pointed a gun at Randy. The old lady tried to break it up and got in between them and the gun went off. She was hit in the head and the shoulder. Well, you can imagine how the son felt and what it was like in the house then, so I guess what happened was that Randy grabbed the gun away from his daddy and shot him. It was a shotgun. Anyway, the old man dropped dead as a doornail. There wasn't even no use in taking him to the hospital. We just called the coroner and took him over to the funeral home."

A sheriff's deputy tells you that Randy Clancy is being held in the county jail without bond. His arraignment will be sometime this afternoon.

You call the hospital and a spokesman

there says Mrs. Clancy has died. She died just a few minutes after she arrived at about 11 o'clock last night.

James Clancy, another son and an employee of the local Stokley canning company, tells you the following things about what happened: "No, Randy never was exactly right, but he was a good kid. I wasn't there. I just talked with him a little while after it happened. He says he don't remember much, but he said he couldn't live without mama. He was always her favorite, but he and daddy hadn't gotten along too well lately. I guess it happened about like the sheriff told you. I had talked with Randy earlier in the day, and he told me he was going up to see mama and daddy because he needed some money 'cause he was getting into some trouble with some people he had borrowed from. I think he was going to ask them for about $200. Daddy used to get really mad when he would ask for money. He got there about 9 o'clock. He told me that after the shooting he went upstairs to what used to be his bedroom and tore all the pictures off the wall. Then he went out into the yard and smashed the shotgun on a fence post. I found it later and showed it to the sheriff. As I understand it, after he had done that, he went to a neighbor's house and called the sheriff and told him to come get him."

The neighbor, Will O'Reilly, who lives next door to the Clancy couple on Caney Creek Road, tells you thats what happened: "I heard a lot of arguing coming from their house, I guess it was about 9 o'clock or maybe a little afterwards. Then I heard these shots, and I told my wife, 'There's trouble up there,' but she said I'd better not leave the house. Pretty soon, Randy come knocking on the door and asked to use the phone. I remember he was wearing a tee shirt with the words 'Gospel Baptist Church' on it. He was pretty calm, but I heard him tell the sheriff what happened and for them to come and get him."

Employee records at the Stokely plant show that Darris Clancy was 64 years old and had worked as a driver at the plant off and on for more than 20 years. He quit seven years ago because of arthritis and had been drawing disability payments ever since.

Bertie Clancy had lived all her life in the Pigeon Forge area but had never been employed anywhere for any length of time.

Caney Creek Road is a winding mountain road, and the dead couple had lived there for about 25 years.

Prosper

Prosper is a mining town of 909 people in the northeast corner of Crocker County. Since the deep-shaft coal mine was opened in 1901, it has provided a major source of employment for the town's people, and in the last 18 years has brought more than 800 people from other towns to work every day at the mine, United Coal Company's Mine No. 3, known locally as Hellpit. The company announced yesterday that the mine will close in two weeks for an indefinite period. Since 1980, when Propser was incorporated and became eligible for coal tax revenue, its budget has risen from $40,000 to $300,000 ($125,000 in coal severance tax monies, $125,000 in federal matching money for capital improvements.) Mayor Lester Jenkins tells you that "With the mine closed, our revenue is just about gone." Some tax money will continue to dribble in as stockpiles of coal are depleted, but Wilma Foster, the city clerk, forsees a cutback for the fiscal year, which starts in 30 days, to $60,000. "That will cover essential services like police protection and utilities at city hall and at the new ball park," she adds. Councilman Ed Barnes tells you that most of the coal money went into building projects. "And we've got the city hall and the park paid for, so at least we're not in debt." The town council will talk about a new budget at its meeting tomorrow night. The mine employed 1,000 people. The shaft is a quarter mile deep, the deepest in the state. Company officials cannot be reached by phone, but a statement delivered to you gives the reason for the closing as a severe cutback in demand for coal because of a shutdown in manufacturing nationwide. It quotes Wilson Standridge, company president: "We hope to see an increase in demand, but until we do, the mine will remain sealed."

Murder

Francie Franklin, proprietor of a small bakery in Pleasant Grove, was killed during the night. Police Chief Wilburn Cole tells you over the phone that Miss Franklin did not deliver a wedding cake as expected this morning and when the bride's mother went to the bake shop in her home to check, found the front door open and a display case smashed. "She didn't go no further," Cole says. "When we got there we found Miss Francie in the kitchen. She was shot dead." The little shop is in a shambles when you go by to check and you note the contrast to the neat tidy operation the woman kept. You can't find the chief, but the radio dispatcher reads this memo to you: "Francie's body was taken to Smith's Funeral Parlor where they'll do an autopsy. It must have happened before midnight because her television set was still on and she always turns it off after Johnny Carson. She was shot once in the chest and her pistol is missing from the drawer under the cash register. Money was scattered around but they probably got away with some." Kenton County Homicide Investigator Kelton Kelly says she was shot with a .22 calibre bullet and that they didn't find any fingerprints but that a strange, unidentified red wool ski cap was found under the body. Kenton Couny Coroner Ransom Cranwell tells you that death was from a single gunshot wound and that there were no other injuries. "It was crazy the way they messed up the place though," he adds. "She was always so proud of it. She was just an old maid who loved everyone and everyone loved her." Arrangements are pending. No known survivors. Age 68. Address, 504 Ash St. She started the business 20 years ago under the name Francie's Fancies. She recently expanded by building on a small showroom at the front of the house.

Sit-in

Black students are angry because black candidate for Homecoming Queen did not make Homecoming Court in election held yesterday (Monday)

Homecoming Court of five girls is selected through a general election; girl with highest number of votes is Homecoming Queen

Protesting students have staged a sit-in in front of administration building

Began this morning; plan to continue throughout the week

About 10 students are participating

All have handmade signs - "Black is beautiful," "No Homecoming this Year," "We want equal representation," and so on.

University President Jimmy Wilson has issued a statement warning other students to leave the protesting students alone. Here is an excerpt from the text:

"These students have chosen a non-violent form of protest against something they think is unfair. They are not excused from classes and will not be allowed to make up work they miss. However, they will not be punished in any other way unless violence erupts. Any students harrassing these protesters will be punished with immediate expulsion."

Wilson is a former president of the local NAACP

Yvonne Dees, the defeated candidate for Homecoming Queen: "I don't feel that the election was fair. We (black students) are 35 percent of the student body, and we should be represented on the Court."

Wendy Thomas, president of the Student Government and chairman of the campus Election Committee: "It was absolutely fair. I don't think they have a cause at all. The black students just didn't get out the vote for their candidate, that's all, and they want to be represented without trying."

Bobby Dean Willis, a senior who organized the protest: "We are going to stay out here until something is done. We are tired of being treated like we don't exist in this school. We want representation on that court, and we will bring some real attention to this problem. I want all the media in here; I want the public to know what's going on."

Student government election

Student council elections were held yesterday

35 percent of student body voted

Votes were counted by a student-faculty committee last night

Four people ran for president:

Carol Lyndis, last year's Student Government Association secretary, won with 53 percent of the vote

Daughter of Mr. and Mrs. Ben Lyndis, 449 Holly Lane, Hollyville, Tx.

21-year-old junior, cheerleader for two years, on school team, majoring in biology

Other candidates for president were Johnny Haynes, a junior who is president of the Lambda Delta Honor Society; Tania Wilson, last year's Student Government vice-president, a junior; and I.J. Weisburg, a sophomore who writes an advice column on love for the school paper

In the vice-presidential election, Gene Johnson was unopposed

His parents are Mr. Phil Johnson, 776 Union St. and Mrs. Sally Osborne, 2103 South Donley Rd., Johnsonville, Neb.

Johnson is a junior, 21 years old, Boys State Rep, president of Alpha Omega fraternity, majoring in political science

For secretary, there were two nominees: Freda Hance and Reba Wilkes

Hance won. She is the first freshman ever elected to a major Student Government office

Wilkes, a junior, was SGA treasurer last year

Hance is the daughter of Mr. and Mrs. Hanly Hance, 807 Queen St. (in the town where the college is located); She was president of the freshman class this year and was features editor of the student newspaper last year; majoring in journalism.

Keith Nelson was unopposed for treasurer. A sophomore, he was a Student Government senator for two years. He was Homecoming chairman this year and fundraising chairman his freshman year

Lyndis: "I am really happy about the new officers we have. I think they will all do well in their jobs and all. I do want to thank all those who supported me in so many ways, especially my parents."

Here are the vote totals:

President:
Lyndis 1,126
Haynes 135
Wilson 612
Weisburg 232
Write-ins 125

Vice-president:
Johnson 1,854
Write-ins 39

Secretary:
Hance 1,169
Wilkes 954
Write-ins got 2 votes

Treasurer:
Nelson 1,966
Write-ins got 20 votes

Russel

Last New Year's Eve, John Page was found shot to death in his home. At first, the police and the coroner ruled the death a suicide, but that changed when they later found that Page had withdrawn a large amount of money from his bank account on the day that he died. Page is the owner of Page Auto Parts Store. He is also a real estate developer, a deacon in the First Baptist Church, a city councilman and generally thought to be one of the wealthiest citizens in town. The amount of money Page withdrew from the bank that day was $10,000. Page's wife told the police that he had been depressed for some weeks before his death, but she didn't believe that he committed suicide.

Page's death and all of the subsequent events, including the police investigation and the trial, received a great amount of publicity from the city's newspapers and television stations.

A month after Page's death, the police arrested William Russel and charged him with first degree murder. William Russel is owner of Russel Realty, and even though they were competitors in business, Page and Russel were known to be good friends.

They grew up together, and their families had been friends. Police said that several clues pointed to Russel as the murderer. Russel had been seen leaving the Page home late New Year's Eve by a neighbor who had been walking his dog. The bank provided the police with serial numbers of the money it had given to Page, and most of that money was found in Russel's house.

During the trial, which began a month ago, it came out that Russel had been having an affair with Page's wife, Geneveve. The district attorney, Hix Bradfield, tried to paint Russel as a desperate man whose business was failing and who was blackmailing Page. The key witness in his case was Page's wife, who said that Russel had threatened Page by saying he would "tell everybody in town about your slutty little wife" if he wouldn't pay. She said Page was worried that his reputation in the community would be damaged and it would mean the end to his political career. She said he had been planning to run for Congress next year.

Russel took the stand in his own defense and denied killing Page, and he denied having an affair with his wife. He said Page had asked him to keep the money because of a business deal he was about to make, but he didn't know any of the details. He said Page had been despondent because he had found out that his wife had been having affairs with other men. "I felt sorry for John," he said. "He married a little slut. I suspect that she was blackmailing him." Russel said he went to talk with Page on New Year's Eve but found him too depressed to talk. When he left, Russel said, Page was drinking heavily. Russel said he didn't tell the police about the visit or the money because "I got scared. It was a stupid thing to do."

Yesterday, after three days of deliberating, the jury found Russel guilty. Russel broke down and cried when he heard the verdict.

This morning, Judge Cecil Andrews sentenced Russel to death in the electric chair. In handing out the sentence, Andrews said, "This was heinous crime — one that merits swift and severe retribution. The victim was a leading citizen in the community, a man who had made many contributions. In a cold blooded way, the defendant ended his life while posing as his good friend. He was shown no remorse for his deed and has, in fact, lied about it. He showed no mercy to his victim, and I, in turn, can show no mercy to him." Russel, who looked pale and puffy-eyed when he came into the courtroom, had to be helped out.

Outside the court, Regina Wright, Russel's lawyer, said she would file an immediate appeal both of the verdict and the sentence. "Mr. Russel didn't get a fair trial. The massive amount of pretrial publicity surrounding this case prevented that. Early on, we asked for a change of venue, but that motion was denied. There was just no way that a person accused of killing a popular man like John Page was going to get a fair trial in this town." Asked about the sentence, Wright said, "I just can't believe he was given the death penalty. I believe Judge Andrews had it in for my client. He should have disqualified himself because he was a friend of John Page. He should have granted our change of venue motion. He did neither, and then he winds up sentencing my client to death."

After the sentencing, Bradfield said, "The sentence was a harsh one — not the one we would have recommended. We would have preferred a life without parole sentence, but I'll go along with what the judge said. It was an awful crime, and John Page was one of our leading citizens."

You try to get a comment from Mrs. Page, but her attorney, Frank Story, tells you she left immediately after the sentencing for New York to discuss writing a book about the trial and her experiences.

Write a story for tomorrow morning's newspaper.

Tornado

Yesterday afternoon was unseasonably warm for this time of year. Early in the afternoon, the temperature reached 70 degrees, and the people at the Weather Bureau became concerned. There was a lot of moisture in the air, and the conditions seemed just right for a tornado. At two o'clock they issued a tornado warning because of some buildup of moisture west of here.

At three p.m., after receiving several reports of funnel clouds, Lee Harper, chief metereologist at the weather bureau, issued a tornado warning. Funnel clouds had been sighted just south of Midville, and there was one report that a barn had been damaged and some cows had been killed. The tornado watch was to stay in effect for an hour.

At 3:33 a tornado touched down on Cleveland Street, a street with a lot of businesses and homes on it. The tornado damaged the following businesses: the Cleveland Street branch of the Trust National Bank; Red Cedar's used car lot; the Jiffy-Kwik 24-hour food store; and the Big Bank Sound Record Shop, which is located in the same building as the food store. Also several homes were damaged, including that of Robert T. Mellon, the mayor. The bank was being housed in a mobile home while a permanent building was built. There was no damage to the building site, which was located nearby. The mobile home was lifted completely off its foundation, however, and was totally destroyed. Clyde Plenty, vice president of the Trust National Bank said the following: "Thank goodness, the tornado hit when it did. We had closed up about three o'clock, and nobody was in the building." Some of the records housed in the building were destroyed, but Clyde said nothing of importance had been lost permanently, and all the records could be duplicated. There was also no money in the building to speak of.

The people at Jiffy-Kwik and the record shop weren't so lucky. At least four people had to go to the hospital to be treated for injuries due to flying debris and broken glass, according to hospital officials. Mr. and Mrs. George Jones -- his wife's name is Thelma -- were treated for minor cuts and lacerations and then released at the Good Hope Hospital, and Irving Smalley was being kept overnight because of more serious cuts. He's listed in good condition. He lives at 123 Urban Street. The Joneses live at 1311 13th Avenue. Anna Patton had major injuries after being buried by an aisle of canned goods; she had just come out of surgery at 8 o'clock last night and was listed in critical condition. She lives at 12 Pinto Avenue. Killed was Evelyn Morrison as she was coming out of the record shop and getting into her car. She was a teller who worked at the Trust Bank, the same one that had been damaged by the tornado. She was on her way home. She lived at 67 Kent Street. She was dead on arrival at the hospital and her body was taken to Green Acres Chapel. None of the funeral arrangements have been set.

Holbert Morrison, manager of the Jiffy-Kwik, said his store was not a total loss, but the damage was several thousand dollars worth. "The worst thing was the looters," he said. "I just couldn't believe that some people would steal from us after something like this had happened." Police Chief Robert Sykes said they had arrested several youths for looting after the tornado hit, but they weren't going to release their names yet. Bill Belson, the manager of the record store and a noted area record collector, also said the damage to his shop would go into thousands of dollars. "Fortunately, none of my most valuable records were damaged."

Red Cedar said that one of his cars was damaged when some limbs fell on it, but otherwise nothing was hurt. Three homes in the next block of Cleveland Street were damaged, including that of Mayor Mellon. The roof was torn off of his home. "We were lucky because no one was home. I just feel awful about Miss Morrison, though. She was an old friend and a life-long resident of the town. Lots of people knew her, and I think it's tragic. You know, she used to be a teacher -- was a teacher at Elmwood Elementary School about ten years ago. She taught there for about 20 years before retiring and going to work for the bank. She didn't have much family, but everybody in town knew her." The roofs of the other homes on Cleveland Street were damaged by flying limbs, but none of the owners reported serious damage.

The police chief said the total amount of damage done by the tornado would come to about $150,000. "That part of Cleveland Street looks like a bomb has been dropped on it. It's going to take us several days to get it all cleared. It's amazing that all this damage was done in less than 2 minutes. I feel awfully bad about Miss Morrison, but we were lucky that more people weren't hurt. There were quite a few people in the area at the time." One of the people who was in the record store at the time said the noise right before the tornado hit was the "scariest thing." He was Josh Gibson. "It was like the loudest drum roll I ever heard. Then there was sounds of glass breaking and things crashing around you."

That night Dan Rather devotes about 30 seconds to the tornado. Your editor tells you that it is the first time the town has ever been mentioned on a network newscast.

Harper said this tornado was the only one that did any damage. At least three others were sighted during the afternoon.

City council

Here's what happened at the city council meeting last night.

The meeting started about five minutes late because city council member Harvey Haddix couldn't find a place to park. He came rushing in and made a comment about how the city police were going to have to crack down on illegal parkers. That brought a laugh from the overflow crowd of over two hundred people there. Mayor Ray Sadecki called the meeting to order, and the minister of the Vinegar Bend Baptist Church, Wilber Mizell, started the meeting with prayer. The minutes of the last meeting of the council were read, and no one had any additions or corrections to them.

The first item of business was a report from the Metropolitan Zoning Commission. Bobby Thompson, who is the chairman of the Zoning Commission, said the commission had met two days ago to consider a request by a local developer to move a cemetery so that he can build a supermarket. The developer's name is Carl Erskine. The cemetery is located in the 2800 block of Forbes Street, much of which is zoned for commercial purposes now. Erskine told the council that he will pay all the costs of having the graves relocated in Peaceful Rest Cemetery, which is located about a mile away from the present site. "I think rezoning will be good for the neighborhood and good for the city," Erskine said. "There's not another supermarket for at least a mile and a half in any direction." Thompson said: "We've studied the traffic patterns along Forbes Street, and we don't believe the supermarket will cause any problems." After several more questions by various council members, the mayor asked for any questions or comments from those in the audience. About twenty people spoke, and all but two of them were against the rezoning. It took about an hour. Here are some of the comments:

Early Wynn, 122 Forbes Street: "This thing is going to destroy our neighborhood. It's pretty quiet there now, but if you get this thing in there, it's going to turn noisy."

Dick Groat, 1811 Polo Grounds Road: "Nobody on my street wants the supermarket. We have plenty of places to go to shop. We don't need this. Besides, some of those graves are pretty old, and I don't think it would be the same if you moved them."

Sarah Yawkey, 555 Bosox Drive: "I just can't believe you'd do this. Anybody who'd do this would steal the dimes off a dead man's eyes."

Walt Dropo, 611 Forbes Street and president of the Forbes Street Residents Association: "We've been fighting this thing for two years now. All the zoning commission did was study the traffic patterns. They didn't consider what it would do to the neighborhood. Besides, that cemetery has some of the oldest graves in the city in it -- some of those people helped found this city. I'm sure that if you tried to move some of those stones, they would crumble in your hands. I can promise you that we will mount a campaign to recall any councilmember who votes for this thing." (That comment drew lots of applause from the people who were there.)

Harry Walker, 610 Forbes Street: "I'm afraid Walt's gone overboard on this one, like he usually does. I think our neighborhood needs a supermarket. We've got lots of people who have trouble getting around. Walt's one of these people who's against anything that is progress. He just wants to get some publicity for himself."

When the speakers were done, the council voted 5-2 against the rezoning petition. At that the crowd cheered, and most of them filed out, leaving a small audience of only about 35 or 40 people.

The next item of business was a one-cent sales tax proposed by councilwoman Wilma Rudolph. "The city desperately needs this money," said Rudolph, "or there is a chance that we'll have to start laying off workers next year." Mr. Joe Black, the city treasurer, agreed, saying the city's financial condition was pretty bad. A one-cent sales tax would raise about $400,000 for the city next year, and not only would that mean there would be no layoffs, but it's possible that the city could expand some services, such as having garbage pick-ups twice a week instead of just once a week, he said. "Besides, we figure that such a tax will only cost the average family in the city about $75 a year," Black pointed out. Mayor Sadecki is against the tax. He said, "I believe the people are taxed too heavily now. I don't believe they want this. I think they want to look at our budget and see where we can cut back." But the majority of the council didn't agree with the mayor, and they voted for the tax 5-2. Those voting for the tax were Rudolph, Haddix, Sam Jones, Eddie Matthews and Lew Burdette; those against were Sadecki and Bill Mazeroski.

The last item of business was a proposal from councilman Mazeroski to license morticians in the city. "The state gives us the power to do this, and I think we should take advantage of it," he said. He said his proposal would assess an annual license fee that morticians would have to pay every year. Mazeroski said, "We've got more than 30 mortuaries in the city now, and assessing a fee from them would bring in a considerable amount of revenue." His bill calls for a $150 fee per mortuary per year. Several morticians were in the audience and spoke against Mazeroski's proposals. Don Blasingame, who owns Blasingame Mortuary and who is president of the city's Mortician Society, said: "We don't believe Mr. Mazeroski is correct when he says the state gives the city the power to do this. the state licenses morticians and gives the city the power to enforce this licensing proce-

dure if it chooses to do so. Otherwise, the state enforces the licensing. I believe that if the city did this, it would just have to turn the money over to the state." Harold Reece, the city attorney, said there is some question about this in the law, and he has asked the state attorney general to give an opinion on it. Mazeroski said, "I don't believe we should wait for the opinion. I think we should go ahead and do it." Burdette made a motion to table the proposal, and that passed by a vote of six to one.

With that, Mayor Sadecki adjourned the meeting.

You find out later that when councilman Haddix got to his car after the meeting, there was a parking ticket on it.

Features

Write a short feature story on each of the following sets of information.

Bank robbery

Man named Jesse James tried to rob First Fidelity bank this morning

caught by passing policeman as he backed out the door

had $20,000

same bank had been robbed nearly 100 years ago by real Jesse James and his brother Frank; they too had been caught suspect says: "Jesse James was my great-great uncle. I was just trying to finish the job he sarted."

Police Chief Weldon Freeman: "This man has no sense of history."

Noise abatement

City Civil Court this morning
Judge Jan Sommerfelt
suit involved Lakeshore subdivision residents suing Weatherford Construction Co.
Company was building a road near subdivision
residents complained that noise the construction company was making violated city ordinances against loud noises
Judge ruled in favor of the residents but refused to stop the construction; said con-

struction company would have to give ear-plugs to anyone who complained about the noise

Student sit-up

Local high school student Bobby Lott, junior at City Central, now sitting in tree in front of school

will sit there until Friday's football game with County Central, City's arch-rival; winner of the game goes to state championship

climbed into tree at 9 a.m.

Principal Dick Barrett says Lott is a good student, "has his parents permission to do this," and "I won't make him come down. I don't think he'll get behind in his school work." friends taking class notes for him, handing him food

Lott says this is his way of showing support for the team; he won't come down except to go to the bathroom; says he won't stay in the tree if there's a lightning storm. "I may be crazy, but I'm not stupid."

Features II

Write feature stories based on the following sets of information.

Tennis player

Bucky Haskiell is a tennis pro who graduated from your college two years ago. While in college, he led the team to the conference championship during his senior year and was named the conference's best player. When he graduated, he turned pro.

During this year's Wimbledon tennis tournament in London, England, Haskiell held the limelight briefly when he had to play John McElroy, the eventual champion, during the first round. Haskiell lost to McElroy, but only after he and the champion had played five full sets. The match was also highlighted by one of the fiercest temper tantrums McElroy had ever thrown. At one point during the match, McElroy stormed around the court cursing the officials and nearly got himself eliminated.

Haskiell has returned to the college for an exhibition tournament to raise money for the college tennis team's travel expenses. You are sent to interview him and here's how the interview goes.

What was it like playing John McElroy during the first round at Wimbledon?

Very hard (he says, laughing). In some ways McElroy is much like any other tennis player — only he's very, very good. When he concentrates on tennis alone, there aren't many people who can beat him. When he gets distracted, he tends to let down. But even then, he's hard to beat. I guess I found that out.

Was it the first time you had played him?

No, I had played him once before in a tournament in South Carolina. I beat him the first two sets, but he came back and won the last three to take the match.

Did he throw any tantrums that day?

No, he was pretty calm.

Do you think that the fit he threw at Wimbledon hurt your game that day?

I'm not sure. I've thought about that a lot. I don't think I played as well after he had finished his argument with the line judge as I had been playing. But I don't know if I was tired or what. I didn't really think about it at the time. I was trying to concentrate on my game.

Do you know McElroy personally?

Yes, I've been with him on several occasions. He's really a nice guy off the court and doesn't deserve his 'bad boy' image. He even gave me some pointers about how I was serving once that really helped my game.

What was Wimbledon like? Everybody says it's a great place to be.

Well (laughing), I really wasn't there that long. As a player, it's not a great tournament because of the grass courts, which most of us aren't use to, and the accommodations aren't as good as some we've had at other tournaments. But the atmosphere at Wimbledon is hard to beat. There's so much tradition there — it makes you feel good just having a chance to play. Of course, next year I would like to win a match or two.

Do you expect to be invited back to Wimbledon next year?

I hope so. I'm having a pretty good year. I've won one tournament and have finished in the semi-finals in at least four others. My ranking with the tennis association is better than last year, so maybe I'll get back there.

What's it like having been a tennis pro for two years?

I really enjoyed it, but it's not what people think. Tennis pros aren't pampered people. All of us have to work very hard just to maintain our forms. And we're required to travel a lot — it's not like being a tourist either. It's just one hotel or motel after another. The time you might spend seeing the sights is time you should spend practicing — and you do if you want to be any good. For instance, I saw relatively little of London when I was there for Wimbledon. I'd like to go back sometime when there's not a tournament.

Oldest tree

A plaque marking the oldest tree on campus will be dedicated today. Ceremonies for the dedication will take place under the tree at 10 a.m., and they will also be used to announce a fund raising drive by the alumni association for the school. A news story has already been written about this event. Your job is to write a feature story about the tree which will be used as a sidebar (a journalistic term for a secondary story) with the news story. You gather the following information about the tree:

The tree is a water oak and is thought to be about 100 years old. University records show that the tree was probably planted by students who had been hired to do some work on the campus. One record says that during the spring 50 trees were planted in that area of the campus.

Marcus Maxwell, professor of history and University historian: "The University used to hire students to do odd jobs around the campus, so we think students planted this

tree. There is no exact record of what was planted and by whom, so we're not sure about it.

"A number of buildings have been built in the area of the tree, but none has come so close to it that the tree had to be destroyed. The tree has some significance in university history. the first troop of soldiers that gathered at the University to fight in World War I assembled under that tree right before they left by train to report to their army base. A crowd of people gathered, a band played and some politicians made speeches. It was a pretty festive occasion.

"Likewise, when the first of the University's reserve units was activated right after the beginning of World War II, they also gathered under the tree for a send off. I understand that it wasn't such a festive occasion then."

Elmer Hinton, a retired bicycle repairman in the town, was among the soldiers who started for World War I at the tree. He tells you: "It was hot as blazes that day, even though it was April. Fortunately, we got to stand in the shade, and I remember being thankful of that. I enjoyed the music the band played, but I coulda done without the speeches. Lots of people thought this war was going to be a lark — that all we had to do was show up and the Germans would fade away. It turned out not to be like that at all. The part of World War II I saw was pretty rought."

A number of legends exist about the tree. One is that a man was lynched on the tree around the turn of the century. He had killed the family of the mayor of the town, and one night an angry crowd broke into the jail, took him out and hung him. Newspaper accounts say that a man named Josiah Lindy was hung by an angry crowd in 1901; he was accused of killing the family of Mayor Tyree Jones — Jones' wife and two daughters after the wife had let him in the house and given him something to eat. The news account doesn't say exactly where the lynching took place. Nor does it say that Mayor Jones was part of the crowd.

Another legend that was once popular with students is that the girl who walked under the lowest branch of the tree on the night of the full moon before the homecoming queen election would win that election. That legend became so popular in the 1920s and 1930s that students had a ritual of requiring all homecoming queen candidates to walk under the tree on the night before the election. That ritual died out during World War II.

Flora Handle, a professor in the biology department, says: "The tree is a good example of one of the major types of trees of this area. It is in remarkably good shape for a tree of its age. Usually a tree that old will have too many limbs and not enough foliage to support the whole system. That's not the case with this one. If something doesn't happen — if the tree isn't struck by a disease or by lightning — it should live another 50 or 75 years. It must be trimmed properly."

Your story should include a description of the tree and its location. (For that, you may pick any large tree on your campus.)

Hiker

A local high school teacher, Will Henderson, was lost for four days last week while hiking in the Great Smoky Mountains National Park. Henderson has been hiking along the Appalachian Trail and had gotten off the trail near a place known as Gregory Bald. After a couple of hours of walking off the trail, Henderson tried to cross a stream when he slipped and broke his leg.

Henderson is an experienced hiker. He is a member of the National Hiking Association. He had plenty of food with him at the time. He had been hiking for about 10 days before the accident. He had started in Georgia and was in Tennessee at the time of the accident.

After his fall, Henderson used some sticks and string to make a splint for his leg. He then began four days of crawling, pushing his 40-pound hiking pack in front of him. He crawled through a lot of thick underbrush. Finally, he made it back to the main part of the Appalachian Trail and was soon found by two other hikers.

The Appalachian Trail is nearly 3,000 miles long, stretching from Georgia to Maine. It is one of the most popular hiking trails in the country.

Henderson teaches biology at Jefferson High School. He is 39 and has been hiking since he was a boy of 10.

Henderson was hospitalized for several days in Knoxville during which time a number of stories were written about his ordeal. Now he is back home, recuperating in a local hospital, and your newspaper sends you to interview him. Here's some of what he tells you:

"I never doubted that I would be found. I got discouraged sometimes, but I figured that I had plenty of food and thought that if I could get back to a trail -- particularly the main Appalachian Trail because it's so busy -- somebody would come along before long.

"I'll tell you though, I sure was happy when I heard those first footsteps coming up behind me. Those guys thought I was some kind of animal at first. I guess I looked pretty rough. They kind of hesitated in approaching me, but when I said, 'Help' a couple of times, they came running.

"One of the guys stayed with me while the other went for help. They kept telling me not to go to sleep, and I didn't. I was so happy then that I probably couldn't have even if I had wanted to. I'll never forget the feeling I had when they found me, not if I live to be a hundred. Those guys are going to get mentioned in my will.

"The hardest thing about being lost was thinking that other people might be worrying about me. I was supposed to meet some friends in Gatlinburg a couple of days after I got lost. As it turned out, they weren't worried but said if I had been gone another day, they would have contacted the park rangers and started a search.

"After a day or so of crawling, I had to discard most of my clothes and most of the other things in my pack. They had gotten too wet and heavy for me to push. Of course, I kept all of the food I had. It was mostly dry stuff -- crackers, fruit, peanut butter, things like that.

"The mountain foliage was like a jungle. There had been a lot of rain up there this year, and it was really thick. If I had stayed where I was when I fell, I probably would still be there. At least, that's what one of the park rangers said. I think I knew that instinctively when I fell, so I never thought about staying put. I knew that I had better get somewhere where people could find me.

"Besides food, I did manage to keep a few small things with me. I had several pictures of my wife and two little girls. I looked at them a lot, especially when I got discouraged. I would spend a little time looking at those pictures, and then I would crawl a little bit more.

"I broke the first rule of hiking, of course. I hiked alone. If you're on the Appalachian Trail, it doesn't matter because you're not really alone. There are so many people on that trail. But when you get off the beaten track -- that's when you need to be with somebody. I learned my lesson about that. My goal is still to hike the entire trail, but I guess I'll have to wait until I get my leg in shape.

Magazine writing

Travel article

A travel magazine is running a series of short pieces on several cities in your area. The series is geared toward college students and is trying to tell them things they would want to know if they visited them. Write about 300 words about the city where your college or university is located. Include some basic information about the city and the colleges and universities located there; also tell about places which are popular with students; finally, include something about places in the city which any tourist would want to visit.

Student budget

Write a short article (about 300 words) on how to live on a limited budget during your first year in college. This article is for a

magazine which goes to high school students. You should talk about some of the unexpected expenses a new college student encounters as well as give some advice on how to save money on books, food or other expenses.

A Story with a Moral

Write a short story, possibly based on some incident in your life, that has a moral to it. The story, which should be about 300 words long, is for a religious publication which is geared to teenagers. The story should not be heavily theological, but it should contain some moral message. The story can be completely fictional or based totally on a real happening.

Professor

The alumni magazine of your college or university wants stories on file about the professors who have been selected as the school's outstanding teachers, and you have been asked to write one of them. (You will have to select the professor on whom you do the story.) There are four professors who have been awarded the Outstanding Teacher Award, and the editor wants a 400-word article on each of them. Be sure to include information about the teacher's background, research, personal activities and interests and what makes this teacher outstanding.

"My Most Unforgettable Character"

Reader's Digest runs a regular feature article called "My Most Unforgettable Character." It is a character sketch about the author's encounter with an unusual and interesting character. Write a 400-word article on your most unforgettable character. What was your relationship with the person? What makes the person unforgettable?

6

Writing for Broadcast

Many people believe that broadcasting is the most important medium of mass communication in the world today. Certainly it is the most pervasive. Underdeveloped areas which cannot get access to even a small newspaper will usually have a transistor radio which serves as a link with the rest of the world. On another level, satellite broadcasting is far advanced from what it was just a few years ago, and in many ways it is drawing the world closer together (although not always with positive results). The airwaves are filled with a wide variety of messages which are cheap and convenient to receive.

In America, broadcasting is arguably the most widely used and influential mass medium for receiving information. Americans get their news and information from a variety of sources, and it would be a mistake to believe that broadcasting is always the dominant medium in this regard. Newspapers and newsmagazines deliver a large amount of information to the American public and will continue to do so, but broadcasting is perceived to be the dominant medium. There are more than 6,000 radio and television stations in America (and thousands more shortwave radio operators), as opposed to 1,700 daily newspapers. More people watch the network's brief newscasts during prime time television than read newspapers on any given day.

The opportunities for working in broadcasting are great for those who are willing to apply themselves. The qualities that a person needs to be a success in broadcasting are intelligence, diligence, dependability — and the ability to write. Even though broadcasting is an audio-visual medium, just about everything you hear or see in the way of news or entertainment (except for the broadcasting of live events such as baseball games) has been written down. The occasions for ad libbing before the cameras are rare; broadcasting time is too valuable for such chancy moments. The broadcasting industry is always looking for people who can write clearly, concisely and precisely. Very rarely will the industry hire or promote people who do not have this ability.

Broadcasters look for the same basic qualities in writers that we have discussed earlier in this book. They want people who know the language and its rules well, who are willing to research their subjects thoroughly and understand them well enough to report on them with clarity, who do not mind working hard and who are willing to rewrite their work and have it rewritten by others. In addition, they are particularly interested in people who can write under pressure and can meet deadlines.

Much that is written for broadcasting is like that which is written for the print media, but there are some important differences which we will discuss in this chapter. Those differences concern the way news is selected for broadcast, the characteristics of writing and story structure and the style with which the information is presented.

Selection of news

Most of the same news values discussed in Chapter 4 apply to news selection for broadcasting. Broadcast news reporters, like print journalists, are interested in events which have an impact on many people, prominent people who are often in the news, current issues, events which happen close to home and events which have conflict or an unusual element. Because of the opportunities and limitations of their medium, however, broadcasters are likely to view events in a slightly different way than do print journalists. Some of the factors which broadcasters use to select news are discussed below.

Timeliness. This news value is even more important to the broadcaster than to the print journalist. Print journalists tend to work on daily cycles; broadcasters work on hourly, or less than hourly, cycles. A news broadcaster has to "go to press" many times a day, particularly if he or she is working in radio. The news must be up-to-the-minute. News that is more than an hour or two old may be too stale for the broadcaster. When you listen to a news report on a breaking news story, you expect to hear the very lastest news, and that is what a broadcaster must try to give.

Information, not explanation. Broadcasters look for stories which do not need a lot of explanation in order for listeners or viewers to understand them. They prefer stories which are relatively simple and which can be told in a simple, straightforward manner. The maximum length for almost any story on a television newscast is two minutes; the more normal length is 20 to 30 seconds. This is not enough time to explain a complex story in detail. It is only enough time to give the listener or viewer a few pertinent facts. Of course, some stories are complex and important and explanation cannot be avoided. These are the ones the broadcaster must wrestle with, and it takes practice and talent to condense these stories to their essence.

Audio or visual impact. Broadcasters want stories that their audience can hear or see. Playing a part of the president's state of the union address (called an "actuality") is much more dramatic than a news reporter talking about it; pictures of a flood are more likely to be watched than an anchorman's description of it. Broadcasters often choose stories for their newscasts *because* they have sound or pictures, even though the stories themselves might not merit such attention otherwise. This is one of the major criticisms of broadcast news, but it remains one of the chief factors in broadcast news selection.

Characteristics of writing

The UPI *Broadcast Stylebook* says that while print journalism has the Five Ws, broadcast journalism has the Four Cs — correctness, clarity, conciseness and color. These four Cs serve as the basis for broadcast writing and form a good framework for talking about broadcast writing styles.

The broadcast journalist is a journalist, and the first commitment of a journalist is to accuracy, or correctness. Everything that a broadcast journalist does must contribute to the telling of an accurate story. Even though the broadcast journalist must observe some strict rules about how stories are written, these rules should contribute to, not prevent, an accurate account of an event.

Because of the factors discussed in the previous section, writing news for broadcast has some important characteristics which are different from those of print journalism. These characteristics require the broadcast journalist to approach stories in a slightly different way.

One important characteristic of writing for broadcast is *the emphasis on the immediate.* As we mentioned earlier, broadcast news must be up-to-the-minute. It should also be written as if it is up-to-the-minute. While the past tense for verbs is preferred in the print media, the present tense is preferred in broadcasting. Consequently, while a newspaper story might begin something like this:

```
        The president said yesterday that he will
    support some limited tax increase proposals
    when Congressreconvenes this week. . . .
```

the broadcast news story would begin like this:

```
    The president says he's for high taxes. . .
```

Another way of emphasizing the immediate is to omit the time element in the news story and assume that everything happened today. As we can see in the example above, the broadcast version has no time element since it would probably be heard on the day the presdient made that statement. Of course, news which does occur on a day other than the day of the broadcast should have a time element.

Another important characteristic of writing for broadcast is the *conversational style* which broadcasting requires. Even the clearest, simplest newspaper style tends to sound a little stilted when it's read aloud. Broadcast writing cannot sound this way because people wil be reading it aloud. Broadcast news should be written for the ear, not the eye. The write should keep in mind that someone is going to *say* the words and others will *listen* to them. The writing should style can then be a little more casual than it would be for print.

This casual or conversational style, however, does not give the writer

Slug	SHUTTLE LANDS		Page	1

Directions	Script	

TWO SHOT
 	
ON HALL/ FF
SHUTTLE LAND-
ING
 	
ROLLCSS--VO---
---FT. EDWARDS
AIR FORCE BASE
 	
ON HALL/CU
	(2 shot) (s)
	GOOD EVENING, I'M SCOTT
	RICHARDS.
	   (J) AND I'M JANET HALL.
	*****
	   DISCOVERY WELCOME BACK.
	THOSE WERE THE SWEET WORDS
	FROM MISSION CONTROL TODAY
	AS THE SPACE SHUTTLE
	DISCOVERY MADE A PICTURE
	PERFECT LANDING IN THE
	CALIFORNIA DESERT.
	   THIS WAS THE MOMENT NASA
	HAD WORKED SO HARD FOR
	FOLLOWING THE CHALLENGER
	DISASTER.
	   THE SHUTTLE CREW STEPPED
	OUT OF THE SPACE SHIP WAVING
	A LARGE AMERICAN FLAG AS
	SOME 340 THOUSAND SPECTATORS
	CHEERED.
	   VICE PRESIDENT GEORGE BUSH
	AND SEVERAL NASA OFFICIALS
	WERE THE FIRST TO GREET THE
	ASTRONAUTS.
	   NASA ADMINISTRATOR JAMES
	FLETCHER SAID QUOTE, "THIS
	IS A BANNER DAY FOR ALL OF
	US AT NASA AND WE'RE VERY
	HAPPY THIS ONE WORKED SO
	WELL."
	(2 SHOT) (S)
		1

Figure 6-1
This is the script sheet for the beginning of a local news broadcast that leads off with a national story. The directions on the left indicate that videotape or film is being shown while the announcer is speaking.

Thanks to Janet Hall
WBRC-News, Birmingham

freedom to break the rules of grammar, to use slang or off-color phrasing or to use language which might be offensive to listeners. As with all writing, the broadcast writer should try to focus attention on the content of the writing and not the writing itself.

The *tight phrasing* which is characteristic of broadcast writing is one of its chief assets and one of the most difficult things for a beginning writer to achieve. Because time is so short, the broadcaster cannnot waste words. The broadcaster must work to constantly simplify and condense. There are a number of techniques for achieving this:

Eliminate all but the most necessary adjectives and adverbs. Broadcasters know that their stories are built on nouns and verbs, the strongest words in the language. Avoid using the passive tense. You may say either that a meeting "is held" or that an organization "holds a meeting." If broadcasters had to choose between them, they would choose the latter — and the good broadcast writer would then change the verb to "meets."

Use short, simple sentences. Broadcasters do not need the variety of length and type of sentences which print journalists need to make their copy interesting. Broadcasters can more readily fire information at their readers like bullets in short, simple sentences.

One of the most admirable characteristics of good broadcast writing is its *clarity*. Clarity is an absolute requirement for broadcast writing. Listeners and viewers cannot go back and re-hear a news broadcast as they might be able to re-read a newspaper (although print journalists shouldn't count on their readers to do that either). They must understand what is said the first time. Broadcast writers achieve this kind of clarity by using simple sentences and familiar words, by avoiding the use of pronouns and repeating proper nouns if necessary and by keeping the subject close to the verb in their sentences. Most of all, however, they achieve clarity by thoroughly knowing and understanding their subject.

A final characteristic of broadcast writing is its almost complete subjugation to *deadlines*. Deadlines are far more important to the broadcast writer than to the print journalist, and the act of writing must be done with the knowledge that a deadline is imminent. Unless broadcast writers are able to meet deadline, their compact, understandable prose will never be heard.

Story structure

In Chapter 5, we learned that most straight news stories for the print media are written in an inverted pyramid style — that is, the most important information is presented at the beginning and information of lesser importance is given later in the story. If necessary, a story may be cut from the bottom and the essential parts of the story will remain.

Broadcast journalists do not use the inverted pyramid story structure. In its place, they use something known as *dramatic unity*. The dramatic unity structure has three parts: climax, cause and effect. The climax of the story gives the listener the point of the story in about the same way the lead of a print news story does; it tells the listener what happened. The cause portion of the story tells why it happened — the circumstances surrounding the event. The effect portion of the story gives the listener the context of the story and possbily some insight about what the story will mean for the future. The following example will show how dramatic unity works:

Climax

```
    Taxpayers in the state will be paying an
average of 15 dollars more in income taxes
next year.
```

Cause

```
    The state senate defeated several delaying
amendments this afternoon and passed the gov-
ernor's controversial revenue-raising bill by
a 15 to 14 vote. The bill had been the sub-
ject of intense debate for more than a week.
```

Effect

```
     The bill now goes to the governor for his
sginature. Estimates are that the measure
will raise about 40 million dollars in new
revenue for the state next year. Most of that
money has been earmarked for elementary and
secondary education. Passage of the bill is
seen as a major victory for the governor and
his education program.
```

Broadcast journalists should think of their stories as completed circles rather than inverted pyramids. While the pyramid may be cut without losing the essential facts, the broadcast story, if written in this unified fashion, cannot be cut from the bottom or anywhere else. It stands as a unit. Broadcast journalists and their editors are not concerned with cutting stories after they have been written to make them fit into a news broadcast. The reason for this is that the stories should be written to fit into an amount of time designated by the editor or news director. For instance, an editor may allot 25 seconds for a story. The writer will know this and will write a story that can be read in 25 seconds. If the story is longer than it should be, the editor will ask that it be rewritten. We say more about writing stories to fill a certain amount of time later.

Broadcast news stories, however, must gain the attention of the listener from the beginning. The first words in the story are always extremely important. Getting the attention of the listener is sometimes more important than summarizing the story or giving the most important facts of the story. The broadcast news lead may be short on facts, but if it draws the reader into the story, it has served its purpose. Here's an example:

```
     The lame duck keeps limping along.
     Congress met for the third day of its lame-
duck session today, and again failed to act
on the president's gas tax proposals.
```

The first sentence has very little in the way of facts, but it gets the listener into the story. This sort of story structure is only appropriate for certain stories, however. If the facts of the story are stron enough to gain the listener's attention, they sould be used to open the story. For example:

```
     The five-cents-a-gallon gas tax is law.
     The president signed the bill authorizing
the tax today while on vacation in Califor-
nia.
```

In both of these examples, the writer has not attempted to tell the whole story in the first sentence. Rather, the stories are structured so that they have attention-getting leads and are supported by facts and details in subsequent sentences. This structure for broadcast news writing is a common one which should be mastered by the beginning student.

```
Slug    SOCIAL SECURITY         Page      1

   Directions              Script

TWO SHOT              2-SHOT (J)                        1
                      GOOD EVENING. I'M JANET HALL
                      (S)
ON SCOTT FF/          AND I'M SCOTT RICHARDS.
SOCIAL                ***
SECURITY                IF YOU HAVE A PROBLEM WITH
                      YOUR SOCIAL SECURITY
                      BENEFITS, YOUR PROBLEM COULD
                      BE SOLVED BY JUST PICKING UP
                      THE TELEPHONE.
                        BIRMINGHAM IS THE NEW
                      CENTER FOR A SOCIAL SECURITY
                      TOLL-FREE PHONE SERVICE.
                        NOT ONLY IS THE CENTER
                      CREATING A MUCH-NEEDED
                      SERVICE FOR PEOPLE ALL OVER
                      THE COUNTRY, IT'S ALSO
                      CREATING 350-JOBS FOR
                      BIRMINGHAM.
                      LAURIE KUEHENRT HAS MORE.

TAKE CSS PKG--------- CSS PKG
```

Figure 6-2
This is the script sheet for the beginning of a local news broadcast that leads off with a local story. What you see here is a lead-in for one of the station's news reporters to present her story.

Here are some more examples of newspaper stories and the attention-getting leads that could be written for broadcast:

Newspaper story

Americans overwhelmingly oppose the taxation of employee benefits, and congressmen who tamper with such tax-free worker benefits may fact trouble at the polls, two Roper Organization surveys say.

Broadcast lead

Keep your hands off employee benefits.
That's what Americans are willing to tell congressmen who want to tax things like retirement payments and educational allowances.

Newspaper story

```
    The United States is turning out inferior
products that are priced too high for foreign
customers and the problems go beyond a strong
```

Broadcast Copy Preparation

Copy is prepared for one person, the announcer. The copy should be presented in a way to make the announcer's job as easy as possible. The examples in this chapter should give you an idea of how you should prepare broadcast copy. Here are a few tips:

1. Type only one story on a page. A story should have some ending mark, such as "—30—", at the end.

2. Use caps and lower case. An old style of broadcast writing was to type in all caps. This style is hard to read, however.

3. Don't carry over a paragrpah to another page. If a story is more than a page long, end the page at the end of a paragraph; begin the next page with a new paragraph.

4. Don't hyphenate at the end of a line.

5. Broadcast copy should contain no editing marks. X-ing through a mistake is acceptable, but if any other editing is necessary, the story should be retyped. Remember, the announcer (and it could be you) needs to be able to read through the copy easily.

Broadcasters often want to work tapes (either audio or video) of interviews into their stories. The following example shows you how to indicate this on your copy.

People who want to buy a Chevrolet next year are going to have to pay more. That's what company spokesman John Smith said today in Detroit. The new cars will cost about seven percent more than last year's cars. Smith blamed the increase on the new contract recently negotiated with the United Auto Workers.

```
        ROLL TAPE: The workers are getting more . . .
        END TAPE: . . . really no way of avoiding this.
    [ :15]
        Labor  leaders  disputed  this  reasoning,  however.
    Local auto workers president Stanley Porter said Chev-
    rolet was raising its prices just to make the union
    look bad. At a separate news conference in Detroit, he
    called on Chevrolet to roll back its prices.
        ROLL TAPE: The union gave up a lot . . .
        END TAPE: . . without good reason.[ :18]
```

The number in each of the sets of parentheses indicates the number of seconds of each tape.

dollar, high wages and high taxes, a presidential commission reports.

Broadcast lead

Many American products aren't worth what we are asking for them.

Newspaper story

A lone juror, a city sanitation department supervisor, forced a hung jury and a mistrial of Midville Mayor Reggie Holder's trial on perjury and conspiracy charges involving alleged illegal campaign contributions.

Broadcast lead

One man has made the different in the perjury and conspiracy trial of Midville Mayor Reggie Holder.

The broadcast writer should remember that stories are measured in *time* — minutes and seconds. What a newspaper can devote 10 column inches of type to, a broadcaster may have to say in 20 to 30 seconds. The broadcast writer should keep this time element in mind during every stage of the writing and editing process. Broadcast news stories cannot go into the detail and explanation that print stories can. The broadcast writer must remember that certain facts and explanations must be omitted from the copy if the story is to fit into the time allowed for it.

Style and writing tips

Broadcast writing style differs somewhat from the style you have learned for print journalism. While the *AP Stylebook* is still consulted for many usage questions, broadcast writing takes a different form than writing for print. The following is a list of some of the major differences in form and style.

Titles usually come before names. Just as in print stories, most people mentioned in broadcast stories need to be identified. This identification is handled differently in broadcast news writing, however. Titles almost always precede a name. Consequently, while a print story might have "Alexander Haig, former secretary of state," the broadcast journalist would say, "former Secretary of State Alexander Haig."

Avoid abbreviations, even on second reference. Only the most commonly known abbreviations should be used in broadcast writing. The FBI and UN are two examples. FTC, however, should be spelled out as the Federal Trade Commission.

Avoid direct quotations if possible. Unless a direct quote is es-

| Slug | GADSDEN POLICE CHIEF | Page | 1 |

Directions	Script	

ON HALL/ FF SKYLINK 6	(J)
	  THE CITY OF GADSDEN HAS A NEW POLICE CHIEF TONIGHT DESPITE THE CONTROVERSY THAT SURROUNDED HIS HIRING.
	  FORMER BIRMINGHAM POLICE INSPECTOR JOHNNY MORRIS WAS SWORN IN AS POLICY CHIEF THIS AFTERNOON.
		1

ON HALL/LIVE RON	WE SENT OUR NEW SKYLINK 6 SATELLITE TRUCK TO GADSDEN TODAY . . . RON FUDGE JOINS US NOW VIA SATELLITE. RON, WHAT'S THE REACTION THERE TO THE NEW CHIEF TONIGHT?	
TAKE LIVE FULL SPR: SKYLINK 6 / GADSDEN SPR: SKYLINK 6 / RON FUDGE	(LIVE FULL)	

Figure 6-3
This script sheet shows a lead-in for a live report. The reporter will appear live on camera via satellite and give his report.

sential to accurately tell a story, a broadcast writer won't use it. Paraphrasing quotes is preferred. Direct quotes are hard to handle in broadcast copy because it is awkward to signal the listener that what the broadcaster is saying is a direct quote.

Sometimes, a direct quotation is essential and should be used. When that is the case, the writer needs to tip the listener off to the fact that a direct quote is being used. The use of the phrase "quote . . . unquote" is awkward and should be avoided. Instead, phrases like "in the words of the speaker," "in his own words," "used these words," and "as she put it."

Attribution should some before a quotation, not after it. The sequence of direct quote-speaker-verb which is common in print journalism is not useful for the broadcast writer. Tagging an attribution onto the end of a direct or paraphrased quote is confusing to the listener. The listener should know where the quotation is coming from before hearing the quote.

Use as little punctuation as possible but enough to help the

newscaster through the copy. Remember that broadcast news copy will be read by only one person, the person who is reading it on the air. That person should be able to read through the copy as easily as possible. The excessive use of commas, dashes and semicolons will not help the newscaster.

Numbers and statistics should be rounded off. While a print journalist will want to use a figure which is as exact as possible, a broadcast journalist will be satisfied with a more general figure. Consequently, $4,101,696 in print becomes "more than four million dollars" in broadcast copy.

Numbers themselves are handled somewhat differently than the *AP Stylebook* dictates for print journalists. Here are a few rules about handling numbers in broadcast copy: numbers one through nine should be spelled out; numbers 10 through 999 should be written as numerals; write out hundred, thousand, million, billion, and use a combination of numerals with these numbers where appropriate (for example, 15-hundred, 10-billion); don't write "a million" or "a billion," but rather use the word "one" ("a" sounds like "eight").

Personalize the news when possible and a appropriate. One of the story examples above might have begun, "Gas is going to cost you five cents more a gallon . . . ." Personalizing is a good way of getting a listener interested in a story and of telling the listener how a story affects him or her.

Avoid extended description. "President and chief executive officer of International Widgets John Smith said today . . ." would become "International Widgets President John Smith says . . ."

Avoid using symbols when you write. The dollar sign should never be used. Nor should the percent sign be used. Spell these words out so there will be no mistake on the part of the news reader.

Use phonetic spelling for unfamiliar and hard to pronounce names and words. Again, you are trying to be helpful to the newscaster. Writing "California governor George Duekmejian (Duke-MAY-gen) said today he will propose . . ." will help the newscaster get over a difficult name. Notice that the syllable which is emphasized in pronunciation is written in captial letters. Difficult place names should be handled in the same way. "A car bomb exploded in downtown Caracas (ka-RAH-kus) today . . ." Writers should also be knowledgeable about local pronunciations of place names. For instance, most people know that Louisville, Kentucky is pronounced (LU-ee-vil); but most people do not know that residents of Louisville, Tennessee pronounce the name of their community as (LU-iss-vil). Pronunciation to the broadcast writer is like spelling to the print journalist. It should always be checked if there is any doubt.

Avoid pronouns, and when you have to use them, make sure it's clear to whom you are referring. The broadcast writer needs to strive for absolute clarity in writing. The listener gets only one shot at hearing a broadcast news story, and that story must be easily understandable. Putting too many pronouns in a story can be an obstacle to that kind of clarity. For instance, in the following sentence, it is unclear to whom the pronoun is referring: The president and the chief foreign affairs advisor met yesterday. They discussed his recent trip to the Mideast.

Avoid apposition. An apposition is a word or set of words that renames a noun. In "Tom Smith, mayor of Midville, said today . . ." the phrase "mayor of Midville" is an appositional phrase. These phrases are deadly in broadcast writing. They slow the newscaster down, and they are often confusing to the listener. Appositions, when they are found in the middle of sentences, are surrounded by commas. Listeners to broadcast stories do not have the advantage of those commas, however. Consequently, they may hear the example above as "Midville said." Broadcast writers should keep subjects and verbs as close together as possible.

Use the present tense when it is appropriate. Using the present tense ("the president says" rather than "the president said") is one way broadcast writers have of bringing immediacy to their writing. That is perfectly proper in broadcast writing. Care should be taken, however, that using the present tense doesn't make the broadcaster sound foolish. For instance, if the president made a statement yesterday, a broadcast news story probably should not have the attribution in the present tense. The past tense would be more appropriate. The present tense should be used for action that is very recent or that is continuing.

Avoid dependent clauses at the beginning of sentences. These clauses are sometimes troublesome to print journalists because such clauses must refer to the subject of the sentence. They are troublesome to the broadcast writer for that reason, too, but also because they are confusing and tend to hide the subject of the sentence. For instance, "Stopping on the first leg of his European tour today, the president said he . . ." can be very confusing for the listener. The broadcast writer should always remember that the simple sentence — subject, verb, object — is the best format to use.

Putting together a newscast

Broadcast journalists work with time and against time. They use time to measure their stories, but they are also always working against the clock. Their Stories must be done in time for the next newscast. People working in radio feel this pressure keenly because of the hourly news shows which many radio stations produce. Television journalists are more subject to these pressures today because many television stations have increased their news offerings. Instead of simply the evening news and late-night news reports which TV stations once scheduled, many stations now have morning and noon news shows and news briefs throughout the day. For the broadcast journalist, the clock is always ticking toward a deadline, and the deadline cannot be delayed.

Many broadcast journalists—even those who are fairly new in the business—must worry not only about writing their stories but also about putting together a newscast. Producing such a news cast whether it is a 45-second news brief or a half-hour telecast, involves many of the skills learned as a news writer.

The first such skill is that of exercising news judgment. In Chapter 4 we discussed a set of news values which may be apparent in any news story. Writers must use those values in deciding what events constitute nes. Editors and producers use those same values in deciding what goes into a newscast. Since we have emphasized the element of timeliness and the importance of time in broadcast writing, it should come as no surprise that the key element in putting together newscasts is the timeliness of the stories. A newscast producer looks at the stories available and often decides which ones to run based on how recent the stories are. Since broadcasting is a medium that can emphasize the immediate, news producers often take advantage of this quality by telling listeners and viewers what happened only minutes before a newscast.

Timeliness is not the overriding news value, however. Just because a story is the most recent one available does not mean that it will be the one which is used first in a newscast. Stories which are older but have more impact or involve more prominent people may take precedence. All of the other news values come into play in putting together a newscast, but timeliness is the most important one.

Another element which news producers use in deciding what to put into a newscast is the aids available for a story, such as audio tapes, slides, film and video tapes. One of the criticisms of broadcast journalism is that decisions about what to run and what not to run are based on the availability of such aids. It is true that often such decisions are made, but broadcast journalist — especially television journalist — feel that they must take advantage of their medium to show a story rather than just tell it. Pictures compel viewers to watch, and the feeling of many in television is that the "talking head," the news announcer with no aid, is not as compelling

Finally, in discussing the newscast, we must come back to the element of time. Not only must stories be timely in themselves, but they must be written to fill a certain amount of air time. The producer or news director is generally the one who assigns the amount of time for a story to fill up. The writer must then write a story which can be read in that time. The producer, of course, must have enough copy to fill up the time allotted for the newscast. Sometimes, however, even with the most careful planning, a newscast producer will come up a few seconds short. The producer should always give the announcer one or two more stories than he or she will need in order to fill this time.

Conclusion

Writing for broadcast places a difficult set of demands on the writer. Broadcast news is written is a different form—dramatic unity—than the inverted pyramid structure that we discussed in Chapter 5. Broadcast copy is written for the ear rather than the eye; that is, writers must be aware that the consumers of broadcast news will be listening to what they write rather than reading it. Finally, in writing broadcast copy, the writer is less concerned with relating the details of a story than with making sure that a story is told as completely and clearly as possible in a short amount of time.

All of these characteristics of broadcast writing place a heavy burden on the writer of broadcast copy. Producing such copy is no easy task. The person who can do it consistently and well, however, is likely to have a large audience for his or her work.

Points for consideration and discussion

1. The author begins the chapter by saying that many people believe that the broadcast medium is the most important medium of mass communication. Do you agree or disagree?

2. List the major differences between writing news for broadcast and writing news for print. Which of these differences makes writing for broadcast more difficult than writing for print? Which makes it easier?

3. Take a story from the front page of your local newspaper. Read it through completely. Now list, as briefly as possible, the three major facts of that story. That's the kind of thing a broadcast journalist must do. Try to write a 30-second story using the three facts that you have listed.

4. Look at the lead paragraph of each of the stories in the figures in this chapter (pages 140, 143, and 146). What devices did the reporters use in writing these leads? Do you consider these leads good one?

5. Make a list of names of local personalities that might be hard to pronounce for broadcasts. Then write their phonetic spellings.

Further reading

Edward Bliss and John Patterson, *Writing News for Broadcast*, New York: Columbia University Press, 1971.

Irving Fang, *Television News*, New York: Hastings House, 1971.

Robert L. Hilliard, *Writing for Television and Radio*, 4th Ed., Belmont, CA: Wadsworth, 1984.

Peter E. Mayeux, *Writing for the Broadcast Media*, Boston: Allyn and Bacon, Inc., 1985.

Mitchell Stephens, *Broadcast News*, New York: Holt, Rinehart and Winston, 1980.

EXERCISES

The following section contains a variety of broadcast writing exercises. You should follow your instructor's directions in completing them.

Broadcast leads

Write a broadcast lead—the first one or two sentences of a story—based on the following information.

FFC official

James Graybeard, congressional liaison for Federal Communication Commission
Speaking to meeting of State Broadcasters, meeting in town today
"We are on a brink of new era in communication...new technology are not all that new-what's different is that costs are lower. Many more people can now use technology because the prices are going down and because equipment is easier to operate. Every day, engineers are making technology more accessible. Direct broadcast satellites (DBS) will be available to everyone in the U.S. for the price of a television set by 1995."

Car telephones

Survey by local telephone company
Number car telephones in area doubled last year
948 last year; 2110 last year
Survey shows mostly used by businesses for business purposes; personal use of car telephone limited but growing

Homecoming

Pep rally on Friday right before Saturday's homecoming football game
Begins at 7:30 p.m.
Featuring bonfire and music by pep band
For the first time this year a fireworks show, produced by fireworks artist Larry Lain, who designs fireworks for world's fairs
Fireworks to begin about 9 p.m.

Country music songwriter

Bill Gillespie, country music song writer; resident of Nashville; spoke to university music appreciation class today
Told student to "write if you feel like it; don't write if you don't"
Gillespie has written hit songs for Dolly Parton, Buck Owens, Charlie Pride
Most recent hit: "Sell Your Soul to the Devil"

House fire

House valued at $150,783 burned completely this morning
Address : 716 Ruppert Street, in Woodland Lake subdivision
Owner: George Mason, vice president of the First Trust Bank
No one at home at the time of the fire
Three engines fought the fire for more than an hour
Don Kerlinger, photograher for local paper, hurt by falling timbers as he tried to take pictures of the blaze; in satisfactory condition at local hospital with minor burns and bruises

Historic document

Letter signed by Robert E. Lee found by local woman this morning
Mattie Harrington, 718 Donald Avenue
She was going through some papers in a trunk in her attic
Says letter was written to her great-grandfather after the battle of Gettysburg
Says Lee talked about the battle, saying he had made some mistakes during the battle but still expressed optimism about the outcome of the war
Letter dated August 17, 1863
Letter now in the custody of the university history department;
Dr. Robert Weir checking its authenticity

Absence policy

New absence policy being considered by university

More than four absences from class during the semester will result in automatic failing grade

Neil Hendron, president of the Student Government Association, said today the policy is "unreasonable" and "outrageous." "I don't think it can or will be enforced."

Faculty senate last week passed a resolution endorsing the policy.

Newscast I

Construct a two-minute newscast based on the following items.

Capsize

A 15-foot boat capsized in rough waters off Point Lookout yesterday evening. Two men—Terry Reston, 23, and Will Bendix, 25—were in the boat. The men said offshore winds increased wave heights and capsized their boat. The men were picked up by a Coast Guard boat after an hour in the water. Both were hospitalized for observation, but the hospital lists their condition today as good. The men say they were hunting sharks about 200 yards offshore.

Basketball death

A 15-year-old freshman basketball player died this morning during practice at Central High School. The freshman, Todd White, collapsed while running during a practice game. White had not had any known illness, according to trainer Mike Way. White was pronounced dead at Central Valley Memorial Hospital after all efforts to revive him failed. An autopsy will be performed by the county coroner today.

Energy plan

The secretary of the interior announced a new $800 million energy plan while traveling through the Western United States on a busy three-day tour. The secretary of the interior announced his plan at a Western Governor's Conference meeting in Salt Lake City. The plan calls for a five-year program to ease strains brought on by strip mining and other energy ventures.

Abuse acquittal

A fourth-grade school teacher in Midville has been acquitted of child abuse for spanking a 10-year-old girl with a wooden paddle after the girl lied about having gum in her mouth. The District Court jury returned a verdict of not guilty after deliberating three hours. Lynda Kristle had been charged with child abuse after parents noted bruises on the child's buttocks.

Hotel opening

The world's largest casino-hotel opened yesterday in Reno, Nev. The MGM Grand is on a 145-acre site and will accommodate more than 1,500 persons. It has 19 bars. Prices for rooms range from $50 to $250 per day.

Newscast II

Construct a two-minute newscast based on the following items.

Retirement

The speaker of the state House of Representatives, Milton Bradford, has announced that he will not seek re-election. He has served in the state house for 27 years and has been speaker for the past 10 years. He is a Democrat from Logansville. He has always been closely aligned with the state's education lobby and has recently worked for substantial pay raises for the state's elementary and secondary school teachers.

New runway

The Airport Authority has announced that a new runway will be built some time next year. The airport now has three runways, and this fourth one will increase the airport's capacity. The new runway is being built to meet increased demands from airlines that want to schedule more flights into the city. The costs of construction for the new runway will be about $3 million, but Sam Peck, chairman of the Airport Authority, says the airport should recover the costs within about three and a half years.

Strike

Machinists Union Local 333 has called for an indefinite walkout of all local members against the city's General Motors plant. The walkout was called because the contract that GM has with the machinists expired last Friday. Since then, workers have been working without a contract, and Barney Olive, president of the union, said this situation cannot continue. "We have bargained in good faith, but we can see no evidence that General Motors is doing the same thing." General Motors spokesmen refused to comment about the walkout but said the plant will maintain its operation. The plant manufactures hubcaps for GM tires.

Concert

The City Community Orchestra and the City Chorus will combine forces this Sunday and present a joint concert which will feature the last movement of Beethoven's Ninth Symphoy. Lister Banks and Quenton Hill are leaders of the orchestra and chorus, respectively. Banks said this is the first time the two organizations have performed jointly. In addition to the Beethoven symphony, the chorus will perform works by Bach and the symphony will play works by Brahms. The concert will be at the City Auditorium at 3 p.m. Sunday. Admission is two dollars for adults and a dollar for students.

Custody battle

Bobby Ray Hacks, a native of the city and now a famous songwriter in Nashville, has said he will try to disprove a child- molesting charge and regain custody of his 12-year-old son. In a Nashville courtroom, Hacks vowed to fight the charges brought against him by his former wife. They were divorced last year. He was convicted of child molesting last week, and his sentence hearing was today. He received a six-month suspended sentence but was also told that he had to give up custody of his son.

Newscast III

Write a two-minute newscast using the following information.

Bank robbery

The city hasn't had a bank robbery for six months. That changed this morning when two men, both wearing ski masks, entered the Fidelity Federal Bank, the downtown branch, just after it opened this morning. Police Chief Arthur Shultz said the men must have been waiting for the bank to open. They took $22,000 in cash and an undetermined amount in checks and securities, according to the bank's manager Jack Sherry. The men came into the bank brandishing shotguns, and one of them fired a couple of shots into the air. They made all the people in the bank lie down on the floor except for Sherry. "Fortunately, we hadn't taken all of the money we would have out of the vault, and they seemed interested only in the money they could see." Both men were tall and wearing leather jackets. They ran out of the bank and jumped into a red, four-door Chevrolet with a New York license plate. The county sheriff, Pat Gibson, said that roadblocks have been set up on all main roads leading out of the west of the county. That's all you have right now. A reporter from your station is working on the story.

Donations

The county's United Way drive has been going on for three months. Today it was brought to a close officially by this year's chairman, Sara Morris, a local attorney. She said that a record had been set. The county United Way raised $455,789.03. More than a hundred thousand people contributed. That's a record, too, according to

Morris. "We couldn't be happier with the progress that we have made in this year's fund drive. The people of this city and county have responded far beyond our expectations." Last year's drive netted just over $400,000, and the goal this year was $400,000 again. United Way helps various community charitable and service organizations. Morris said the United Way board will meet soon to decide on how the money will be allocated.

Reactions

Don Seigel, the press secretary to the mayor, says that the mayor's office has received "literally hundreds" of phone calls this morning. Most of the people calling are mad because of the increase in property tax the city council voted last night. The council voted to increase property tax 10 percent across the board. That means everyone who owns property in the city will have to pay 10 percent more in taxes. "Actually, a 10 percent increase isn't that much because our property tax base is so low now," Seigel said. Mayor Lyle Fester proposed the tax, and after a heated debate, it passed 5-2. A number of people have called the radio station this morning complaining about the tax. It will go into effect next July 1. One citizen's group, the Taxpayer's Union, has announced that it is planning a recall movement against the mayor because of the part he played in proposing the tax. Seigel says, "We knew people would be upset. It was a tough decision, but it was the right thing to do. Most of this new money will go the the city school system, and they need it bad."

Books gift

Stanely Minion taught journalism at the local university for more than 30 years. He retired last year. Yesterday, the university announced that he had donated his entire collection of books and newspapers to the library. Minion was a noted collector of newspaper front pages, and his collection includes many pre-Revolutionary War newspapers. Quincy Mundt, the university librarian, said he is "thrilled" about the gift.

"Dr. Minion has some newspapers that aren't available anywhere else that I know of. His collection is one of the best. We are looking into plans to remodel one floor of the library to house the collection. We would like to make the newspapers available to the public for viewing as well as to researchers." Minion's donation includes more than 7,000 books and 10,301 newspapes. Mundt said the collection is worth at least $133,000.

Traffic lights

A violent rainstorm passed over the city early this morning. It didn't last long, only a few minutes. But lightning struck one of the power company's substations and knocked out the traffic lights on one of the city's busy streets, McTerril Boulevard. Traffic backed up for several blocks during rush hour, and several accidents were reported. At least three of them were caused by the lights being out, according to the police chief. Your reporter on the scene says traffic delays of up to 45 minutes were reported in some areas. "The wet streets from the rainstorm didn't help us any," the police chief said. The power was restored and the lights were working by 8:30.

History of the county

The county historical society has been working on a comprehensive history of the county for several years. This morning, Lila Bancroft, president of the society, announced that the project has been completed and that a history of the county will be published some time early next year. She said many of the members of the society contributed to the work, but the main author was John Widner, a retired history professor at the university and a native of the county. The book will cover county history from the earliest settlers in the 1700s to the present day. "It's going to be a beautiful book-very well written and with lots of illustratons," according to Bancroft. The pre-publication price will be $17.50; after publication, the price will be $25. It will be available in all the local bookstores.

Newscast IV

Write a two-minute newscast using the following information.

Canine pacemaker

Last week, Marie Bruton's dog was sick. This week it's better. In fact, it's up and running around—"chasing the cat," she says. The reason is because the dog has had a pacemaker inserted to keep its heart going. Dr. Charles Eulau, a local vet, did the surgery, and he says it's the first time anything like this has been done in this area. Mrs. Bruton: "Wrangler had been pretty listless. Then last week he just collapsed. I didn't know he had a heart problem until I took him to the vet. Now he's doing fine. I think he knows that something has happened to him—that he's been given a new lease on life." Eulau says he used an old pacemaker provided to him by the local hospital. It cost about $100, and he charged $50 for the operation. Mrs. Bruton is a legal secretary for a local law firm.

Sentencing

A local man has been on trail for several months, accused of poisoning some Halloween candy. His name is Sam Gather. Two days ago a jury convicted him after a week-long trial. His attorney argued that he was insane, but the jury did not accept that defense. Less than an hour ago, Judge Harvey Eagle sentenced him to five years in prison. This was the maximum sentence the judge could give him since he wasn't trying to kill the children, just make them sick. At least ten children got sick from eating the candy given to them by Gather. He had put some cleaning fluid onto some hard candy, which he then gave to the kids.

Beerless St. Patrick's Day

M.A.D.D. stands for Mothers Against Drunk Driving. This organization is working to get drunken drivers off the road and to strengthen laws against them. It also helps victims and families of victims of drunken-driving accidents. Denise Clearly, president of the local chapter, has announced a "beerless St. Patrick's Day party." The party will be on March 17 at Palisades Park. It will feature a cookout and entertainment by a local bluegrass group, Ham'n Eggs. It will start at 5 p.m., and according to Clearly, "Everybody is invited. We want to show people that they can have fun without having to drink." She said that information about M.A.D.D. will be available at the party, and interested people may join. The annual dues are $10 a year.

Stabbing deaths

Frederic Church, a local contractor, and his wife, Sarah, were found in their $300,000 home Sunday, beaten and stabbed to death. Their home is on Lake Smith. Police say they think the couple surprised a burglar because some jewelry and other valuable items were stolen. This morning the police announced that they had arrested and charged a 15-year-old boy with the crimes. They said he is a local youth, but his name is being withheld at this time. His name should be available from the district attorney's office later in the day. The police said he was seen by neighbors leaving the house on Sunday, and they said footprints in the mud outside the house matched a shoe belonging to the boy.

Depositers

Two months ago the Trust National Bank was declared bankrupt by the U.S. government. The bank was a state bank and not federally insured, so a lot of people lost their money. A number of people had their life savings invested in the bank, and they have been wondering about it ever since. Today the state claims board, which handles these kinds of things, announced that the state would provide about $60 million to pay back the investors. This amount of money would mean that investors would get about 40 cents back for every dollar they had in the bank. The money would be paid out over a period of three years. The state legislature must still approve the plan.

Resignation

The state treasurer is a man named Manness Manford. He has been state treasurer for 20 years, which means that he has been elected to the post four straight times. Today, at the state capital, Mr. Manford announced that he is leaving office at the end of this month. He had just been re-elected to the position last November. He is leaving to become president of Fidelity National Bank in the capital city. Mr. Manford is from your town and a lot of people there know him. He is credited with revising the accounting procedures for the state, making it easier for the state legislature to predict the amounts of funding that will be available for the upcoming fiscal years. There have been rumors that he has been ill and not able to do his job. The governor made the following statement: "We believe that Manness Manford has served the state well. He has approached his job with imagination and foresight, and he has made the job of everyone in state government easier. He's my good friend, and I hate to have the state lose his services, but I can understand his desire to go into private business. We all wish him well."

More broadcast writing

Rewrite into radio and television style these stories from the UPI newspaper wire. Make a special effort to boil them down into capsule form. Watch for errors in style.

Hurricane

MIAMI, FLA.—Hurricane Nancy lurched toward the United States today after a brief pause last night during which she whipped up 160-mile an hour winds and developed into the most intense storm since 1935.

As the huge storm swung into motion, hurricane watchers warned persons in the target area of the possibility of monster tides being pushed ahead of Nancy.

Officials at the National Hurricane Center here said the storm was about 325 miles south of Pensacola, headed for the Florida Panhandle at a speed of 12 mph. At that speed she would strike the mainland tonight.

She was expected to hit the Panhandle with wind speeds of up to 156 mph.

Residents and travelers were told to move from low and exposed places which the up-to- 15-foot tides could cut off from escape routes.

"Nancy is now very similar to the 1935 storm," said Dr. Robert H. Simpson, head of the National Hurricane Center. "She has a very large fury concentrated in an exceedingly small area."

Seismography report

WASHINGTON, D.C.—One hundred seismograph stations could keep Russia from violating an atomic test ban and at the same time provide new knowledge of how the earth is put together. This view was expressed by seismologist Frank Press of the California Institute of Technology at the annual meeting of the National Academy of Sciences.

Earth waves generated by quakes or large explosions provide science with a tool for studying the planet's structure from crust to core. Such waves are recorded by seismographs. Dr. Press said a network of 100 special seismograph stations could be established in a country the size of the USSR for less than $10 million and "operated at an annual cost of several million dollars." Such a system would spot any sneak atomic tests and at the same time, by recording earthquakes, provide a scientific bonus which "would justify much of the cost."

Authorities agree that no nation could start undetected tests of large nuclear weapons. But in the absence of a monitoring system small underground shots "present the possibility of evasion," Press said.

Collision prevention

SACRAMENTO—A device that has the capability of preventing in-flight airplane collisions through use of infrared rays has been described to a radio engineers conference here. The gadget, designed and developed by the Aerojet-General Corp. of Sacramento, uses invisible heat rays received from the oncoming aircraft to trigger an alarm.

Robert G. Richards, operations analyst for Aerojet's Avionics Division, told the Seventh Regional Conference and Trade Show of the Institute of Radio Engineers yesterday that the invisible heat rays are sent out by all engines, motors, electrical apparatus, or anything having a source of heat as part of its makeup.

It took about 14 years of research to develop the device which, Richards explained, would have provided a warning in the case of the Grand Canyon disaster more than three minutes before the collision.

Interviewing for broadcast

Highway deaths

The State Department of Transportation today said that the total number of trafic deaths on the state's highways was 120. This is the lowest total in 10 years. Your station sends you to do an interview with the State Transportation Commissioner Dick Blocker about why this occurred.

Having the lowest highway death total in 10 years is quite an accomplishment.

That's right, it is. I think the people of the state are to be commended for it. I think we must be doing something right.

What do you think we are doing right?

Several things. For one thing, I think people are just being more careful, observing the speed limit, having their cars checked, watching out for hazardous conditions-things like that.

The 55-mile-an-hour speed limit-do you think that's had an effect?

Well, the 55-mile-an-hour speed limit has been in place for more than a decade, so last year's low figure wouldn't necessarily be due to that. You know, it's interesting about the 55 limit. It was originally established to conserve fuel, but it's real effect has been to save lives. It's not that everyone is observing the 55 limit per se. But I think the 55 limit has made people drive more slowly than they would otherwise. So now, instead of the average speed being 75, it might only be 65-and that's an improvement.

Do you know of any specific reason that the death total should have been so low last year?

We're looking into that. One reason has to be the good weather we had generally last year. Hazardous weather conditions create a lot of accidents, and we didn't have much of that last year. Another reason has to be the tough new car safety inspection law the governor proposed and the legislature passed three years ago. I think that's gotten a lot of cars off the road that might have caused accidents.

Is drinking and driving a problem in the state?

Yes, definitely. Eighty out of the 120 people who were killed in automobile accidents in the state last year were killed in accidents where alcohol was involved. Alcohol is still the major safety problem in this state.

What's being done about that?

As you probably know, the governor has sponsored legislation to increase the penalties for those convicted of drunk driving. We were joined in this by M.A.D.D., Mothers Against Drunk Driving. We have also sponsored legislation that would raise the legal drinking age from 19 to 21. Unfortunately, neither measure was passed by the legislature this session, but we'll be trying against next session.

Hall of Fame

A local resident, George M. "Bucky" Barnett, has just been elected to Baseball's Hall of Fame. Barnett spent most of his career as a shortstop for the St. Louis Cardinals, from 1923 to 1936. He also played with the Boston Red Sox before he retired in 1939. He then spent 20 years as a coach and minor-league manager and has been living in your city since leaving baseball. Barnett was best known as a fielder. Grantland Rice, the famed sportswriter, once described Barnett as "personified lightning" on the field. In fact, he had the highest fielding percentage of any shortstop, .993 (fielding percentage is the number of chances handled without making an error). He had a lifetime batting average of .310. Your station sends you to interview him.

How did you get interested in baseball?

When I was growing up, you didn't get interested in baseball. Baseball was just there-kind of like milk. I don't guess it ever occurred to most of us not to be interested in baseball.

What's different about kids growing up today? Why aren't they as interested in baseball as your generation seems to have been?

There are a lot of distractions, I think. When I was growing up, baseball was about all you had, and you simply tried to survive the winter waiting for spring training to begin. Now kids have television and basketball and football to look at if they want to.

I take it you don't think much of football?

I don't have anything against football. It's just that I love baseball so much. Nothing comes as close to being a perfect game as baseball. A good baseball game has lots of little dramas going on on the field at the same time, and it takes a keen, intelligent eye to see just a few of them. I'm sorry that many kids today seem to have adopted another sport. I think they're settling for second best.

What was the greatest thrill of your baseball career?

I think it was when the Cardinals won the World Series from the New York Yankees in 1926. The Yankees of 1927 were supposed to be the greatest team in the history of baseball. They had essentially the same team in 1926, and we beat them. I don't think anything in my playing career gave me so much joy as beating the Yankees that year.

People have said that you were the greatest fielding shortstop in the history of baseball.

That's flattering, but I'm not sure it's true. The game has produced several great men at short. It's funny because I always thought fielding was the easiest part of the game. It was just a matter of staying alert, knowing the hitters, and moving with the pitch. Usually, I just wound up where the ball was. Hitting was always the hardest part of the game for me-something I really had to work at. I think I was lucky to have such a high hitting percentage.

7

Writing Advertising Copy

Advertising pervades every part of our society. The products we use in our homes, the clothes we wear, the programs we watch on television, the books we read, the places where we shop and go for recreation–all of these things are affected by advertising.

Advertising is one of the country's major industries. One estimate put the money spent on advertising in 1984 at $85.4 billion. One company alone, Procter and Gamble, the nation's largest advertiser in 1982, spent $726 million in 1982. By 1988 that figure had gone up to more than $1.4 billion, and Procter and Gamble was no longer the nation's top spender. Philip Morris Companies had taken its place, spending $1.5 billion. Major companies routinely spend thousands of dollars on the production of advertisements, and the costs of buying time in the mass media can be astronomical. In just one product category, soft drinks, Coca-Cola spent $141 million in 1987 to promote its chief product; Pepsi spent $135 million; and 7-Up spent $62.8 million. The entire retail soft drink market that year generated revenues of $40 billion. When Procter and Gamble introduced a new product, Citrus Hill, into the frozen orange juice concentrate market in 1983, the company was prepared to spend $100 million in advertising.

Charges for network television advertising time during the National Football League Super Bowl are among the highest prices any advertiser can pay. In 1983, 30 seconds of air time during the Super Bowl cost $330,000. For the 1988 Super Bowl, those charges had risen to nearly $650,000. For the 1989 Super Bowl, Anhauser-Busch spent $5 million to become the sole beer advertiser during the Super Bowl and then spent another $1 million to produce six 30-second spots, which company officials planned to show only once. One of the most watched programs in television history, the final episode of "MASH" in the spring of 1983, cost advertisers about $450,000 for 30 seconds of air time. An average 30-second prime-time television announcement costs more than $100,000 and about $200,000 to produce.

People who spend that much money obviously expect a return, and they often get it. Most companies recognize the need to advertise and the benefits of doing so, and they are willing to pay a price for it. Because advertising is so costly, however, there is little room for error or waste. In this chapter we will discuss the writing of advertising copy, but we must always keep in mind that the writing of the ad is only a part of the marketing strategy of a company. Writers of advertising copy must have more on their minds than how the ad will look and what the ad will say.

A love-hate relationship

Americans have a love-hate relationship with advertising. Many people claim that they never pay attention to advertising. They say they leave the room when a commercial comes on television, and they never read the ads in newspapers or magazines. Most will tell you they never make consumer decisions based on the ads they see, as if to do so would be to admit something is wrong with them.

More sophisticated critics of advertisements put them down as insulting and degrading. They say that ads create desires and needs which are often wasteful and unhealthy. Advertisers, they believe, use false, misleading, or deceptive measures to foist their products on an unsuspecting public. They pollute the public's mind and its environment with their messages.

Despite these criticisms, advertising is one of the vital links in the modern economic chain. It is a major way of getting information to a consumer, information that a consumer often wants and needs. For example, a billboard near an interstate highway telling the location of a gas station may be an eyesore to some, but to the driver who is low on gas, it provides a vital piece of information.

Those who say that they never pay attention to advertising are not being honest. To live in today's society means receiving the messages of advertisers. There are few places people can go where advertising will not reach them. Even the "non-commercial" public broadcasting system contains advertisements, in the form of credits to those who contribute to its programming and promotional spots for upcoming shows. One estimate has the individual consumer confronted with 1,600 advertising messages every day.

Not only do people pay attention to advertising messages, but they often act according to those messages. Advertising works. Check around any room in your house, and you will find plenty of items purchased, in part at least, because of the advertising you have encountered.

Figure 7-1
The process of writing an advertisement takes into account many factors, as pictured in the figure on the opposite page. We will discuss each of these factors in this chapter.

Developing an Advertisement

Needs and Desires

Food and drink
Shelter, security, comfort
Sex, intimacy, and social contact
Independence, privacy, self-fulfillment,
 and power
Stimulation
Acquisition

Audience

Age
Income
Sex
Education
Marital status

Product

Working characteristics
Physcial characteristics
History
Manufacturer
Price

Advertising situation

key fact
advertising problem
advertising objective

Unique Selling Proposition

Copy Platform

product characteristics
audience
appeals
benefits

Writing

A-I-D-A
Use clear, simple English
Pay attention to verbs
Be specific
Be precise
Use personal pronouns
Don't be afraid of contractions
Inspire confidence
Give audience information it needs

Print

Headline
Subhead
Body copy
Illustrations
Closings
Logo & signatures
Mandatories &
 legals

Broadcast

Voices
Sound effects
Music
Graphics
Formats

Other media

Point of purchase
Outdoor
Direct mail

The field of advertising

The person who wants to enter the field of advertising has chosen an exciting and challenging profession. Advertising copywriters must be willing to work long and difficult hours researching their products and audiences and straining their creative forces to be successful. Like other writers for the mass media, they must love and understand the language and must be willing to be caretakers of it. They must be willing to change their creativity into forms that others are willing to pay for and support. The rewards to the few who are able to do well in this profession are great.

Two concepts should form the base of a student's thinking about writing advertising copy.

Advertising copy is a different form of writing than the ones that we have studied in other parts of this book. Its purpose is to persuade and motivate. The basic precepts of good writing-simplicity, brevity, accuracy, word precision-remain in force with writing advertising copy as they do with all other forms of writing.

Advertising is based on the assumption that words have the power to produce a change-a change in thinking, attitudes, beliefs, and ultimately, behavior. Advertising that does not accomplish this, or aid in accomplishing it, is worthless. Copywriters must select the words and ideas that will help produce this change.

The process of advertising copywriting is in many ways the same as the process of news writing. The copywriter must process information and put it into an acceptable form for its medium. Just like the newswriter, the advertising copywriter must conduct research before the writing begins. He or she must decide what is important enough to use and what must be left out. The copywriter must choose the words and the structure for the copy that will best fit the product, media, and purpose for the advertising. The copywriter, like the newswriter, is subject to many editors–not the least of whom is the client who is paying for. the advertising and whose ideas about advertising copy may differ radically from those of the copywriter.

> *Advertising is based on the assumption that words have the power to produce a change—a change in thinking, attitudes, beliefs and ultimately behavior. Advertising that does not accomplish, or aid in accomplishing this, is worthless. Copywriters must select the words and ideas that will help produce this change.*

But what about the "creative process?" Doesn't advertising copy require more creativity on the part of the writer than newswriting? In some respects, it does. Ad copywriters have a greater variety of forms for their work than do newswriters, who are often confined to the inverted pyramid or dramatic unity.

Those entering the field of advertising make a serious mistake, however, if they believe that because advertising requires creativity, they have complete license to write what they want when they want. A prime example of what many would consider a lack of creativity is found in the advertising for many Procter and Gamble products–household items such as Tide and toothpaste such as Crest. Advertisements for these products rarely win awards given to the more "creative" or attention-getting ads for the competition. Yet many of these products– backed by a large advertising budget–take a lion's share of their market, and Procter and Gamble remains one of the biggest spenders in the advertising industry. The evidence at the cash register is that the ads for these products, despite their lack of creativity, work, and that's the kind of evidence that a client wants.

On the other hand, highly innovative approaches for ads are often effective, especially when products have established and well-rooted competition and the purpose of the ad is to gain the consumer's attention. Possibly the leading proponent of the off-the-wall approach is Joe Sedelmaier of Sedelmaier Productions in Chicago. In 1984, Sedelmaier created an ad for Wendy's fast food chain that had a little old lady in front of a fast food counter (at the competition's store, not Wendy's) shouting, "Where's the beef?!" That cry was taken up by a presidential candidate that year and became part of the national lexicon. More importantly for Wendy's and Sedelmaier, revenues for the fast food chain jumped 31 percent, net income 24 percent, and average sales per restaurant 13 percent from the previous year. Much of the credit for these increases was given to Sedelmaier's off-beat approach — one that he has repeated for clients such as Federal Express and General Motors Acceptance Corp.

Sedelmaier demands total creative control as a condition for taking on a client. His agency is one of the few that can do that. Most clients, whether they are spending a larger or small amount of money on the advertising, want a say in the final production of the ad. A copywriter often has to justify his or her copy, a process that demands a great deal of research and discipline. The creative process is a part of the process of producing copy, but it is only a part, and sometimes only a small part, of it.

Beginning the process: needs and appeals

The process of writing advertising copy begins with a recognition on the part of the copywriter that all humans have certains needs and desires. Effective advertising appeals to these needs and desires in a way that will make people act positively toward a product or an idea. We live in a consumer-oriented society where the list of needs and desires is a fairly long one. Our first step, then, is to examine some of the needs and desires of humans in a very general way.

Food and drink. The need for food and drink is among the most basic and universal needs that we have. We must have food and water daily to sustain our selves. Beyond that, we want food and drink that is nourishing and palatable.

Shelter, security and comfort. Next to food and drink, one of our most basic needs is for shelter. We need a way of protecting ourselves from the elements.

Following closely on to the need for shelter is the need for security, the need to feel that we are protected from various dangers that might befall us. Rational people understand that they cannot insulate themselves from every danger, but they can take some steps to ensure that they are not victims of calamities.

Once shelter and security are established, people want to feel comfortable. Physically, they want to be without pain, they want to be warm when it's cold and cool when it's hot. They want to live, work, and play in a comfortable and pleasing environment.

Sex, intimacy and social contact. Most people need to have contact with other people. That contact can take various forms in various stages of our lives. Our social relationships are very important to us, no matter what form they take. They can be based on sexual intimacy, friendship, or casual contact. Whatever they are, we remain social beings, and contact with other people is a very real need (except for a few who become hermits). Lack of such contact can have physical as well as emotional consequences.

Independence, privacy, self-fulfillment and power. While we need

Figure 7-2
The two ads below try to accomplish the same thing with the same audience. They make very different appeals, however.

social contact, we also have a countervailing need for independence and privacy. We need privacy even from those to whom we feel the closest. We have the urge to "get away from it all," and occasionally we do that, even if that means we simply draw inward rather than removing ourselves physcially.

Related to this need is that for independence. Although we are social beings, we are also individuals, and we need to feel that we can develop our own personalities. This need for individual development continues through adulthood and governs many of our actions. We are all different from one another, and we need to confirm that to ourselves.

Independence is part of a greater need for self-fulfillment, much of which is met for many by their work. We need to be engaged in constructive activity that will give us satisfaction and confirm our worth as individuals. For many, the highest fulfillment of this need lies in the work they choose as adults.

At its best, the need for power means that we are able to make our own decisions and in some way control our own environments. Child psychologists argued that this need is one of the most important that children have. At a very early age, children need to be able to make choices–even if they are very small ones–so that they can develop their individuality. Adults also need to feel that they are in control of their lives and their surroundings. This need, of course, can develop into a need to control the lives of others. Many of us have this tendency to some degree, and our places in society may dictate that we exercise this power. Parents, particularly, feel the need to control the environment and actions of their children.

Stimulation. The need to be stimulated–to find life interesting–is one of the most important that we have. Despite the habits and routines that we design for ourselves, we need to feel that life holds a variety of experiences for us. We read books, watch television, go to parties, shop, and engage in a variety of other activities in part to entertain ourselves. Occasionally, we need to be excited, to have the feeling that something is going to offer us special enjoyment or a unique feeling. Individuals meet this need in various ways, but we all have the need.

Acquisition. We mentioned earlier that we live in a consumer-oriented society. The number and variety of goods and services that are available to those in Western industrial societies in particular would boggle the minds of people in other cultures and from other centuries. The availability of those goods and services has stimulated within many a need to acquire things. Part of our development as individuals is the acquisition of good that go beyond those that meet our basic needs of food, clothing , and shelter.

On occasion the need overcomes common sense and the bounds of rationality. For instance, news reports coming from the Philippines in 1985 said that Imelda Marcos, wife of the deposed dictator of that country, had a closet full of shoes—more than 3,000 pairs. Her shoe collection became one of the standing jokes of the year, and she became a symbol of a consumer who was beyond conspicuous. What possible use, many wondered, could she have had for so many shoes?

Yet there is some of Imelda Marcos in many of us. Many people acquire things for the sake of acquiring them—not because they are useful or because we need them for basic purposes. Children "collect" things like dolls, baseball cards, rocks, etc., and that collecting syndrome carries over into adulthood.

The foregoing list contains just a few of the needs that we all have. It is by no means complete. Probably you can think of a dozen or so related needs after reading each of the foregoing paragraphs. The consideration of needs is one of the most important parts of the process of developing effective advertising copy. To understand that people need, or feel they need, certain things is vital to formulating the appeals that advertising can use.

Appeals are the words, phrases, and ideas used by advertising copywriters to tap into the needs of the audience. It is in formulating these appeals that copywriters must be creative and must choose their langue carefully. They must understand that certain words, even those they may have similar meanings, can evoke strikingly different images. The copywriter must have a highly developed ear for the language to couple with an understanding of the needs of the audience.

Just what needs are most salient to an audience? In the next section, we will discuss how marketers find this out.

The audience

Most manufacturers and advertisers want to sell as many units of their product as possible. They recognize, however, that most products are not universal; that is, not everyone will want what they sell. In addition, distributing a product to a massive audience can be costly. Consequently, it is not efficient to try to sell most products to everyone. Marketing a product or service begins with deciding what part of the population is most likely to buy it.

In considering the audience for a product, advertisers need to think about two groups. One is the people who are already using the product. They cannot be taken for granted. Many advertisements are directed at reinforcing the behavior of people who have already bought a product. (For instance, readers of car advertisements in magazines are often those who have already bought the car; they are simply trying to reinforce their belief that they made the correct decision.) Advertisers need to have some idea of how strong a user's loyalty is to a product.

The second group of people advertisers must consider is those who do not use the product but are most likely to. These potential users provide the greatest opportunity for a product to grow. Finding out who they are and what kind of advertising message is most likely to motivate them is the job of market research, and the answers have a direct effect on the advertising copywriter.

How does an advertiser get this information? Researchers can employ a variety of methods for this purpose. They may include personal interview surveys, telephone surveys, mail surveys, focus-group interviews, consumer product testing, intercept interviewing (the kind of interviewing conducted by people in shopping malls), and many other methods. Our purpose here is not to study the research methods that might be used but to understand the kind of data that they produce and how it is useful to the advertising copywriter.

The major concept that the beginning advertising copywriter must understand is that of **demographics.** Demographics is a way of dividing the population into groups. We assume that people who share many of the same demographic characteristics are likely to share many consumer behaviors. In the 1980s, the term "yuppie" was coined to describe an important segment of the population. A yuppie is a young, upwardly mobile professional. All of these categories are demographic characteristics, and they provide researchers with a way of looking at different segments of the population.

There are hundreds of demographic categories. As an introduction to this area, we are going to discuss some of the most basic demographic characteristics in this section.

Age. How old people are is one of the most common determinants of how likely they are to use many products and services. Our needs and desires change as we get older, and often they change in the same way for most of us. Most children want toys, but as they get older, the desire for toys decreases and the desire for other products increases. The changes that accompany age are not only physical but also psychological and emotional.

Sex. Boys and girls are different; men and women are different. That's obvious, but these differences are of primary importance to the advertiser. These groups have different needs and desires, due not only to different physical characteristics but also to differing roles they are likely to play in society. For instance, within a household, a man is more likely to earn more money, but a woman is more likely to make most of the household buying decisions.

Income. How much money people have to spend is an important determinant of how likely they are to buy a product, again for obvious reasons. Some products and services are marketed to people who do not have as much income as others, and the appeal the advertisers use is often based on price. This kind of appeal is likely to motivate potential customers. On the other hand, many producers want to direct their advertising toward an "upscale" audience, those who have high incomes or whose incomes are likely to increase.

Education. Education is an important demographic variable for two reasons. One is based on the assumption that education changes people; it changes their attitudes and values. (For instance, the more education people have, the more likely they are to place a value on getting an education.) The second is that education is often related to the demographic characteristic of income. The more education a person has, the more likely that person is to have a higher income.

Martial status. If a person is married, that means he or she is in a household. That inevitably leads to different consumer behavior than if that person were single. Knowing whether or not a person is married is important for the advertiser because of the different appeals that may be used to sell a product.

There are many other demographic characteristics that advertisers may need to consider in finding the consumers for their products. For instance, race, home ownership, number of adults and children in a house-

Figure 7-3
The design of the Macintosh, unusual for a computer, helped establish its place in the market.

hold, occupation, place of residence, and type of housing are just a few of the many variables that can be examined by researchers.

As a step in developing an advertisement, an advertiser might want to draw a "demographic profile" of those who use the product already or those who are potential users. For instance, a manufacturer might find that those who have found the product are women between the ages of 18 and 30, single, with at least a high school education. Chances are that not all consumers who fit this profile are buying the product, so advertising directed at this group might not only persuade others to buy it but also reinforce those who already do. On the other hand, an advertiser may decide that the product could be marketed to older women as well as to those already likely to buy it. In that case, the advertiser might use a different appeal—one that would work for women 31 to 40 years old.

In addition to these demographic factors, advertisers must also take into account psychographic variables. In general, psychographic variables refer to the values and attitudes of people and how they feel toward various things in their environment. Market researchers want to know what people feel is important and valuable. If people use a product, they want to know how they feel about that product and if they are likely to use it again.

As you can tell, making decisions based on just this small amount of information is not a simple task. An advertiser may take a variety of routes in marketing a product. Good research is essential to making the correct decisions about marketing and advertising. But the audience is only one factor to be considered in trying to sell a product. Of equal importance is the product itself.

The product

Along with knowing who the audience is for a product, the advertising copywriter must know the product itself. Again, to say this is to state the obvious, but knowledge of the product—particularly from the standpoint of developing advertising for it—is not as simple as it might first seem. (Note here that when we talk about a product, we are speaking of anything the advertising is designed to promote. It could be a product, such as a vacuum cleaner, a business, such as an auto body repair shop, or an idea, such as quitting smoking.)

The advertising copywriter must ask, "What is it about this product that I am try to sell?" The answer may come from a close examination of the product, and it may be surprising.

First, the copywriter should know **what the product does.** A vacuum cleaner may clean a floor, but how it cleans the floor may be important to the advertising of the product. Does it introduce some new cleaning method—something that no other vacuum cleaner on the market does? A line of sofas may come in 15 different patterns; it may also be comfortable to sit on. Which one does the copywriter emphasize? A copywriter may find that there are a number of advertiseable facts about any product, and someone—the copywriter, the advertiser or a combination of them—will have to decide what it is about the product that will be advertised.

The **physical characteristics of the product** also provide the copywriter with some useful considerations in developing the advertising. Sometimes a product will be designed to do a job more efficiently than competing products. Sometimes it will be designed to do a part of a job. Small, hand-held vacuum cleaners are vacuum cleaners, but they're not meant to vacuum an entire house, or even an entire room. They're for small jobs that need to be done quickly. The physical characteristics of the product help promote the feeling that the product can do the job.

Sometimes the physical characteristics of a product can have little to do with how the product works, but they can still be useful in helping to sell the product. When the Macintosh computer was introduced by the Apple Computer Company in 1984 (with an engrossing set of surreal commercials aired only once, during the Super Bowl that year), one of the characteristics that helped set the Macintosh apart from other computers was its unique, small, box-like design. That design helped establish the Macintosh as "the computer for the rest of us," as its advertising slogan said. One of the most legendary campaigns in the history of advertising, the 1960s promotion of the Volkswagen Beetle, also used the car's

Social aspects of advertising

Advertisers must recognize how their products and advertising fit into society and whether or not the approaches they use are appropriate. For example, many women feel that much of the advertising for and about them is degrading. One watchdog group, Women Against Pornography, annually gives awards to advertisers who use non-sexist approaches in their advertising, and at the same time the group criticizes advertisers who, according to the group, degrade women. In 1983, the group criticized the Hanes company for the way it implied in its hosiery ads that men preferred women with "shapely, sexy, silky legs."

More recently, the British auto maker Austin Rover received many compaints about an ad that focused on the walnut interior of one of its models and quotes an old English saying, "A woman, a dog, a walnut tree, the more you beat them, the better they'll be." The makers of Opium and Obsession perfumes have also been criticized by those who believe that the names of these products and their advertising glamorizes degrading conditions within society.

The Center for Science in the Public Interest has criticized the alcoholic beverage industry for ads which it said were aimed at starting young people to drink and at inducing alcoholics to return to the bottle. Ethnic minorities are often sensitive to the way in which they are portrayed, and advertisers are wise to be aware of their concerns.

This is not to say that advertising should always avoid controversy and that advertisers should construct ads so bland that absolutely no one will be offended. Controversy might well be an advisable marketing strategy, as when Burger King directly criticized McDonald's in a recent advertising campaign. The point here is that advertisers should never be surprised at the effects of their ads. They should know what society, or groups in society, expect of them, and they should have thought through their advertising campaigns well enough so that the ads produce the intended results.

unique shape to distinguish it from other cars. Some of the ads even poked some good-natured fun at the car in order to establish this difference in the minds of the consumers.

The **history and reputation of a product** are characteristics that also need to be considered when formulating advertising. A product may have a long history, and that may be something that a copywriter will want to emphasize. Many businesses use the phrase, "Established in — — (year)" to let people know that they have been around for a long time and thus can be considered reliable and stable. If a product has existed only a short time but has gained a good reputation, the advertisement may reflect that reputation.

Sometimes an advertising campaign will be designed to overcome the history or reputation of a product. It could be that the product has not worked particularly well, and a manufacturer has taken steps to correct that. Or, it may be that manufacturers want to sell the product to a different audience. One classic case of this redefinition of a product was done by Miller Brewing Company. For many years, its main product had been known as the "Champaign of Bottled Beers". The slogan had little appeal for the Sunday afternoon, football-watching crowd, who were up mostly of men. When Miller began making a lite beer, Miller Lite, the company sponsored a series of commercials that had ex-jocks arguing as to whether the product "tasted great" or was "less filling." The commercials were good entertainment in themselves, but they also established Miller Lite as a beer that could be enjoyed while watching a football game.

Another classic advertising campaign that reestablished a product was the one the Chicago-based advertising agency Leo Burnett developed for Marlboro cigarettes. Marlboro had been a red-filtered cigarette when filtered cigarettes were thought to be products for women. Marlboro also had the slogan "mild as the month of May." Burnett developed a series of ads that put the cigarette in the hands of men and put those men outdoors. Eventually, the Marlboro Man, a rugged outdoorsman (usually a cowboy with a horse), became a stable of the advertising industry. The campaign was so successful that the Marlboro Man is still with us today, more than 30 years after he was created.

The **manufacturer of a product** is another characteristic about a product than an advertising copywriter may want to give attention to. Many products are indistinguishable from their competition, but if the manufacturer is well know and has a reputation for reliability and stability, that can help set the product apart. International Business Machines (IBM) has a reputation for servicing its products, and that has established for IBM a broader reputation for reliability. IBM often uses this reputation in advertising its individual products.

Many advertising and marketing campaigns emphasize the brand name of a product. This emphasis occurs for a number of reasons. Consumers often exercise what is called "brand loyalty." Having made a decision to buy a product at some point in the past, many are reluctant to change. It could also be that a brand is associated positively with other products that carry the name. Nabisco, for example, appears on a number of crakers and cookies because of the strong brand identification that name has. Such identification makes a product, especially a new one, easier to sell.

One of the most important product characteristics is price. People want to know how much something costs. They also want to believe that they are getting the best product for the money they spend. Sometimes, price is the most notable factor about a product, and it will be the characteristic the copywriter will want to feature. This is not always the case, but copywriters should never ignore the price of a product as a possible advertising vehicle.

Finally, copywriters will want to consider the **competition** that a product has. Much of what we have said already has made reference to a product's competition and the means by which advertising can distinguish it from others like it. Rarely is a product the only one of its kind. It may have some individual characteristics, but there are usually other items that will accomplish the same task. One of the copywriter's main jobs is to set a product apart from its competition.

The list of product characteristics just discussed is only an indication of the many variables that may be considered in developing advertising for a product. They key here is that the copywriter should know as much about the product as possible so that the best characteristics may be selected for the advertising.

In advertising terms, this process is called finding the Unique Selling Proposition (USP). A product's USP will give potential consumers their first clue as to why they should want to buy that product. Once a USP has been identified, the selling process has begun.

The advertising situation

The marketing environment is an all-important consideration in the development of an ad. This environment is created by the audience and product–factors which have already been discussed, but also by the more immediate situation surrounding the advertisement. We are at the point where the copywriter is beginning to make decisions that will determine the content of the ad.

First, ad writers must know and be able to state the **key fact** about an advertising situation. This key fact sets the stage for the thinking about an ad, and writers who do not have a key fact clearly in mind will be confused and prone to wander in several directions. The key fact may involve the competition: A new product may have entered the market two years ago and now accounts for more than 50 percent of the sales in the market. The key fact may involve the audience: Few people know about the product. The key fact could involve the product itself: Some improvements have been made in the product. Discovering this key fact is sometimes difficult and time consuming. It often takes extensive research and discussion with the manufacturers. But being able to write down the key fact of the situation orders the thinking of the advertiser and helps to produce effective ads more efficiently.

Distilling the key fact of the advertising situation leads directly to the next step in the process of ad development: **stating the problem that the ad should solve.** The problem statement should be a specific one and should evolve from the key fact. For example, the key fact may be: A product's percentage of the market is down. The problem then would be: The product's share of the market needs to be raised. Problems may also involve the product itself: The product has a bad reputation; or the product costs more than its competitors.

A prime example of a problem to be solved occurred in 1982 for the Johnson & Johnson company and its product, Tylenol. After it was discovered that several people had died after taking Tylenol that had been laced with cyanide, Johnson & Johnson conducted a nationwide recall of the product. Tylenol, which had been one of the top sellers of all headache remedies, was suddenly no longer available, and its reputation had been damaged. The company first had to decide to try to revive the product when the controversy about the arsenic deaths subsided. Then the problem it faced was restoring the damaged faith people had in the product. An entire marketing strategy was designed to solve this problem. Part of that strategy was an ad which featured a woman looking straight into the camera and telling the audience, "My first experience with Tylenol was in a hospital, after my son Christopher was born. Since then, it's become one of the things we can count on." Within a year after the arsenic deaths, Tylenol had recaptured 80 percent of the market share it had held previously, although at enormous cost to the company.

Not many companies are faced with the kind of crisis that Johnson & Johnson found itself in. Still, the problems can be daunting. After years of pitching its product to consumers more concerned with quality than price, Curtis Mathes cut prices on its television sets in 1987 and tried to compete with the larger discount electronic companies. The strategy was a disaster. Sales dropped from $250 million annually to $165 million. At the end of 1988, Curtis Mathes had decided to return to its high-end marketing strategy. The problem it faced was how to regain its previous market.

If the key fact and the problem of the advertising situation are clear in an advertising copywriter's mind, the third step in the process should follow: **the objective of the advertisement.** The objective needs to be stated clearly and precisely. Just what is the advertisement supposed to do? The following are some statements of advertising objectives: the ad should make people aware of the product; the ad should change people's attitudes toward the product; the ad should tell consumers of the product's improvements; the ad should encourage people to shift from buying another product to buying this product.

Once an advertiser has thought through to this point—and assuming that the proper amount of research has been done—the next step is to develop a copy platform.

Copy platforms

A copy platform is a way of getting the ideas and information of an advertising situation down on paper and of organizing those ideas in such a way that effective advertising copy can be produced from them. A copy platform is not an ad itself, but it will contain many of the ideas that will later appear in the ad, and it will provide valuable information for the ad copywriter. One version of a copy platform is found in this book, but it is not the only one. Copy platforms vary according to the advertising agency and the advertiser, but most contain this basic information.

Copy Platform

Ad Subject: General Motors Spinout
Ad Problem: This new model needs to gain some identity and find its place in the market.

Product Characteristics:
 reasonably priced against competing models
 dependably built (experts say it should
 have an excellent maintenance record)

Advertising Objective: Help model establish itself by building on brand loyalty to GM.

Target Market: Young, single people who are just graduating from college, ages 21-24.These folks have just taken their first job and need transportation.

Competition: Toyota Tercel, Honda Civic, Ford Escort.

Statement of Benefit or Appeal:
 1) Spinout is reasonably priced.
 2) Spinout is a member of the GM family.
 3) Spinout is dependable.

Creative Theme:
 Take the spin -- Spinout.

Supportive Selling Points:
 1) Depreciation in 3 years expected to be only about 30 percent.
 2) Part of GM, so it's built in America.
 3) Priced so that someone starting out can afford it.

Figure 7-4
The copy platform to the left (for a fictitious product) shows how a copy platform can be put together.

The copy platform is where many of the factors in developing an ad begin to come together. The copywriter must finally commit what he or she has learned about a product and about an audience to paper and develop ideas from the information that is there.The examples of the copy platforms on this page show you some of the elements that make up the platform. (The form of a copy platform will vary from agency to agency.) Note that the advertising problem is the first piece of information that is called for in the copy platform. Stating this problem directly and simply sets the stage for many of the other ideas that will appear on the copy platform. A problem may be encountering a number of different advertising situations, but generally the copywriter will zero in on just one—the one that the advertiser considers the most important.The product characteristics are usually a list of items about the product that might be helpful in formulating the ad. This list cannot be all-inclusive; the copywriter will have to limit the list to those items that relate directly to the advertising problem and items that might otherwise make the product distinctive and beneficial to the consumer.

As we mentioned earlier, the advertising objective is drawn directly from the advertising problem. The objective should be a way of solving the problem.

The target market is the audience to whom the advertising will be directed. A description of this audience should be stated as simply and specifically as possible. Knowing exactly whom the audience is will help the copywriter in coming up with the next, and most important, part of the copy platform—the statement of benefit and appeal.

Advertising should tell its audience the benefit of a product—the "what's in it for me." That is, the advertising should state, implicitly or explicitly, why the product or service is good for the consumer, why the consumer should buy it, or what the consumer can expect from it. This statement of benefit and appeal is the most persuasive part of an advertisement, and its importance cannot be overestimated. Here are a few examples:

You'll save money if you buy our product.
You'll be safer if you use our product.
You'll live in more comfort if your have our product.

These benefits relate direct to the discussion of needs and wants at the beginning of this chapter. Such appeals are highly potent ones for advertising, and they have been highly effective in many advertising campaigns.

The creative theme in a copy platform allows the copywriter to use some imagination in formulating the appeals of the advertising. The creative theme might be a slogan, or it might be a description of the way in which the advertising will be presented.

Supportive selling points is a list of product characteristics or factors about the advertising situation that will help sell a product. They may vary somewhat from the main statement of benefit, but they can be used to reinforce a tendency to use the product.

Writing the ad

With the copy platform in place, the copywriter is almost ready to write an ad. Among the decisions that still need to be made are which medium the advertisements will appear in, how many ads there will be for a product, when they will be placed, how large or long the ads will be, etc. All of these are marketing decisions that go beyond the scope of this book. Our focus here in the writing of the advertisement.

In this section we will look at some common ad writing practices and guidelines. (We'll look at writing for a particular medium in the next section.) There are few "rules" in the writing of an advertisement, and there are no dominant structures for ads as there are for news stories and for broadcast news. Instead, each ad is a combination of the factors that we have already discussed in this chapter, plus the limits and opportunities provided by the medium in which the ad is placed.

Still, there are some things that we can say generally about the writing of advertisements. One of the oldest advertising copywriting formulas is A-I-D-A: attention, interest, desire, action. According to this formula, an ad should do four things, in this order. It should gain the attention of the viewer or listener. An ad that doesn't do at least this is not going to be able to do anything else.

After getting the consumer's attention, the ad must hold his or her

Now You Don't Have to Go Out of Your Way To Be Good

You know frozen yougart is good for you. Better than ice cream. But until now, you had to travel more than a mile from campus to get it.

Now there's Milo's — just two blocks from the center of campus.

All the frozen yougart you want, any time you want it.

New flavors every day, plus all your old favorites.

See how good being good can be.

Milo's Frozen Yougart

**323 Elm Street
Open 11 a.m. to Midnight every day.**

Figure 7-5
The headline of the ad to the left offers a benefit to the reader; the headline of the ad below—combined with the illustration—are designed to get the attention of the reader.

Notice the liberal use of pronouns in both ads, particularly the one on the left.

Notice, too, the short, direct sentences. Each one builds on the previous one.

The ad to the left gives the location of the store and the hours of operation.

Do I look that stupid?

You think I don't know it when you buy me cheap dog food. You think I don't understand that you're trying to save a few pennies at my expense. I'm the guy who's here every day when you get home – giving you a lift, no matter how I feel. Think about that the next time you reach for that cheap dog food at the grocery store, and ask yourself, "Is this what he deserves?"

A message from the dog's point of view, brought to you by
Gino's Dog Chow
"The best there is for your dog."

interest. The ad should use words and pictures that will draw the reader or listener into the ideas that the ad is trying to present. An ad may be about an interesting or important subject, but it can be so dull that the consumer is lost before the message gets across.

The ad should create a desire for the product, service, or idea presented in the ad. It is important for the copywriter to choose the appeal, the benefits, and the proper words that will develop this desire.

Finally, the ad should stimulate the consumer to some action. In most cases, what you want the consumer to do is go out and buy the product.

With this formula in mind, let's look at some of the commonly accepted guidelines for writing effective advertisements.

Use clear, simple English. This rule reappears throughout this book. It is basic to communication in the mass media. Obscure words and complex sentences will not encourage people to read an advertisement. You can't impress someone with your wide vocabulary in an advertisement.

Another reason for using simple language, particularly in advertising, is that it is more believable. People will tend to believe advertising messages that are presented to them in language they use or are used to hearing.

Pay attention to the verbs. Verbs are the most important part of the language. If your ad has mostly "to be" verb forms (is, are, was, were, etc.), the ad will probably sound flat and lifeless. If it contains mostly action verbs, it will be alive and interesting.

Here's an interesting thought. Use verbs, rather than adjectives, to describe your product. What verbs are associated with how the product looks, what it does, and how it makes the user feel? If you can come up with a list of those verbs, you are on your way to developing some good advertising copy.

Another rule about the verbs in advertising copy is to stick with the present tense (whenever appropriate) and the active voice (almost always). The present tense implies immediacy and puts the reader into an advertisement more quickly. Earlier in this book, we discussed the strengths of using the active rather than passive voice in writing for the media. Those strengths are just as applicable to advertising copy as they are for any other kind of writing.

Be as specific as possible, but don't let too many details get in the way of the advertising message. This is not a contradictory guideline. It argues for a balance. Facts—specifics—are more likely to sell a product than general ideas of concepts. Yet too many facts are likely to confuse the reader or listener. Consumers like to have reasons to buy a product, and an ad should give them enough of those reasons that they will be motivated to do so.

Be precise in the use of the language. Here's where intelligence, art, and creativity mix together for the copywriter. The copywriter needs to know the language intimately. He or she should be sensitive to the subtle meanings of words—not just their dictionary meanings but the images they provoke.

Here's an example. The words "laugh," "giggle," and "guffaw" have essentially the same meaning, but they provoke different images. For instance, most of us laugh; little boys and girls giggle; old men don't usually giggle; old men guffaw; and so on. Writers need to understand the subtle differences between words and to take unusual care with them. They need to select the words for their copy that evoke exactly the images that they want to convey; that will describe the product in exactly the way they mean for it to be described. You should select the words that related directly to the benefit you are presenting with the product.

Use personal pronouns when appropriate. Let the reader, listener, or viewer of an advertisement know that you are talking directly to him or her. Using personal pronouns, especially "you," is an effective way to do that, but like any good idea, it can be overdone. Occasionally, you should ask a question (although only occasionally; we'll discuss this more in the next section).

Don't be afraid of contractions. Contractions are a good way making sure that your tone is informal, and the informal tone is preferable in most advertisements. Like personal pronouns, they can be used too much, particularly if they sound forced. A copywriter should develop an "ear" for the language and should recognize when a piece of copy "sounds" right or wrong. If a contraction sounds right, use it.

Inspire confidence in the product and the advertiser. Ads should contain messages that will help people believe and trust a product. They should not sacrifice a long-range trust for a short-term goal. They should, however, tell an audience that the product being advertised is one which will benefit them and will live up to expectation. Not only should the messages in an ad inspire such confidence, but the ad itself should contribute toward this goal. Ads that are in good taste, that use English properly, that are not cutesy or smart-alecky, and that do not insult the audience are the kinds of ads that build confidence. A manufacturer should be as proud of the ads commissioned for a product as of the product itself. Advertisement writers should feel that same pride in what they produce.

Give the audience all the information it needs. An ad doesn't have to tell everything about a product or a manufacturer, but it should not leave hanging any major questions about the product or service being advertised. For example, a power company recently advertised that energy audits were available to its customers. These audits involved representatives of the power company coming to the home, inspecting it, and recommending actions to increase the efficient use of energy. The service was free. What the ad did not say was how a customer could get this service: Whom should the customer call or write; what was the procedure? The ad left the clear impression that the power company wasn't very interested in having customers take advantage of this service.

Elements of a print ad

Unlike the newspaper reporter, who generally does not have anything to do with the physical appearance of a story in the newspaper, an advertising copywriter must always be aware of the design of an ad. Design is an

Invest your cash where you can get to it. But taxes can't.

Here's a better way
to manage
your money

Amazing!

Be all that you can be

There are a million reasons to celebrate the New Year. Here are three.

We've figured out a new way to look at the bottom line

While others talk about the future, we deliver it.

How fast can you make it through the grocery store these days?

Saturday and Sunday Specials

Entire Stock 50% Off

Figure 7-6
These headlines demonstrate the wide variety of techniques available to
get the attention of the reader.

integral part of the ad writing process, and it often is a determining factor in what the ad says. In this section we will discuss the different parts of a print ad, keeping in mind that, depending on the work situation, it may or may not be the copywriter's job to design the ad as well as write the copy.

Illustration. The illustration an ad uses is often the most important attention-getting item in that ad. It is the part of an ad most likely to achieve the attention-getting part of the A-I-D-A formula. While we are not concerned here with the design of the ad or the selection of the illustration, the copywriter will often write the copy based on the kind of illustration that is used. The illustration, the headline and the body copy—the three most important parts of the ad—must be closely tied to one another. If the relationship between these three elements is not readily apparent, the ad runs the risk of losing the reader who will not want to figure it out.

Headline. The headline is often the most important part of an ad because it gives the reader the first solid information about the advertise-

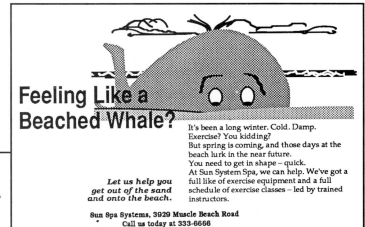

Copy Sheet

Product: Sun Spa Systems membership
Medium: Newspaper
Client: Sun Spa Systems
Writer: Smith

Headline: Feeling like a beached whale?

Subhead:

Body copy:
It's been a long winter. Cold. Damp.
Exercise? You kidding?
But spring is coming, and those days at the beach
lurk in the near future.
You need to get in shape – quick.
At Sun System Spa, we can help. We've got a full
line of exercise equipment and a full schedule of
exercise classes – led by trained instructors.

Subhead or slogan
Let us help you
get out of the sand
and onto the beach.

Signature: Sun Spa Systems, 3929 Muscle Beach Road
Call us today at 333-6666

Figure 7-7
This figures shows how copy is
translated from a copy sheet to the
completed ad.

ment. The headline will most often achieve the interest part of the A-I-D-A formula and will determine whether or not the reader's interest is aroused enough to read the rest of the ad.

The most effective headlines appeal to the self-interest of the reader – the "what's in it for me?" The copywriter must decide what appeal is being made and what benefit is being offered.

The headline should consist of just a few carefully chosen words (many ad writers say the limit is eight words) that will set the tone for the ad and implicitly promise some reward to the reader for reading through the ad. Many advertising copywriters believe that headlines in ads should be treated much like headlines for news stories in newspapers. That is, they should give the reader some information that the reader does not already have. Although this approach is not the only one to writing headlines in ads, it is a useful one for many ads.

A headline may deliver a promise about a product. It may challenge an assumption on the part of the reader. It may make a claim about a product. It may play on the reputation of the advertiser. It may simply try to provoke a mood for the reader.

Above all, headlines should involve the reader in the ad quickly.

They may do this by asking a question ("When will you get an opportunity like this again?"), offering some information ("How to save money"), or making a provocative statement ("Not all men are created equal").

Finally, caution should be exercised when writing headlines. Some headlines are clearly misleading and inappropriate, and an advertiser will use these at his or her peril. Misleading or deceptive headlines can get an advertiser into legal trouble, and inappropriate headlines can destroy the advertiser's credibility with the reader.

Subheads. Subheads allow the copywriter an opportunity to expand on what has been said in the main headline. They also allow the writer to introduce new material that may draw the reader into an ad. Subheads are set in a smaller size of type than the main headline, and they are generally longer. Most often, the thoughts presented in a subhead are tied to those presented in the main headline. For instance, if the main headline poses a question, the subhead may answer it, as in the following example:

IS NOW THE TIME TO BUY A NEW CAR?
Most experts agree that it is.

Not every advertisement needs a subhead. They are not attention-getting devices; rather, they are informational devices, and they should be used only when necessary and appropriate.

Body copy. The body copy is the heart of the advertisement. If the art and headline get the attention of the reader, the body copy is where the reader should be rewarded for taking the time to read the ad. That reward should come in the form of information about the product being advertised and answers to questions raised explicitly and implicitly in the headline.

Writing body copy can take a number of approaches. The factual approach is a direct one. Essentially, it says: Here is some information about the product; here is why you should buy it. The narrative approach is a less direct one. It generally tells a story about the product, emphasizing the selling points of the product. The narrative approach is used when the ad needs to hold the attention of the reader. The stories or situations used in a narrative approach should be projective. That is, they should be situations that the readers can relate to or imagine themselves in.

The rules for writing body copy are the same ones that we have emphasized all along for writing in any part of the mass media—simplicity, brevity, word precision, etc. Ad copywriters should take special care with the verbs they use and think of them as the chief descriptors of a product.

Avoid mistakes in grammar. Mistakes call attention to the writing and not to the message. Sentence fragments—one or two words or short phrases that do not make complete sentences—can be acceptable, but they must be deliberate, and the writer should exercise complete control of the language.

Avoid exaggeration. Saying that something is the "greatest in the world" or even "the cheapest in town" is not likely to help sell a product. Readers are more likely to want facts and specifics.

The writer should have a simple message in mind, and everything in the body copy should relate to that message.

Tell the reader what you want him or her to do. "Call today," "Go out and buy it," "Clip this coupon"–whatever the action is, don't assume that the reader will know it.

Above all, the copy should be interesting (if not compelling).

Closings. Closings may be thought of as subheads that come after body copy rather than before it. A closing will make a fairly strong point for the reader. Often it will summarize what the body copy has been implying. Sometimes, it will give a direct command to the reader; at other times, it will only suggest that the reader do something. Like the subhead, a closing may not be necessary for every advertisement.

Mandatories, including legals. Mandatories are items that must be included in the advertisement. For instance, an advertiser may want an ad to mention the name of the company president or that a product is manufactured in a certain area. The words, "an equal opportunity employer," are a mandatory for the employment ads of many organizations.

Legals are items that are required by law to be in an ad. For instance, all cigarette ads must give the Surgeon General's warning; all automobile ads must include the mileage ratings. The Federal Trade Commission and other federal agencies, such as the Food and Drug Administration, have issued many regulations about the content of advertisements. These regulations often require that certain things be in an advertisement. A professional copywriter must be familiar with these regulations if the ads he or she writes are to remain legal.

Slogans, logos, signatures. These items may be included in an ad, although none are necessary in every advertisement. Slogans are short phrases that become identified with products. A slogan should be short, easily understood, and appropriate to the product. Sometimes, whole advertising campaigns are built around slogans, such as Coca-Cola's slogan, "The Real Thing," or that of McDonald's, "We do it all for you."

A logo is a design that represents a company. The Volkswagen logo, for instance, is a "v" sitting in the middle of a "w," all of which is in a circle. Volkswagen has been using this logo for years. It has become a symbol of the company. Advertisers will want to use well-designed logos in their ads because of the distinctiveness they add to the advertisement. Signatures generally refer to the name and address of the company, which are often necessary or useful in an ad.

Writing advertising for broadcast

Much of the advertising that we pay the most attention to comes from the broadcast media—television and radio. Broadcasting has advantages over print in being able to deliver a message with immediacy and impact. It can bring a product to life and show it in action. But broadcast advertising is expensive to produce and air, especially on television. And broadcast advertising gets only one chance at a time with the listener or viewer. If the message is not delivered immediately, the consumer cannot turn back the page and listen to it again.

Whereas print ads are space oriented, broadcast ads are time oriented, as we learned in writing news for broadcast. In fact, many of the lessons that we discussed in the previous chapter about broadcast news writing can be applied to broadcast advertising. Copywriters should write for the ear. The visual and oral messages should complement one another. Broadcast ads should be simple. They should be designed to achieve maximum impact in a short amount of time. They should key in on the sounds, words, and pictures that will help sell the product.

The copywriter for broadcast advertising has certain tools available, and it would be useful to take a brief look at what they are and how they can be used.

Voices. The most commonly used tool of the broadcast advertiser is the voice. Talking is the most direct and effective form of communication for broadcasting and the easiest to produce. Most of what the advertising copywriter will write for broadcast advertising is scripts for what people will say. To write conversational language, however, is neither easy nor simple. It takes a great amount of practice, and in real life it takes a good deal of writing and rewriting. The script must be suitable for the voice that is using it as well as the other elements of the ad.

Figure 7-8
A typical radio script sheet.

Radio Script Sheet

Product: Shipler's Soup
Client: Shipler's Soup Company
Title: Home from the Hills
Writer: Smith
Length 20 seconds

Source	Audio
	SDX: Wind blowing, door slams
ANNCR #1	Hi, honey, I'm home.
ANNCR #2	Oh, Jack! You're home. It's been two years. Where have you been?
ANNCR #1	Crossing deserts, sailing oceans, climbing mountains — you know, that sort of thing. I'm hungry. Got any Shipler's soup?
ANNCR #2	No. We ate the last of it yesterday.
ANNCR #1	Well, see ya!
	SDX: Door opens, wind blowing, door slams.
ANNCR #3	Shipler's Soup. Good enough to make them stay home.

Sound effects. Like voices, sounds can be a very effective means of communication. Sound effects are often vital to radio ads. Car engines, crowds cheering, quiet walks in the woods, children laughing—all of these sounds can take listeners to the scene of an advertisement. They provoke pictures and images inside the heads of the listeners. They can "demonstrate" the way a product looks or works.

Music. Like sound effects, music can provide the proper background for a commercial, or it can be the main part of the commercial's message. Selecting the proper music for a commercial's background is an important consideration for the producers of an advertisement. The haunting music of Vangelis (part of which was used in the score for the movie *Chariots of Fire*) was one of the most memorable parts of the famous Ernest and Julio Gallo "Wedding" commercial. The commercial needed only the music, the superb photography, and the tagline, "All the best a wine can be" to gets its message across.

In the days when radio was the dominant broadcast medium, the jingle—the one-or two-line musical message about a product—was one of the most popular advertising technique. The jingle is still popular for radio but has also become a staple of the television commercial. In fact, the

Figure 7-9
A typical television storyboard sheet.

Television Storyboard

Product: Shipler's Soup
Client: Shipler's Soup Company
Title: Home from the Hills
Writer: Smith
Length 30 seconds

Video	Audio
Frame time 3 seconds	SDX: MUSIC; winding blowing, door opens, closes
	MAN: Hi, honey, I'm home.
Frame time 5 seconds	WOMAN: Oh, Jack! You're home. It's been two years. Where have you been?
Frame time 10 secconds	MAN: Crossing deserts, sailing oceans, climbing mountains — you know, that sort of thing. I'm hungry. Got any Shipler's soup?
Frame time 2 seconds	WOMAN: No. We ate the last of it yesterday.
	MAN: Well, see ya!
Frame time 4 seconds	SDX: Door opens, wind blowing, door slams.
	ANNOUNCER: Shipler's Soup. Good enough to make them stay home.
Frame time 6 seconds	MUSIC UP

simple one- or two-line jingle has developed in a number of ways. Some advertisers have produced orchestra-score songs to promote their products, and Coca-Cola's "I'd Like to Teach the World to Sing" became a popular hit when it was recorded and sold to the public.

Pictures. Pictures are not available for radio, of course, but they constitute one of the major advantages of television. Not only can television show pictures, but a well-produced advertisement can direct the eye to exactly the images that it wants the audience to see.

Pictures bring a commercial to life. We can see real people talking to one another and doing real things. While most people realize that commercials are most often dramatic presentations (not pictures of real life), they still have a believability about them that makes people accept them and consider the messages they have to send.

Visual effects. Graphics and special effects have always been a part of television and have proven themselves to be a useful tool in the production of television advertising. Today their value has been enhanced because the computer hardware and software to create complex and eye-popping graphics is readily available and easy to use.

While broadcast commercials can vary widely in approach, there are two basic formats that can be used: dramatic formats and announcer formats. Dramatic formats emphasize the action on the screen or within the script. One of the best and oldest ways to make a point is to tell a story. Radio and television commercials are often small dramas packed into just a few seconds. They may also be just a set of scenes and sounds that lead to a point about a product. While they may use announcers, the announcer plays only a partial role in the ad. There are four types of dramatic formats:

Through the grapevine

In the mid-1980s, a group of California raisin growers undertook an advertising campaign to increase the consumption of their product. The animated raisins that they used spurred a modest growth in the raisin market. The merchandising of the raisin characters, however, reached $500 million in 1988–twice the size of the raisin market itself.

Problem-resolution. Presenting a problem and then resolving it is one of the most common ways of selling a product. The outline for a problem-resolution commercial is a simple one. For instance, a person has a headache; he takes a brand of aspirin; he no longer has a headache. The problem-resolution technique is popular with advertisers because it can make a strong point in a short amount of time.

Whatever the problem is, the commercial is structured so that its solution is directly attributed to the product. You can think of the problem-resolution commercial as a "before" and "after" structure: "Before" using the product, we had this problem; "after" using it, we no longer have the problem.

One of the secrets of the problem-resolution commercial's success is the speed at which a problem can be established. A copywriter can waste no time in letting the audience know what the problem is. Usually, that is done with the very first words and pictures. The idea of the problem has to be clear and simple: The people in the commercial are hungry; or they're uncomfotable; or they're looking for something; and so on. The product then comes to their rescue just as quickly. All this is done usually within the space of 30 seconds, sometimes even 15 seconds.

Slice of life. Normally, the slice-of-life-commercial shows people doing things in which the advertised product is involved. These may be small mini-dramas with a problem and resolution that have little to do with the the product itself, but they show the product in a very good light. Or they may be sketches that revolve around the product. For example, a popular commercial for Coca-Cola shows a baseball team on a bus after a game which the team won; the team is hot and thirsty, and the bus stops at a small diner; the team descends on the diner, and everyone who works at the diner must work harder; finally, the team quenches its thirst with Coca-Cola, and one of the team members gives his baseball cap to one of the waitresses right before the team leaves.

In a similar type of commercial, a father drives his pre-teen daughter and her friends to McDonald's, where they may run into some boys they have been discussing. When they get to McDonald's, the father gets out, and his daughter, horrified, says, "You're not going in, are you?" The father waits in the car, realizing that his daughter is growing up. He takes comfort in eating some McDonald's french fries.

Slice-of-life commercials must be entertaining, but more importantly, they need to identify the product with a situation or feeling that is familiar and comfortable. They try to demonstrate that the product is part of the life that the people on the screen are living, and it should also be part of the viewer's life.

Documentary/demonstration. These kinds of commercials use fewer dramatic techniques than others. They may simply show how a product works (for example, how a fabric cleaner "lifts out" the stain from a sweater). They may try to show how a product works in comparison to its competition. They may show how a product works in an unusual situation to demonstrate something about the product (such as Timex watch's slogan, "It takes a licking and keeps on ticking," or Master Lock's demonstration of the durability of its lock by firing a rifle bullet into one of them). Occasionally, a commercial may show how a product is made in order to demonstrate something about the product.

Fantasy. Putting people and products in unreal or abnormal situations is another way of making a point about a product. Fantasy also includes the use of animation, such as in commercials for Keebler cookies or Jolly Green Giant products, and special camera techniques, such as dancing cats and talking dogs.

Fantasy characters are not always without controversy. During a mid-1980s campaign, Duracell used a fuzzy, pink bunny beating a small drum to say that its batteries lasted longer than those of the competition. One member of the competition, the Eveready Battery Company, took exception to this message and brought out an ad feating a garish, hot-pink bunny with sunglasses pounding a bass drum. "For years, one of our competitors has been telling you they have the longest lasting battery. But they haven't invited us to the party," the voice-over announcer says.

Dramatic presentations have either no announcer at all or an announcer who plays only a minor part in the commercial. Announcer formats are those in which the announcer is the main character, or one of the main characters, in the commercial. There are two types of announcer formats: the spokesperson and the anonymous announcer.

The spokesperson. The spokesperson is another popular format for broadcast commercials. Spokespersons may range from celebrities to unknown but real people to actors. They may or may not be experts on the product they are advertising. The Federal Trade Commission has a wide variety of rules governing the use of spokespersons in advertisements. In general, celebrities who endorse products have some responsibility for the claims that are made about the products; people who are identified as "real people" or "typical users" in advertisements must be who the ads says they are; actors may play the part of "real people" or "typical users" as long as they are not identified otherwise. In other words, if a commercial identifies a speaker as "Joe Smith of Hoboken, New Jersey," that speaker must be Joe Smith of Hoboken, New Jersey.

Famous people (usually actors but not always) can become spokespersons and even symbols for the manufacturers that hire them for their products. Actors Cliff Robertson and James Garner have become identified with ATT and the beef industry, respectively, because of their appearance in commercials. Jesse White has for two decades been the Maytag repairman, "the loneliest guy in the world." The advertising industry took special note when Maytag announced in 1989 that Gordon Jump, a star of the "WKRP" comedy series, would replace White in this role.

Testimonial. Closely associated with the use of the spokesperson is the testimonial commercial. The testimonial differs from the spokesperson commercial because of the credibility of the person doing the testimonial. In the testimonial, the person in the commercial is saying, in effect, "I have some expertise about this product, and I think it's the best there is." Sports figures are often asked to endorse sporting goods products because it is believed that they have high credibility in this area. In some cases, they're endorsements have gone as far as allowing their names to be placed on the product itself.

Anonymous announcers. The anonymous announcer format is the one in which the announcer does not appear and is not identified but is only heard. This format is popular with advertisers who want to direct all the attention of the audience to the product itself. The attributes of the product, not the spokesperson, are emphasized.

One of the most useful tools that writers of television commercials have is the television storyboard. The storyboard allows a writer to begin visualizing the commercial as it is being written. It uses a series of scenes from the commercial along with the words to give the writer an idea of how the commercial will look when it is produced. An example of a television storyboard can be found later in this chapter.

Storyboards are useful in some other ways. Besides helping the writer visualize the commecial, a storyboard can give a client an idea of what a commercial will be like before any expensive production work has begun. It can also give the producer and director of the commercial insights into what the writer has in mind for the commercial.

No one has to be a good or clever artist to use a storyboard. The most basic drawings of commercial scenes, even using stick figures if necessary, will be sufficient for transmitting the visual ideas in a commercial.

Sometimes "anonymous" announcers may not be so anonymous. A number of people have such distinctive and widely recognizable voices that viewers of a commercial will know who is speaking even when they are not identified. Burgess Meredith's voice has become closely identified with Honda cars, and Jimmy Stewart has done the voice-over parts for Campbell Soup commercials. This technique of having a recognizable voice in a commercial can heighten the interest in a product without distracting from the message of the commercial.

Students should recognize that many commercials do not fall strictly within the categories just outlined. They are often combinations of two or more of the types of commercials. They use techniques from a number of sources to help sell their products. On the other hand, you should remember that the most common characteristic of a television ad is its simplicity of structure. The time constraints of a television commercial demand that you get the message across to the viewer simply and quickly.

Other media

Three other types of media should be mentioned briefly as part of our overall discussion of advertising. They are point-of-purchase advertising, outdoor advertising, and direct mail. These are important forms of advertising, particularly in supporting advertising campaigns that are carried on in other media. Because they involve many decisions beyond those of the copywriter, however, we will discuss them only briefly here.

Point-of-purchase advertising refers to the packaging and display of a product. One study by the Point-of-Purchase Advertising Institute indicated that as many as two-thirds of buying decisions are made after the customer has entered the store. All other advertising is useless unless a product can be found. That means that it must be well packaged and well displayed. It must stand out from other products–particularly the competition, which is likely to be displayed beside it on the store shelves.

Point-of-purchase's effectiveness can be found in the history of one product –Hershey's candy bars. For decades, Hershey's declined to advertise in any media except its own packaging. Its market strategy was known as mass availability. That is, the company tried to place its product at as many locations as it could. That strategy worked, and Hershey's products became some of the most popular in its area. It has only been in recent years that the company has produced mass media advertising.

Outdoor advertising is a billion-dollar business. Because the messages on almost all types of outdoor advertising must be brief, this media is also used to supplement advertising campaigns in other media. One of the chief assets of outdoor advertising is its repetitive nature. A person may pass by a poster or billboard many times, and yet the advertiser has made only one advertising purchase.

Finally, **direct mail** advertising offers an advertiser many possibilities and advantages. Direct mail includes a variety of marketing techniques, including sales letters, post cards, pamphlets, and brochures and catalogues. Direct mail allows advertisers to target a very specific audience and to get a message to that audience very quickly. It can carry a great deal of information. One of the problems with direct mail is that it can be very expensive. It can, however, give an advertiser some fairly precise information about how well an advertising campaign has worked.

Conclusion

Writing advertising copy calls for a high degree of intelligence, hard work, creativity, and competitiveness on the part of the writer. It is not a job that everyone can do, but it is one that has great rewards for those who are successful.

Points for considertion and discussion

1. The text lists some major demographic characteristics that advertisers want to know. Can you think of other demographic variables that would be important to advertisers? What would make these important in selling a product?

2. Think of a member of your family. What needs are most important to that person. What advertising appeals would work best to sell a person that product?

3. Take an ad from a magazine. To what audience, in terms of demographic variables, is that ad targeted? What appeals does the ad use?

4. The text says that ads should tell people what they should do (for example, "Go out and buy one today." Find an ad that does *not* do this and then find one that does. Which do you think is more effective?

5. Select an ad that you think is a good one from a magazine. List the verbs that are used in the ad. Does this tell you anything about how the ad was written?

6. What characteristics does advertising copy writing have in common with news writing? How are they different?

Further reading

Advertising Age. For the person who wants to keep up with the world of advertising, this weekly publication is must reading.

John W. Crawford. *Advertising.* Boston: Allyn and Bacon, Inc. 1965.

Donald Jugenheimer and Gordon E. White. *Basic Advertising.* Columbus, Ohio: Grid Publishing, Inc, 1980.

S. Watson Dunn and Arnold M. Barban. *Advertising: Its Role in Modern Marketing.* New York: Dryden, 1978.

David L. Malickson and John W. Nason. *Advertising – How to Write the Kind that Works.* New York: Charles Scribner's Sons, 1977.

EXERCISES

The following section contains a variety of advertising situations for students to use to practice advertising copywriting. The advertising copy sheets contained in Appendix D may be used for these exercises.

Non-product advertising

College promotion

Pick a slogan or theme for an image advertising campaign for your college or university (example: It's a great place to learn.) and write 200 words of copy for three ads centered around that theme. You will also need to write a four- to 10-word headline for each of the ads.

Forestry company

Write an image ad for the Houseware Forestry Company, a national firm which owns two-thirds of the commercial forest land in Alabama. Houseware is 75 years old. It began as a small family business in 1907 near Oshkosh, Wisconsin. It did not stay confined to Wisconsin for long. Frank and Joe Ware were natural entrepreneurs who expanded into Michigan in 1915. By 1920, they had begun to buy up forest land all over the country, planting it with appropriate trees.

Houseware is currently embarking on an image campaign to emphasize the care it takes to replant the land from which it harvests trees, the family beginnings of the company, and the research the company conducts concerning the preservation of the ecosystem in the areas it harvests.

Houseware also takes great pride in its strict employee safety standards and generous employee benefits. Employees working with heavy, loud equipment must wear earmuffs, hard hats, and heavy gloves. No employee words unsupervised until he or she has completed a two-week training course.

Houseware has had only 15 accidents during the time it has been in existence. None of the accidents was fatal.

Houseware replants the areas it harvests and also restocks some of the larger areas with wildlife. The company works closely with environmental protection groups, sharing the results of its research. The 20-person Houseware research staff has found evidence that their company's forestry activities have improved the ecology of areas overcrowded with wildlife and trees.

The current chairman of the board of Houseware is Joseph P. Ware III.

Guns

Several politically oriented groups in your state have begun a lobbying effort with state legislators and city councils to outlaw the sale of handguns. These groups seems to be making some progess. In the last session of the state legislature, a bill to restrict the sale of handguns was passed by the House of Representatives but barely defeated in the Senate.

The state chapter of the National Rifle Association (NRA) has decided to fight this movement through an intensive advertising campaign. The central thrust of this campaign is to oppose the handgun legislation which the state legislature is currently considering. The bill is known as Senate Bill No. 3, and it would outlaw the mail order sale of handguns and require that persons buying handguns in stores fill out a long application stating why they want to buy the handgun and supplying personal information about themselves and the people in their households. This application would then go to the State Gun Control Board for approval.

The state NRA retains your advertising firm for the campaign, and you are asked to design three ads opposing this legislation and urging people to write or call their local state legislators about it. When you talk with the head of the state NRA about the campaign, he tells you, "We think guns are good for people, not bad for them." The ads should have headline, subhead if necessary, and 75 to 150 words of copy

Retail advertising

Baseball team

A National League Baseball franchise has been granted to Washington, D.C. The last time the city had a team was 1971, when the Washington Senators moved to Texas to become the Texas Rangers. The owners of the new team have not selected a name for the team yet, and they want your ad agency to propose a name and design a set of advertisements to promote ticket sales during January and February. Ticket prices are $6.50 for box seats, $5.50 for reserved seats, $4.50 for general admission, and $2 for bleacher seats. Those wanting more information or wanting to buy tickets should write to the Washington National League Baseball Team, Box 3995, Washington, D.C. 20006 or call (202) 555-1212. The owners tell your agency that the ads for tickets should emphasize the advantages of buying early, the excitement of baseball, and the fact that the game is finally back in the nation's capital. Write a headline, subhead, and copy for three ads. The copy should be 75 to 100 words long.

Wedding dresses

A local wedding shop wants to run a series of ads in April and May with the idea that it has "the best prices in town" on wedding dresses and accessories. Wedding dress prices begin at $150, and bridesmaids dresses begin at $100. The shop has lots of sizes and colors, and it also carries many accessories for weddings such as veils, ring pillows, etc. The store, the Bride's Boutique, is going to remain open extra hours during these two months for its sale. It will be open until 9 every night and Sunday from 1-5 p.m. One of the owners says she especially wants the ads to mention that brides who have looked everywhere else in town and

haven't found what they wanted should come to the Bride's Boutique. They'll probably find something they like. Write four ads which include a headline, subhead, and 75 words of copy.

Classical record sale

A local shop, Sound Advice, normally advertises and sells a lot of rock and country recordings. The owner wants to expand his business by offering "the best collection of classical records in the area." He wants you to write some ads promoting this part of his business. But you must be careful, he says, because he doesn't want to drive away his current customers. He is starting the new part of his business by offering all his single classical records and tapes for $1.99 for this weekend only. Come up with a slogan that the owner can use for this expansion in his business and write the ads, which will run in the local paper on Thursday, Friday, and Saturday. The owner says he has a full line of classical music, from Bach to Stravinsky.

Frozen dinners

Good Foods, Inc., is a manufacturer and processor of many foods commonly found in grocery stores. The company produces many canned goods, distributes fresh produce in many areas of the country, and has a large line of individually frozen fruits and vegetables. The company is now seeking to enter the frozen dinner market. The company has done extensive research in this area and has found two major negative characteristics of frozen dinners among consumers. One is that frozen dinners lack taste—the food found in most frozen dinners is simply not very good. The other negative characteristic is that, generally, frozen foods do not have a very good reputation. That is, "good" cooks don't serve frozen dinners to their friends; "good" wives and mothers don't serve frozen dinners to their families. People who serve or eat frozen dinners are thought to be lazy and not very good in the kitchen. Frozen dinners have these reputed characteristics despite the fact that research shows frozen dinners are eaten in the average American home at least once a week.

Good Foods doesn't know which negative characteristic to attack in its advertising and comes to your ad agency asking for prototype ads to help company officials decide which approach to take. Choose one of the negative characteristics above and write some advertising copy designed to counter it. It is up to you to come up with a name for Good Foods' frozen dinners, and the name should help in countering the negative characteristic you choose. Here are some more facts about the advertising situation which are included in a copy platform written by your agency.

Target market: Middle-and upper-middle class women who work but still have the responsibility of fixing meals for their families; age range 25 to 45.

Competition: Two major brands of frozen foods now dominate the market: Swan Foods has a wide variety of frozen dinners, which are generally advertised as the cheapest on the market; their average price is 91 cents per dinner. Wholesome Foods doesn't have as many varieties of dinners but research shows that people generally think they're a little tastier and more nutritious. They cost about $1.03 per dinner. These two companies sell 75 percent of the frozen dinners in America. The rest are sold by a variety of small companies, many of whom specialize in foreign dishes, such as Chinese foods.

Supportive selling points: Good Foods dinners will average about $1.25, making them almost the most expensive on the market. Good Foods will have fewer varieties than Swan but more than Wholesome, with more vitamins and minerals than any dinner on the market. One line of the Good Foods dinners will feature rib-eye steaks which have been pre-cooked "well done," "medium," and "rare." The dinners will also have more vegetables than the dinners now on the market, and Good Foods has come up with a process that will preserve more of the natural flavor of these vegetables.

Writing copy for advertising layouts

On the pages at the end of this exercise section are layouts for print ads for the next five exercises. All of them have illustrations. Spaces are indicated on the ads for the headline, subhead, body copy, slogan, and signature. You or your instructor may want to use these ads as they appear, or you may want to cut them out and change them around. You may also want to photocopy them in case you need to write a series of ads. Below is the information for writing each ad:

Local flower shop

Pearsall Florist Shop, the manager says, "wants to put a flower in every business in town at least once a week." She wants to promote the idea that fresh flowers enliven a business and make both customers and employees feel better about that business. The advertising will be pitched to downtown area businesses where the flower shop is located. (It's at 222 Main Street, and the telephone number is 643-ROSE.) For businesses that order one bouquet of flowers each week for a month, there will be a 20 percent discount. Because the shop is located in the downtown area, it can offer quick delivery to businesses in the area. In fact, they guarantee delivery within two hours of getting a telephone order. The manager says the florists at the shop are experts in designing "specialty bouquets" for special occasions or locations and that they can design something that is appropriate for any business.

Suggested assignment: Design a series of four ads to run in the local newspaper in four succeeding weeks. Each ad should carry the same slogan but have a different headline and body copy. Each block of body copy should be about 50 words long. You may want to keep the same design and illustration for the ads, or you can change things around.

Car repair shop

Wright's Auto Repair, located at 126 Wesley, is the oldest car repair shop in town. It has operated continuously from the same location since 1923. In fact, that makes it one of the oldest businesses in town. The steam engine in the illustration is a 19th century railroad engine, and it represents the kind of longevity that Wright's is known for.

At least, that's what it wants to be known for. Hank Wright, the current proprietor, has just taken over as manager of Wright's from his dad. It was Hank Wright's grandfather who began the business in 1923.

Hank wants a set of advertisements that emphasize the reliability of the work he does. He wants to appeal particularly to those people who have used other repair shops—especially those who use the shops at dealerships where they bought their cars – and who have been dissatisfied with them. Hank says his shop offers not only a guarantee on the work, but also a guarantee on when the work will be finished. If the shop cannot meet that deadline, it will provide a loaner car to the customer if needed. The shop takes care of all types of car work, from car maintenance (changing oil and filters) to engine and brake repair. They also have a specialist trained to repair car radios and sound systems.

Suggested assignment: Write the copy for three ads. The body copy in each should be from 50 to 75 words long.

Local newspaper

For National Newspaper Week, the local newspaper wants to run a series of advertisements about how widespread newspaper reading is. The target audience for this ad campaign is potential advertisers, particularly those advertisers who use other media, such as radio and television.

Here are some supportive selling points: The newspaper is subscribed to by two out of every three households in the area. More than 80 percent of the adults in the area say they read the newspaper regularly. More than 90 percent say they have seen the newspaper in the last week. By contrast, only 30 percent of the adults in the area say they listen to the top-rated radio station. The top-rated television show in the area, "Fly by Night," a syndicated game show, is watched by only about 25 percent of the households each night. Consequently, the argument can be made that the newspaper is the only "mass" medium in the area. If advertisers want a "mass" audience, they should choose the newspaper rather than radio or television. This information comes from a marketing survey that was commissioned by the newspaper within the last three months.

The newspaper wants you to come up with a slogan that would convey this theme.

Suggested assignment: Write three advertisements using the layouts on page 203-207. Use the slogan you have created for the campaign in each of them. The body copy in each should be 50 to 75 words.

Daycare center

Daycare is one of the fastest growing parts of the service sector. As more and more women work outside the home, the demand for quality, affordable daycare has skyrocketed.

The Sunshine Daycare Center is open from 6:30 a.m. to 6:30 p.m. It is located at 1212 Wiltshire Blvd., one of the city's major thoroughfares, so it is convenient to many people, especially to those who work downtown. The center takes children up through kindergarten ages and has a fully accredited kindergarten class.

The center knows that one of the major concerns that parents have for their child's daycare is to make sure that the child is properly cared for and that the child gets a lot of individual attention. Responding to this concern, the center makes sure that there is at least one adult for every 10 children at all times in the center. Most of these adults have some academic or professional training. The center has an open, bright environment inside, with a large, well-equipped playground in the back.

Current advertising should be pitched toward people who work downtown and who are concerned about the quality of care their children receive during the day. These people are not as concerned about price (the Sunshine Daycare Center is one of the most expensive in town) as they are convenience and quality.

Suggested assignment: Write three advertisements using the same theme or slogan. The ads should be at least 75 words each.

Computer store

Computerware, a store that has been in business for nearly 10 years now, specializes in selling and servicing a wide variety of hardware and software for many types of computers, particularly Apple (the Apple II line and the Macintosh line) and IBM and IBM-compatible computers. For the next month, the store is offering special prices on upgrades for many of the models of computers it sells and services.

Computerware is located at 717 Coventry Street, telephone 516-5523.

The folks who run Computerware realize that many people who bought computers for their homes or businesses two or more years ago will have machines that are beginning to get out of date. Because computer manufacturers like Apple and IBM are constantly bringing out new lines of equipment, the people who have owned their computers for two or more years may find that they cannot use much of the newest software that is made for their machine. Or they may find that they need more "internal memory" for their computers. ("Internal memory" is the capacity of a computer to store data and run programs faster.) The upgrade prices vary according to the brand of computer.

Computerware says the price of an upgrade include everything, even installation. There are no extra charges, and satisfaction is guaranteed. People who want an upgrade should call the store.

Suggested assignment: Write two ads for Computerware. Each should be 50 to 100 words long. Use the layouts on pages 211 and 213.

National advertising

Doughboy soft-serve dessert

The Doughboy Company, which produces a variety of frozen foods and mixes, is attempting to broaden its stake in both the dessert and frozen foods markets with a soft-serve dairy dessert. The company has been researching the potential for the product for about two years. It comes in vanilla, chocolate, and strawberry flavors and will be sold in rectangular half-gallon cartons.

Soft-serve frozen desserts typically contain between two and a half and less than 10 percent butterfat, qualifying as ice milk; ice cream must contain at least 10 percent butterfat. The primary ingredients in the new product are skim milk and mellorine (which substitutes vegetable fat for animal fat). The product has the nutritional value of ice cream. Doughboy says it "approximates the texture of soft-serve" desserts sold primarily through food service outlets like Dairy Queen. This product will be sold only in the dairy products section of grocery stores.

Give this product a name and write a headline, subhead, and the copy for three advertisements which will be placed in *Good Housekeeping, Time, and Newsweek* magazines. One of the ads should promote the product's nutritional value, another should promote its taste, and the third should emphasize its convenience. Each ad should be 100 to 150 words long.

Perfume

The Soft Lights Perfume Company has been marketing Wild Abandon perfume for a number of years, and recently it has found that its share of the perfume market has been decreasing. Essentially, the company wants to advertise a "new and improved" Wild Abandon perfume, but company officials are uncertain exactly how to do this. They tell you that this new perfume, which they want to market under the same name, has a slightly stronger scent and that it comes in a variety of colors, including purple, crimson, and gold. (It used to be transparent.) In a radical move, the company has decided to increase the price of the perfume by 50 percent, so that now it costs $65 for a half ounce. Write five advertisements for this product which will run in successive issues of *Vogue*. Each ad should have a headline and about 50 words of copy. The ads will have a common illustration–a gorgeous woman, dressed in a leopard-skin dress and accompanied by a leopard.

College beer

A new brewing company, Real Beers, Inc., is about to enter the crowded beer market with a new product. Company officials have decided that the part of the market they have the best chance of capturing with their new beer is college students. They believe the new beer will appeal to college students for several reasons. In the first place, this new beer is much cheaper than most other beers, with a base price of about $1.50 per six pack. Second, it comes in extremely thin aluminum cans. Finally, this beer will not come in a light version. In fact, the name of the new beer is Not Light Beer. The company wants to base its advertising campaign on the appeal that this beer is "a lot of fun to drink." It wants to advertise in your college newspaper, and you have been asked to write two ads. Each should have a headline, subhead, and 150 words of copy. Write the ads and designate appropriate illustrations.

Smart Tops, Inc.

Most men don't wear hats. That's what the research shows. Smart Tops, Inc., is going to try to change that. Smart Tops is a small firm but owned by the clothes conglomerate Giant Size, a respected name in clothes. Giant Size isn't a charity, however, and Smart Tops has been losing money for years. The managers of Smart Tops fear that Giant Size will close the company down unless they can show a profit in the next two years. They have decided to embark on a major advertising campaign and have come to your agency for help.

The research that your agency has done into why men do not wear hats has come up with two major reasons: men don't wear hats because they don't consider them necessary; and they don't wear hats because they think hats are for "older" men. Smart Tops wants to market its hats to younger men, those in the 25-to-40 range. The managers aren't sure which would be the most effective advertising campaign. Should they take on the "old" characteristic directly and try to convince men that wearing a hat is a "young" thing to do? Or, should they try to counter the negative characteristic that hats are unnecessary with some convincing arguments that hats really are necessary?

Your agency wants you to pick one of these advertising strategies and design some advertising for Smart Tops. The following is some information that the agency research office has provided you which may eventually go into a copy platform.

Competition. Smart Tops now has about a 7 percent share of the market, down from 10 percent two years ago. Almost every other manfacturer of men's hats has seen a drop in sales during the past two years also, so there is no evidence that hat wearers have anything against Smart Tops. The biggest advertiser in the market is Smith, Inc., which manufacturers a line of hats known as Good As Gold. These are some of the most expensive and well-made hats on the market. Other hat manufacturers do relatively little advertising.

Supportive selling points. Smart Tops says that its hats are as well made as the Good As Golds, but they sell for an average of 25 percent less. The hats range in price from $15 to $50. All the hats contain at least 50 percent natural fibers, i.e. cotton and wool. They are extremely well crafted and backed by years of tradition and experience. Smart Tops has been making hats since the 1880s. The hats are guaranteed against any defect in workmanship and against any damage for a year. If a customer is dissatisfied with anything about a Smart Tops hat, all he has to do is send the hat to the company office and he'll receive a full refund. Smart Tops can also be counted on to provide the latest in new styling in men's hats, as well as a wide variety of ztraditional styles.

Audience. The marketing research has turned up the fact that women make about 40 percent of all hat purchases for men.

Your assignment is the following:

Write a slogan for Smart Tops hats that can be used in all their advertising.

Write two print ads, each with a headline and at least 50 words of copy. Be sure to use the slogan you have written.

Write a 30-second radio spot or a 30-second TV storyboard, also using the slogan you have written.

Professional advertising

Hymnals

A publishing house has asked your advertising agency to market a new hymnal which it has just produced. This hymnal is designed for use in all Christian-denomination churches. It has all the classic hymns in it, such as "The Old Rugged Cross," "Onward Christian Soldiers," and "Amazing Grace." It also contains some new songs that have never before been published in a hymnal but that viewers of television religious programs are likely to recognize. The hymnal is organized alphabetically by song title; it has an index; and it has traditional rituals for baptism, dedication, and other services. You are to write two magazine ads attempting to sell this hymnal to ministers and song directors of smaller churches. The name of the hymnal is *Sing Unto the Lord*. If ordered in quantities of less than 100, it sells for $3; more than 100, $2.75. The publishing company is New Life Publishing House, 200 Sixth Street, Dallas, Texas. The two ads you write should have a headline, subhead, and body copy of at least 75 words.

Electronic editing equipment

Signalcorp, a corporation which manufactures computers, is trying to break into the market of selling electronic editing equipment to smaller newspapers-those with circulations between 25,000 and 100,000. A market study has indicated that this is an expanding area and one in which the company can make a lot of money fairly quickly. Signalcorp has manufactured a good line of electronic editing equipment, as good as that made by any competitor. The corporation's problem at this stage is to distinguish itself from the competition. The corporation's management has asked your ad agency to help solve this problem. The management wants you to develop three prospective ads for use in *Editor and Publisher* and other trade magazines. These ads should say little about the equipment and more about the company and the services it offers. Each ad should have a headline, subhead if necessary, and 75 to 100 words of copy. Develop a common slogan that you can use in these ads.

Magazines

The Scientific Media Corporation has recently begun to publish a new magazine called *Working Scientists*. The magazine attempts to interest children in scientific professions. Its publishers feel strongly about the neglect of scientific and technical education in the United States.

The magazine is written simply, perhaps on the traditional ninth-grade level. Its articles, submitted by professionals as well as by staff writers, deal with many subjects, including astronomy, biology, genetic engineering, energy, and geology. The articles discuss advances in each field. Recent topics covered included microsurgery, the Galileo Jupiter mission, and the future of solar energy. Each issue of the magazine includes two feature stories on two professions. The stories may be personality sketches of men and women working in the profession or may simply outline the job opportunities and responsibilities found in the chosen field. For example, one issue spotlighted career opportunities and pitfalls in astronomy. It described the career of a well-known astronomer who had been the first to research the atmosphere in detail. He had named the various layers of the atmosphere, determining their chemical composition and temperature. Later, he worked at the Jet Propulsion Laboratory in Pasadena, participating in the Apollo, Mariner, and Voyager missions. The magazine is careful to describe the problems as well as the benefits encountered in such professions, mentioning, for example, the astronomer's vulnerability to federal budget cuts. Also included in the career articles are approximate salaries and the type of education each requires.

Write an ad for *Working Scientists*. It will appear in such publications as *Time*, *Newsweek*, *Astronomy*, and *Business Week*. A year's subscription costs $15. Each issue is illustrated with color photos.

Selecting advertising problems

The following exercises present situations that have a variety of problems that might be solved by advertising. In reading and thinking about these situations, consider yourself an advertising consultant and not just a copywriter. Follow the directions of your instructor. You may be asked to select one of the problems and produce some advertising for it, or you may need to produce several ads that attack a variety of problems.

Hershal's Department Store

Hershal's Department Store is one of the largest department stores in town. It's located in the same shopping mall as a Sears and a J.C. Penney store, but Hershal's has a larger variety of clothes than either of these two chain stores. The store's line of women's clothes is especially large, and the store has a reputation for having the most up-to-date styles of women's clothing. It is locally owned and has been in operation for more than 50 years. The president of the board is John Hershal, Jr., the son of the founder. The store's general manager is John Hershal III, the president's son. Hershal's is considered to be the major store in the mall where it is located.

Hershal's recently conducted a marketing survey, as it has for several years, but this

survey turned up some surprising results. The survey found that there is a reservoir of goodwill about the store, something Hershal's has cultivated for many years. For instance, people in the survey said they liked Hershal's refund policy, which has always been a very liberal one. However, the survey found that people did not like a number of things about Hershal's: The store hours were not long enough (Hershal's closes at 8 p.m., while the other stores in the mall stay open until 9 p.m.); it takes too long to check out; many of the departments don't have enough people to wait on the customers adequately; there is some feeling that Hershal's has raised its prices more than other stores have; and many younger women try smaller shops, especially those close to the local college campus, before shopping at Hershal's.

In light of these findings, Hershal's has done several things: Store hours will be extended to 9 p.m. beginning next month; new people will be added to departments that have been understaffed; the store, which conducts three major sales each year, will conduct five during the coming year.

Hershal's also wants to increase its advertising and comes to your agency for help.

At this point, you should identify some of the possible advertising problems and follow the directions of your instructor on handling this advertising situation.

Wayfarer Restaurant

The Wayfarer Restaurant was established in 1865 and is the oldest restaurant in town. It has been in several locations but has been at its present location, 505 Sixth Street, for more than 50 years. The Wayfarer is famous for its breakfasts. It has a tradition of serving the finest country ham in the area, but each item on the menu is of exceptional quality. A food critic for the state's largest newspaper once reviewed the breakfast at the Wayfarer and called it the "best place to wake up in the state."

The Wayfarer Restaurant is small and usually crowded, especially in the morning.

It seats only about 30 people, and that's one of the problems. The owners feel that they are losing customers who are put off by the thought that they will have to wait for a while. There is no thought being given to expanding the restaurant, however. There is no room to expand, and if there was, the owners probably wouldn't because they like the cozy, intimate atmosphere the small space affords.

The owners have also noticed that many of the people who eat at the Wayfarer are "regulars," people who come there often. They feel that they should be attracting some new customers, especially younger people, like students from the nearby college.

Finally, one of the "hidden secrets" of the restaurant, according to the owners, is the dinner menu. The owners say they offer the best steaks in town–they reject a lot of the meat the packers offer them because it isn't good enough. Their steaks cost 75¢ to $1 less than comparable steaks in the best restaurants in town.

At this point, you should identify some of the possible advertising problems and follow the directions of your instructor on handing this advertising situation.

Apple Growers Association

Apples are one of the most popular fruits in America, but in the last few years, the Apple Growers Associaton has been disappointed with retail sales and have been somewhat disturbed that growers of other fruits have been advertising so heavily— especially the orange growers. Even raisin growers have gotten into the act lately with a television campaign that emphasizes the various uses raisins can have. Apple producers feel they need to increase the visibility of their fruit and reinforce its top spot in the market.

There are more than 20 major varieties of apples sold in this country, and most of these varieties are available in most parts of the nation. They range from the large yellow Golden Delicious, a very sweet variety, to the traditional tart green apple, used mostly for cooking. There are also varieties like Winesap and Red Delicious. Apples have a wide variety of uses, and the creative cook can do a lot with apples. The problem is that people don't think about apples very much and don't consider the uses they can make of them.

Another thing about the apple is that it is considered a "traditional" rather than an "exotic" fruit. It's old fashioned. It still bears the image of "an apple a day keeps the doctor away." (The apple is packed with a lot of vitamins and minerals and other things that are healthful.) The Apple Growers Association is divided on how to approach this image. Some want to emphasize the traditional image and uses of the apple, while others believe that image isn't attractive enough, especially to gain younger customers.

The Association comes to your advertising agency with these feelings and this information and wants your advice on possible advertising campaigns it can conduct.

At this point, you should identify some of the possible advertising problems and follow the directions of your instructor on handling this advertising situation.

Toyota Tercel

For several years, Toyota has been using the slogan, "Oh, What a Feeling–Toyota!" in most of its advertising. That slogan has been pitched at creating a good feeling, a feeling of excitement about Toyota cars. The slogan has also been a central theme for the advertising of all models of Toyotas, from the smallest Starlet to the most expensive Cressida.

Toyota has decided to change its marketing plan in a couple of important ways. For one thing, the company wants to begin to get away from the "Oh, What a Feeling!" theme for all of its models and wants to emphasize more substantive selling points for each of its cars. Second, it wants to begin to distinguish more carefully one model from another in its advertising. The thinking with company officials is that the name "Toyota" is the only central theme it needs to use in its advertising since the company has built a reputation for producing quality cars.

Toyota wants to begin this new marketing plan with one of its models, the Tercel. It has chosen the Tercel for a number of reasons. The Tercel used to be part of the Corolla model, the smallest in that line. The company found that the car was so popular that it evolved into its own full line, so that now what once was the Corolla-Tercel is now simply the Tercel. A second reason is that while the car is a popular one, it will be facing stiff competition from several American-made models of the same size during the next two years. Toyota wants to cement the Tercel's position in the market.

Your advertising agency has been asked to bid on the Tercel account. Part of the bid is coming up with a central theme and a slogan for all of the advertising and producing some sample ads. Toyota and your agency's research department have provided you with the following information you may use for constructing the ads.

Competition. The three major models that compete with the Tercel are the Honda Civic, the Chevrolet Chevette, and the Ford Escort. The Civic, like the Tercel, is a Japanese-made car, while the Chevette and the Escort are made in America. Tercel's base price is $7,995; Civic's is $7,495; Chevette' and Escort's are both $7,495. (All of these prices exclude taxes, options, transportation and dealer preparation charges—which must be mentioned in the ad if the price is mentioned.) The Honda is a very well-made car, but the Chevette and Escort have had some problems with recalls. Both have had problems with the transmission. Toyota has not had a major recall of any of its models in seven years.

Supportive selling points. Tercel has a higher-than-average price, but the resale value of the Tercel is also much higher. While most cars depreciate about half their value in three to five years, the Tercel depreciates only about 30 percent. The maintenance record for the Tercel is "outstanding," according to *Consumer Companion*, a highly respected consumer and product-testing publication. In a recent article on subcompact models, the magazine said,

"Taking into consideration price, dependability, low running and maintenance costs, and resale value, the Tercel is the best subcompact on the market today. Owners will pay a little more at the beginning, but they will save money in the long run."

Audience. Toyota wants to pitch its advertising for the Tercel to young, single people who are just graduating from college. The age range for this group is 21 to 24, and your marketing research shows that these people are likely to begin looking for a new car soon after they land their first jobs.

Your assignment is the following: Write a slogan that can be used in all the Tercel advertising. Write two ads for the major national newsmagazines. Each should have a headline and at least 50 words of copy. They should also use the slogan you have written. Write a 30-second radio spot or a 30-second TV storyboard, also using the slogan you have written.

**Layout for
Local flower shop
(see page 191 for information)**

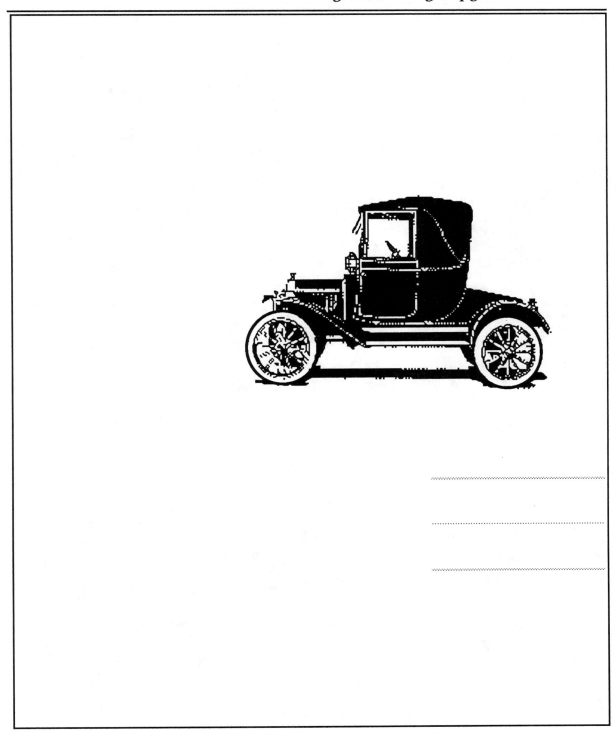

**Layout for
Car repair shop
(see page 192 for information)**

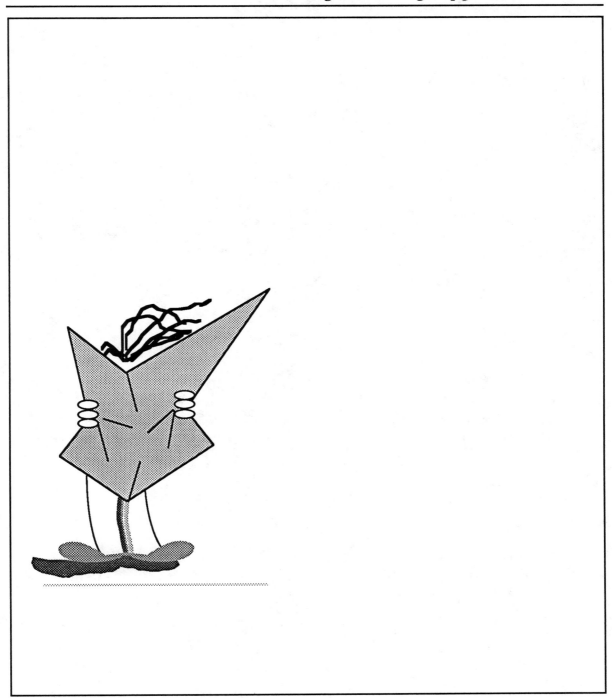

**Layout for
Local newspaper
(see page 192 for information)**

Layout for
Local newspaper
(see page 192 for information)

Layout for
Local newspaper
(see page 192 for information)

**Layout for
Daycare center
(see page 192 for information)**

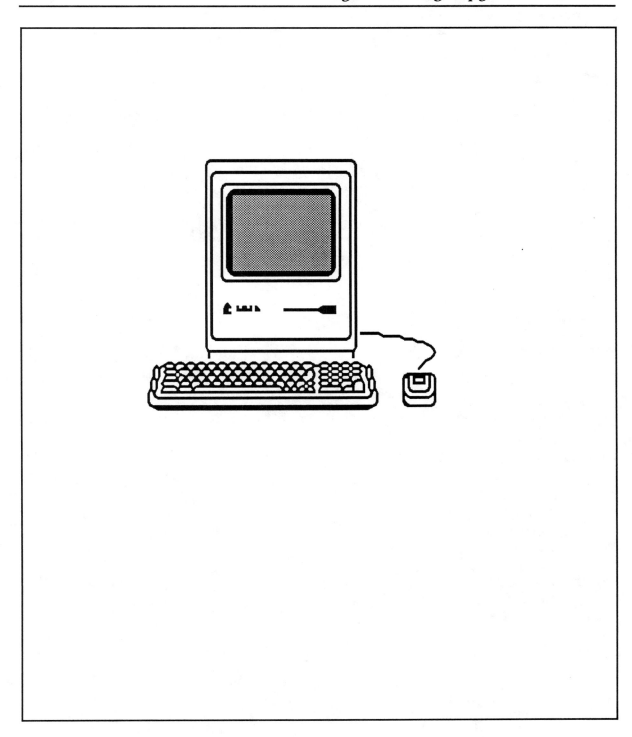

**Layout for
Computer store
(see page 193 for information)**

**Layout for
Computer store
(see page 193 for information;
students should supply illustration)**

8

Writing for Public Relations

The field of public relations ranges across the organizational map. Defined in the broadest terms, public relations means communicating, and in today's business and social community an organization must communicate at every level. Public relations practitioners are communication specialists, hired by organizations to perform and advise on a variety of communication tasks.

Only a few years ago, many organizations saw no need to have such specialists. They sold their products or performed their services for a specialized public, and they were content to believe that they were doing all of the "communicating" that they needed to do. One example is a large corporation that specializes in operating sites around the country that handle toxic chemical waste material for other industries. The company performed this necessary but unpleasant task and did so within the legal regulations that governed such operations. The company felt that it had little need to communicate with the public. After all, it was not trying to sell a service to the general public. It dealt exclusively with other industries. However, in the 1970s and 1980s, when more public attention and concern was focused on the environment—and on dangerous toxic waste sites, such as Love Canal in New York —the company found that it could no longer afford to take such a cavalier attitude about its communication needs. As the issue of hazardous waste disposal has become not only an industrial one but also a political one, this company and many others like it has found itself in the communication business.

This situation has occurred for many organizations, and they are discovering that they need professional communicators on their staffs as well as budget managers, salespeople, scientists, engineers, and secretaries. The field of public relations has expanded a great deal in the last few years, and more and more students are finding excellent employment opportunities in this field. In fact, the public relations major has become one of the most popular fields of study in mass communication.

Traditionally, the career path into public relations has been through

215

journalism programs or working in the mass media. People who had either or both of these credentials were thought to make good public relations practitioners. While this is still the case, many colleges and universities have instituted public relations majors, which study the many specifics of working in the field of public relations. More and more students are obtaining internships in public relations agencies and PR departments within companies and organizations.

Despite these burgeoning opportunities, public relations remains a very competitive field. The person who would enter this line of work must be intelligent, disciplined, and willing to work difficult and long hours. Public relations jobs carry with them a great deal of responsibility, and the people who accept them must be willing to live up to that responsibility.

What do PR practitioners do?

People who work in public relations jobs do a great many things. In fact, that is one of the attractions of a career in PR. The variety of activities that a practitioner can engage in is enormous. On the other hand, that variety requires that a person be skilled in many areas, that he or she be able to deal with many differing and sometimes conflicting assignments, and that he or she be comfortable with many different people.

Here are some of the things that a public relations person does:

Handle the communication with the external publics of an organization. The term "publics" is one that is used often in public relations. It refers to the various groups that an organization attempts to reach through its communication efforts. External publics are those groups outside of the organization that an organization wants to communicate with. They may include the public at larger, buyers of a product, users of a service offered by the organization, potential contributors to the organization, members of the news media on whom the organization depends to distribute its information, or any number of other groups. A public relations practitioner must assist not only in getting information out but also in making sure that information is properly interpreted. Some of the means by which information from an organization is distributed are news releases, letters, brochures, and quarterly and annual reports.

Handle communication with the internal publics of an organization. Just as there are groups outside the organization that must be communicated with, there are also groups within the organization that must receive information from it. These are the internal publics. They can include employees, independent contractors who work with the organization, stockholders, members, and the families of any of these groups. In companies that have a larger number of employees, this communication function is often critical to the organization. Keeping employees properly informed is often vital to the company's health. Associations— those that have memberships that are not part of the day-to-day operation of the organization—also depend on good communication with their members to keep their organizations healthy. Communication with these internal publics can take the form of newsletters, company magazines, letters, notices, memoranda, and periodic reports, among others.

Work with the news media to get information about the organization. In most organizations, one of the chief responsibilities is that of media liaison. The PR person is often called on to help find out information about the organization that would be useful to the news reporter in putting together a story. This kind of information often goes beyond that produced in a press release. The PR person must find the person within the organization that has the information the reporter wants and must often make arrangements for those people to meet. The other side of this responsibility for the PR practitioner is that of advising the organization's officials on media relations. When and how to release information is often the responsibility of the PR person. He or she may also have to give advice on speeches, press conferences, and interviews that the organization's officials may give. In short, any time the news media deal with an organization, there is likely to be a PR person involved.

Help produce public functions and events. Public relations practitioners are often involved in the organization's public activities. A company may announce an advertising campaign; the United Way officials may hold a news conference to kick off its annual fund drive; a local business may make a donation to a school with a ceremony marking that donation; a university may break ground for a new building. Any number of such events may occur, and the PR person is usually a part of the planning. He or she is mostly likely the one who sees that the public is properly informed about them. Almost all organizations have the need to produce public events at some point, and the public relations practitioner will have a major responsibility for their success.

These are some of the day-to-day activities that a PR person might be involved in. On a more general level, a public relations professional can contribute to the organization for whom he or she works by providing a continuing and long-range public relations plan. That plan may have many parts and may certainly be revised as new needs arise and old needs subside. At this level, most experts agree that public relations consists of four parts:

Planning. An organization should develop of plan for how it intends to deal with its publics. Some means of communication are not appropriate for certain publics, while others are. A well-conceived plan will allow the organization's officials to figure out what publics the organization needs to communicate with and how that communication should take place. An integral part of planning is setting goals for the various communications with the organization's publics. Planning is a constant process with many organizations.

Research. Hand-in-hand with planning is research. A public relations practitioner may have to find out exactly whom the organization wishes to communicate with. And that person may also have to discover the best means of communicating. These are often complex questions for which there are no ready answers. A public relations person will need to have these answers if a plan is to be properly executed.

Another part of the research process is finding out what information the organization wants to communicate or should be communicating.

Again, this often is no easy or simple task. The process of research may involve talking with a few people in the organization in order to write a news release; or it may mean pouring over financial and technical papers and holding long discussions with many of the organization's top officials in order to put together an annual report.

Communication. This is the part of the process that we are concerned with most in this book. Putting information into the proper form—and often doing it very quickly—is one of the most important jobs that the PR person can perform. A PR practitioner's ability to do this, more than anything else, will determine that person's worth to the organization.

Evaluation. The evaluation phase of the practitioner's work is when he or she asks, "Did our plan work? Did we get the right information out to the right publics? Did our efforts have the effect we wanted?" Plans need evaluation to see if they are working, and it is often up to the public relations person to devise a means of evaluation for the plan.

> *Essential to all writing for public relations is understanding the purpose of the communication and knowing who the audience is for the communication. In other words, a writer needs to know why he or she is writing and what the audience is likely to do with that information. That knowledge comes not only from the research the writer does on what he or she is writing but from a sensitivity and respect the writer has for the audience.*

Evaluation, of course, is related to the goals of the plan. If the goal of an organization was to gain new members, evaluation is fairly easy. Looking at the number of new members that joined while the plan was being executed is a straightforward means of evaluating the plan. Sometimes, however, goals are much more complex, and evaluation is more subjective.

What does it take to be in PR?

Whether you work for a major public relations firm, a particular company, a government agency, a hospital, a university, or another institution, if you work in public relations the chances are quite good that you will have to write. The overwhelming majority of jobs in the field of public relations are writing jobs. Public relations departments produce brochures, press releases, letters, speeches, scripts, and public service announcements for television and radio, posters, reports, books, formal documents, magazines, newsletters, newspapers, and information directories on a wide variety of topics. While photographers, artists, designers, production managers, and editors may also be required in producing such items, each begins with a writer. Even a flyer announcing a company picnic has to be written by someone.

Gathering information and structuring it into specific formats is the basic process for all writing in the mass media. The best in the public relations profession can take a scribbled set of ideas and produce a 15-minute speech for a vice-president to give at a company dinner in much the same way that a good reporter takes a tip from the telephone and eventually produces a polished story. The differences between public relations writing and news writing are primarily differences created by the intent inherent in public relations writing. A public relations writer must bear in mind a complex set of purposes and interests while producing any piece of copy for any particular publication.

If you wish to write in a public relations environment, you should be prepared to work very hard on a relatively small set of assignments directed at a limited audience. It is not unusual for a piece of writing to be scrutinized by several "editors" (that is to say, your bosses), who will criticize and often change your work. Public relations writing is usually done for an explicit purpose, and the expenditures involved in producing any item must be justified by the degree to which the writing fulfills that purposes. For example, if you are asked to write an article for a company publication outlining a new policy about how raises are awarded, you will be expected not only to write a factually correct story but also to express the attitudes and intentions of management in a manner acceptable to employees.

This idea of intent in public relations writing puts an extra burden on the writer. All of the rules of good grammar, spelling, usage, and structure apply to public relations writing. The requirements of brevity and clarity that help make for crisp news stories also hold for writing brochures. Above and beyond these considerations, public relations writers must constantly bear in mind the interests of the institutions for which they write and the purposes of their writing.

Public relations writers are not merely propagandists for the people who pay them. Rather, the good public relations writer is a professional, able to write honestly and clearly about complex and varied issues in a manner acceptable to people who may know little or nothing about writing but who know a great deal about what they want to see in print.

Public relations writers have a dual role, however. Their responsibilities extend not only upward to their employers but also outward to those who will be reading what they write. In a sense, public relations writers act as translators. They must completely understand the company or institution they write about. If it is a company that makes computer parts, they must know all about computers. If it is a hospital, they must have a working knowledge of medical terminology and procedures. Yet they must write about these things in ways their readers can understand. Their role becomes much like that of newspaper reporters covering particular beats they know intimately.

This intimate knowledge of the institution a writer "covers" engenders a particular problem with the use of language. Public relations writers should take care not to become so immersed in their topics that they take on the jargon of the company to an inordinate degree. Readers of newspapers that use press releases from a hospital may not know what a "cardiovascular microsurgery specialist" really does unless you explain cardiovascular microsurgery in simple terms. The same is true for any highly specialized topic. Central to this concept is the idea of audience. As a public relations writer, you will write for a variety of people—company employees, the general public, management, government officials—and the use of language will change depending on who the audience is. A piece intended for the board of trustees of a university will differ substantially in tone and content from something intended for release to state newspapers, even it the topic (the hiring of a new dean, for example) is the same.

A public relations writer must be something of a verbal acrobat, leaping from style to style with seemingly effortless ability. By the same token, the writer must be skilled at structuring information into a variety of widely differing formats. One person may be required to write speeches, letters, brochures, news releases, promotional copy, and formal reports—all on the same topic and perhaps all in one week! This is particularly true of small firms or departments. Doing this kind of work requires an absolute command of the basic tools of writing, good reporting abilities, and a mental flexibility which allows the writer to think about the same or related topics in a multitude of ways.

A final point should be made about PR writing. Essential to all writing for public relations is understanding the purpose of the communication and knowing what the audience is for the communication. In other words, a writer needs to know why he or she is writing and what the audience is likely to do with that information. That knowledge comes not only from the research the writer does on what he or she is writing but also from a sensitivity and respect the writer has for the audience.

The ability to write—and to use the language effectively—is at the heart of almost all public relations activities, but it is not the only skill necessary for the successful public relations person. That person must also have the ability to deal effectively with many people in various situations. He or she must know how to use tact or persuasion in obtaining information from others within the organization. The PR professional must be able to satisfy the various publics that the organization communicates with. The professional must also be persuasive with the leaders of an organization in advising them on their public relations efforts. The PR practitioner is often one of the most visible persons within the organization and must keep the purposes and goals of the organization in mind during all of his or her contacts.

The successful PR practitioner must have the ability to organize effectively and work efficiently. That means meeting deadlines that are imposed quickly and arbitrarily. That person must be a quick study—that is, one who is able to quickly grasp an idea or situation and give it form and substance. And that person must be able to make sound judgments about the effectiveness of public relations efforts.

The PR professional should combine a belief in the goals of an organization with a high standard of personal ethics and integrity. In the tenth century, so the story goes, Eric the Red sailed west from his native Iceland and discovered a large, desolate land. He wanted to colonize it, but the land was so forbidding that he felt that even his hearty Icelanders would be reluctant to do so. To make the land more appealing, he named it Greenland. With this name, Eric the Red was able to persuade a number of people to follow him to a place that is covered mostly with snow and ice. Eric the Red, many have said, was one of the world's first flacks.

Public relations has had a widespread reputation of being practiced by "flacks." These are people who stretch or ignore the truth to gain something for their organization. They spout the "company line," knowing but not caring that it is self-serving and inaccurate. They seek only publicity, even if it is bad publicity. That kind of person, unfortunately, makes it into almost every profession, and the public relations field has certainly not been immune. Yet, most public relations practitioners consider themselves professionals with high standards of ethics and a deep regard for accuracy. The people who believe in what their organization is doing and make genuine efforts to provide accurate and useful information to the organization's publics make the best PR professionals.

Writing news releases

One of the most common forms of public relations writing is the news release. The news release is information, usually written in the form of a news story, which an organization wishes to make public through the news media. A news release, like a news story, should follow a consistent style; it should be written as concisely and precisely as possible; it should answer all of the pertinent questions about the story; and it should emphasize what an editor will think is the most important part of a story. In short, a good news release differs very little from a good news story.

The last point about news releases--that they should emphasize what an editor will think is the most important part of a story--is one that sometimes gives public relations writers some problems. The first can be overcome by knowledge and application of the news values discussed in Chapter 4. The second problem is that corporate managers, who have very little knowledge of or feel for news values, will often want to emphasize what *they* think is important rather than what rates as important to an editor.

This attitude puts the writer in a difficult position. Most news releases are discarded by editors most of the time. One reason for this is that editors get many news releases every day, and they do not take the time to go through each of them carefully. If a news release does not give the editor some news immediately, the editor is not going to spend much time with it. Another reason that editors discard news releases is a prejudice on the part of many editors against running news releases. News releases are often seen by editors as propaganda or promotion--or even free advertising. The way a writer can overcome these problems is by writing a news release as close to the news story form as possible. Editors are much more likely to use news releases that have the most important information in a simply written lead paragraph and that follow a consistent style than those releases that do not.

Many corporate managers do not understand this, and they often want a non-newsworthy item emphasized in a release. For instance, a manager may want to announce a new plant opening in the following way:

> John Jones, president of the American South Corporation, announced today that American South Corporation will open a new copper-wire manufacturing plant in Midville next year.
> Mr. Jones said the plant will employ about 75 people initially and about 250 when it is fully operational...

The public relations writer will have to convince the manager that this style will not help the news release get used. A better way of writing this release would be the following:

```
        A copper-wire manufacturing plant, which
   will employ about 250 when it is fully opera-
   tional, will open in Midville next year, ac-
   cording to officials of the American South
   Corp.
        The opening was announced by John Jones,
   president of the corporation...
```

While the content of a good news release is the same as that of a good news story, the form differs slightly. Generally, a news release should contain three things at the top of the first page. One is a headline or slug-line telling what the story is about. The styles of various public relations departments are different, and the writer must learn what style his or her department uses. In the example above, a headline might look like this:

```
   NEW PLANT TO OPEN
   IN MIDVILLE NEXT YEAR
```

A second item that should be at the top of a news release is the name and telephone number of a person in the organization who can be contacted for more information. Again, this will differ according to various public relations departments, but it should always be there. Editors who are interested in using a story will often want to know more about it. They are more likely to pursue a story if a name and telephone number are easily available to them. The form this information takes could be as simple as the following:

```
   For more information contact
   James E. Smith
   American South Corporation
   555-1616
```

A third piece of information that should be at the top of a news release is a release time. This tells the editor when the information may be used. Often, the information may be used as soon as the editor gets it, and in this situation the words "FOR IMMEDIATE RELEASE" should be used. Sometimes, however, editors may be sent releases before they should be used. For instance, some sort of a ceremony in the mayor's office may be set up to announce the new plant mentioned in the example above. It may be that corporate officials do not want word of the plant getting out until the official announcement is made, but they still want to cooperate with editors who have deadlines to meet. In these cases, they will put an *embargo* on the release. An embargo is simply a time when a piece of information may be used, and it may look like this:

```
   For release after 10 a.m.
   Friday, October 13
```

Editors will generally abide by embargo times and not release information before they should. There is nothing an organization can do, how-

News from

American
Southern

"Making America Grow"

For more information contact
James E. Smith
American Southern Corporation
(404) 555-1313

For release after 10 a.m.
Friday, October 13

NEW PLANT TO OPEN
IN MIDVILLE NEXT YEAR

John Jones, president of the American Southern Corporation, announced today that American Southern Corporation
will open a new copper wire manufacturing plant in Midville
next year.

Mr. Jones said the plant will employ about 75 people ini-
tially and about 200 people when it is fully operation.

American Southern Corporation has plants in more than 30
states and manufactures a variety of materials that are
used for industrial and technological purposes. The company
employes more than 15,000 people and is headquartered in
Atlanta, Ga.

The copper wire plant planned for Midville will be part
of the industrial parts division of the corporation.

"The computerized rotating process that will be installed
at the Midville plant will be state-of-the-art for this industry," Mr. Jones said in making the announcement in Midville today.

"We plan to hire many people from the Midville area to
work in this plant, but a number of them will have to be
trained in this process. We will be giving those people
that training as soon as possible.

The plant will be located on a 50-acre site on Sherrill
Road, five miles south of downtown Midville. Construction
of the plant will begin immediately, and company officials
estimated that the plant should be fully operational within
three months.

"We looked at a number of sites for this plant but chose
Midville for a number of reasons," Mr. Jones said. "Among
those were Midville's location near some major rail trans-
port sites and the overall quality of life that Midville
offers."

Figure 8-1
This news release has a
number of problems. As
we noted in the text, the
lead emphasizes the
wrong thing. In para-
graph 1, instead of hav-
ing John Jones' name at
the beginning of the
lead, the fact that a new
plant employing as
many as 200 people
should begin the story.

In paragraph 3, the facts
about the company are
too high in the story;
they should be moved to
the end of the story.

In paragraph 5, some
company jargon is be-
ginning to sneak into
this story. The writer
should make sure that
the readers can under-
stand everything that is
in the story.

The location of the plant
is very important, espe-
cially to readers in Mid-
ville, where this story is
likely to get the most attention (paragraph 7).
This fact should be high-
er in the story. Also,
when construction will
start and when the plant
will be operational
should also be higher in
the story.

ever, if an editor chooses to run information before an embargo. Consequently, public relations practitioners should be careful in releasing information with an embargo and should do so only to those editors who can be trusted.

We mentioned earlier that the best news releases are those that exhibit the principles of writing and structure found in a news story. It might be helpful to review some of those principles here. More detail about writing news stories is in Chapter 5.

News stories are generally written in an inverted pyramid form. That is, the most important information is presented first, and the information comes in a descending order of importance. For the writer of the news release, this means that the background information that often must be included about the organization should come at the end of the story rather than toward the beginning.

The writer of a news release—just like the writer of a new story—should keep the commonly accepted news values that contribute to defining news in mind when writing the release. The writer should ask, "Is the story timely? What impact will it have? Is there conflict in this story? Are prominent people involved in the story? Is there something bizarre or unusual about this story?" Reviewing the news values of a news release will help the writer in producing a release that is more likely to be used.

The most important part of a news story—and also a news release—is the lead paragraph. Remember, the first reader of a news release is likely to be a busy editor who must decide whether or not to use it in his or her publication. You should let that editor know quickly what your story is about. Just as a news writer needs to "sell" a story with a lead that is interesting or informative (or even both), the writer of a news release needs to sell an editor on the story in the same way. If the editor thinks the news release is interesting or important, he or she is more likely to use the information.

Another point about news releases should be made here. A news release might have only one reader—the editor or reporter to whom it is sent. Yet, if that person uses the information it contains in a story or uses it as the basis for getting more information, the release has been a success. In most cases—particularly in larger cities—newspapers and trade publications rarely run press releases, so the writer of a news release rarely expects to see his or her own words in print. The purpose of a news release is to get information to the people who work in the mass media. If the information in a news release results in the information being used by the media, the news release has done its job.

The rules about sentence and paragraph structure apply to news releases just as they do to news stories. In other words, keep the sentences short and the paragraphs reasonably brief. Editors, just like newspaper readers, don't like to get involved with long paragraphs.

A news release writer has to pay particular attention to jargon and wordiness that might creep into a news release. Every organization or association develops its own language—abbreviations and acronyms that speed up communication among those with a knowledge or interest in the field. PR practitioners must also know this language in order to communicate within the organization, but they should be careful use only language that is widely familiar in their news stories.

Wordiness is another danger to the well written news release. Wordiness is particularly a problem if a news release must be approved by those who are not professional writers. Those people often believe that the more words you can use — not the fewer words — the more you will impress the reader and the more likely you are to get your point across. Professional writers know that just the opposite is the case. A news release, like all other good writing, should use only the number of words it takes to convey the information you want to convey. Anything more than that is wasted.

News release writers should pay particular attention to proper identification of all the people mentioned in a release. A news release is an official document coming from the organization. Journalists count on a news release to be correct when it mentions information about the organization. Journalists may also want to contact directly the people mentioned in the news release. They assume that those mentioned in a news release are correctly identified and that their names are spelled correctly. A PR practitioner who fails at either of these tasks can cause much embarrassment for everyone involved.

Finally, we should mention a form of the news release that is becoming more popular among many organizations—the video news release. The VNR can range from a short news story produced by the organization on videotape and distributed locally to longer feature items (or even half-hour shows) that large companies distribute nationally. VNRs for news items are written in much the same way as broadcast scripts for news stories are written. They are "reported" by someone within the organization, put on videotapes and distributed to TV news departments in the area. Larger companies produce longer and more expensive VNRs that are likely to emphasize the generic products they sell rather than the brand names. For instance, a soup manufacturer may produce a tape on the nutritional value of soup, or a brokerage firm might produce a piece on the advantages of buying stock.

From the PR practitioner's point of view, the two major problems with producing VNRs are the expense and the uncertainty of their use. VNRs can take a lot of time and money from an organization. The people and equipment involved in producing a high-quality VNR can involve thousands of dollars. For a company with many assets, the costs may not seem out of line, but for smaller organizations, spending several thousand dollars—or even several hundred—on a single item like a VNR is not worth it. The second problem is getting VNRs used by television stations. Many stations are unwilling to use material that is not produced by their own news departments. And even where stations are willing to use this material, they may not have the air time to do so.

Despite these problems, VNRs remain a valid tool for information distribution by an organization. With improvements in video technology, the costs of producing and distributing a VNR are coming down, and more and more companies are finding video a useful means of providing information to their publics.

Letters

Despite increased use of the telephone and advances in other forms of communication, letters are still one of the most important and effective means of communicating in the business world today. The well-written letter is impressive and appreciated by the receiver. The poorly written letter can establish negative feelings on the part of the receiver that are extremely difficult to overcome. PR practitioners are often called on to write letters for their organizations. These letters may serve a variety of purposes, such as selling a product or idea, explaining company policy, answering complaints, and raising funds. Each of these letters must be carefully crafted to accomplish its purpose.

Letters are a good way of directing a message straight to the persons you want to receive that message. Most people read their mail; at least, they begin to read their mail. If a letter does not quickly give its information and make its point, it is likely to irritate or lose its reader—or both. Letters are expensive for organizations to produce and send. They take time and care to write. Like all other communication, they must accomplish their mission for the organization.

Like any other kind of writing, letter writing requires a precise and concise use of the language. Letters require that writers come directly to the point, that they do not waste the time of the receiver. Letter writing requires more, however. The letter is a very personal form of communication. Even if a letter is obviously written for a large number of people, it is still taken very personally by a receiver. Letters, then, should have some personal touch. The reader should get the feeling that the letter was written to and for him or her.

One technical requirement is that letters should *never* contain any spelling, grammar, or punctuation errors. They should also never have any editing marks on them.

The first rule of letter writing is to understand the purpose of the letter. The letter writer should ask, "Why am I writing this letter?" and if necessary should make a list of those reasons. There may be a number of reasons for a letter to be written, but there should be one overriding purpose. If that is not evident from the list the writer makes, then he or she should give some more thought to the letter itself.

Following closely on the purpose for writing the letter is the action expected of the recipient. Again, the letter writer should ask a question: "What do I want the reader to do after reading the letter?" Sometimes the answer is a simple one and comes directly from the purpose of the letter. At other times, the intended action of the reader may not be apparent. Again, the writer should have this clearly in mind before starting to write the letter. In any case, the action of the reader should be as specific as possible.

The table on the next page shows some examples of purposes and intended actions for a letter.

Once the purpose of the letter and the intended action on the part of the reader is established, the writing can begin. One of the first and most important considerations a writer should give to a letter is its tone. The proper tone is essential to the effectiveness of a letter. In most cases of business correspondence, a letter must be both personal and professional; they must show the right mix of these qualities. A letter that is too personal—especially if the writer and recipient are not personal friends—may offend the recipient as an invasion of privacy. A letter that is too formal may make the recipient feel that he or she is not very important to the writer.

What do we mean by being "too personal" in a letter? Here are some things to do to avoid that:

Don't be obsequious. The dictionary defines obsequious as "exhibiting a servile attentiveness or complaisance." In letter writing , this means don't thank someone too much (twice is the maximum for a letter; once is better); don't keep apologizing; don't say "please" more than once in a letter; don't use or repeat phrases like "I hope you'll understand." All of these things irritate the reader; most people want to be spoken to, or written to, in a straightforward manner.

Don't be too complimentary. Depending on the purpose of the letter, compliments can ring hollow very quickly. In a letter telling a job applicant that he or she didn't get the job, this might be appropriate:

```
The experience listed on your resume shows
that you are very well qualified for a number
of positions.
```

But this would be too much:

```
The experience listed on your resume shows
that you are very well qualified for a number
of positions. You made an excellent impres-
sion on all of us when you interviewed for
the position, and we were glad that you know
so much about our company. People like you
```

Letters: Purposes and Intended Actions

The purpose of the letter is	The intended action on the part of the reader is
to answer a complaint from a customer	to understand why the situation occurred
to explain a policy to a member of the organization	to know what the policy is
to announce a new procedure for applying for promotion	to follow the new procedure when applying for promotion
to persuade someone to subscribe to our magazine	to fill out the subscription card
to ask someone to join our organization	to fill out the membership card
to get someone to pay a bill	to send the payment
to tell someone that he or she didn't get a job	to know that he or she didn't get the job but still to feel that he or she received fair treatment

```
would be a credit to our company, and we're
just sorry that we had only one position to
fill.
```

A letter like that is likely to leave the reader asking, "If they thought so much of me, why didn't I get the job?" In that case, the letter would not have accomplished its purpose. Long compliments are usually reserved for friends. They have only limited effectiveness in a business letter.

Generally, don't try to be funny. Humor is not expected in business correspondence and is likely to get in the way of your purpose for writing the letter. In addition, few people can write humor well enough to be understood, so the best rule is: don't try.

Avoid referring to the personal characteristics, habits, or feelings of the reader. If you are dealing with someone on a professional basis, you probably don't know much about their personal habits or feelings. And even if you think you do, you shouldn't make too many assumptions about them. Let's go back to the letter telling a person that he or she didn't get a job. What if the writer had said:

```
I know this news will disappoint you.
```

It's possible that the recipient will be glad that he or she didn't get the job. The recipient may have gotten a better offer from another company. In that case, the writer will look pretty silly.

To avoid sounding too formal in your letters, here are some things you should consider:

Use personal pronouns. Used appropriately—that is, not too much—personal pronouns can humanize a letter without letting it become too personal. A reader wants to be recognized as a human being with attitudes and feelings. Using personal pronouns, especially "you" to address the reader, is a good device for business correspondence.

Avoid impersonal constructions. Impersonal constructions are those such as "It is . . ." and "There is . . ." These constructions also include those that place the blame on "it," as in "It has been decided . . ." Obviously, "it" did not decide anything; some person did. (Using "it" in a letter when it refers to something specific is certainly appropriate.) Writers use these constructions in the hope that readers will not attribute an action to a particular person (especially themselves). Readers are usually sharper than that, however, and can see right through this ploy.

Avoid the passive voice. The passive voice—in business letters as in all other forms of writing—deadens writing. It robs any piece of writing of its vitality. A letter is much more likely to be read and understood if the verbs are active.

Be careful about referring to policies, rules, and regulations. If a policy or rule is the reason that something occurred and that needs to be explained in the letter, the policy or rule should be stated in the simplest terms possible. In many large, bureaucratic organizations, such rules are written in an obscure form of bureacratese. The writer needs to translate this for the reader into the plainest terms possible. In most cases, the writer should not make technical references, such as "Regulation 33.b states . . ." unless that is something the reader will readily understand.

Avoid using technical language that may mean nothing to the reader. A person who has a complaint will not be pacified by a letter that he or she doesn't understand. In fact, it is likely to confirm the feeling that the complaint is valid. Such a letter is also likely to offend the reader by its condescending tone.

Avoid wordiness. Lots of words, long sentences, and long paragraphs will obscure the message of the letter. They may sound impressive to the person who writes them, but they will not impress the reader. One of the best ways of striking that mix of the formal and personal necessary to a good letter is to write in simple, down-to-earth language.

Company publications

News releases and letters are very important and common forms of public relations writing, but they are by no means the only ones. We should return to a point which we have made before: Public relations practitioners must know how to write, and they must be able to write in many various forms. Public relations people are often called upon to write in a variety of situations, and in this section, we will be discussing the different kinds of organizational publications for which public relations people may be responsible.

In dealing with these publications, the public relations practitioner may often be responsible for more than writing. He or she will be called upon to know something about editing, typography, layout, photo selection and cropping, and other parts of the publication process. We will not be dealing with any of that here. Rather, our focus will be on the basic writing skills that are a part of any of these jobs.

Three major kinds of publications that organizations produce are newsletters, pamphlets and brochures, and company reports.

Newsletters. The newsletter is a basic term for a wide variety of publications a company may produce. The newsletter may range from a single mimeographed sheet to a slick, full-color magazine. The form that a newsletter takes will depend on the company, the amount of money that is spent on it, and, most importantly, the audience.

Newsletters are directed at a particular audience, and a writer for a newsletter must keep this in mind to be successful. Most company newsletters are internal; that is, they are targeted for audiences within the company. One of the most popular types of newsletters is the employee newsletter. This one is directed toward the employees of an organization, giving them information about the company and focusing on their interests and concerns. Newsletters may be specialized to the point of aiming at a certain set of employees in a company. The point is that newsletters should always be directed at a particular audience, and they must be written and edited with that audience in mind.

The style of writing a newsletter uses will depend on the audience

The Bartlett Company

ANNUAL REPORT

Employee Benefits at Oakdale University

What reporters should know about public opinion polls...

Southern Opinion Research

Southeastern Watercolor Association

NEWSLETTER

Juried set fo

Pearsall Company's

Spring Catalogue

THE Sentinel

College recruits 4 for key positio   ns

College graduation set for conference center

Thompson, Boone dontate major gifts

Bryant, others in college national telecommunications confer   ence and its purpose. Many newsletters are purely informational. They simply try to get as many facts to the audience as quickly as possible. Others may have the purpose of entertainment. Either way, the writing in a newsletter must be concise and precise. No newsletter should waste the reader's time. Few companies will *require* that their employees read a newsletter. Rather, they are encouraged to do so, and one of the means of encouragement is an efficient writing style.

Because of the advent of desktop publishing (DTP) technology, organizations are more likely to produce newsletters for their publics. Desktop publishing technology is computerized editing equipment that allows the users to write, edit, and design a publication at the same computer screen. With DTP, newsletters are an even more efficient means of getting current information to an audience quickly. DTP allows newsletters to be produced efficiently and at a lower cost than was possible just a few years ago. The leading computer for this activity is the Apple Macintosh, but many other computer hardware and software companies are designing products for the DTP market. Knowing what this technology is and how to use it is becoming more and more necessary for the person wishing to become a PR practitioner. That person needs to know how to write but in addition needs to know how to design and lay out a publication.

Newsletters are most effective when they are consistent in their writing, design, and publication schedule. Those who read them should know what to expect in them and when to expect it. The PR practitioner who publishes a newsletter must understand the value of this consistency to the effectiveness of the newsletter.

Pamphlets and brochures. Unlike newsletters, pamphlets and brochures are usually directed at external audiences—people outside an organization. These kinds of publications are very important because they are often the first and sometimes the only contact a person may have with an organization. It is important that these publications be attractive in appearance to catch the eye of a potential reader, but it is equally important that they be well written. Like an advertisement, the appearance of a pamphlet or brochure will promise something with its appearance; that promise should be kept with the content. Public relations people are often put in charge of producing as well as writing these publications.

There are two kinds of pamphlets and brochures: informational and persuasive. The informational brochure tells about an organization or procedure. The writing in this kind of brochure must be down to earth, practical, and efficient. A brochure on how to hang wallpaper, for in-

Figure 8-2
The examples on the opposite page show a variety of kinds of publications that a company may produce. Every company has to deal with a "public" in public relations terms, and most have more than one of these constituent groups. Targeting them with a variety of publications is a common way for an organization to communicate quickly and efficiently.

stance, should take the reader through a step-by-step process, giving the reader enough information to do the job but not wasting the reader's time. The persuasive brochure is one that tries to make a point, to sell an idea, or to persuade readers to adopt a certain point of view. Many examples of this kind of brochure exist: An American Cancer Society brochure on the evils of smoking is one. Writing style may vary in this kind of brochure, but one thing the writer should remember is that opinions should be based on information. A writer may express opinions very strongly, but these expressions are not nearly as persuasive as facts. For instance, a writer may say, "You ought to give up smoking because it is bad for your health." The writer would be more effective by saying, "Doctors say more than half the cases of lung cancer that they treat are caused by smoking." The second statement is much stronger because it gives the reader facts, not just opinions.

(For the rest of this section, we will use brochure to refer to both pamphlets and brochures. The terms pamphlet and brochure are often used interchangeably, as we will do in this chapter. A pamphlet is usually smaller than a brochure, has a narrower purpose, and often has a shorter life. Beyond that—for our purposes here, at least—the differences between a pamphlet and brochure are not significant.)

The brochure is a common means of introducing an organization to the public. It's strength is that it can be designed for and delivered directly to an audience of the organization's choosing. That means that it is efficient in holding the attention of a particular audience. It can be designed for maximum effect on the audience.

The design is a very important part of a brochure and has a great deal to do with the writing in it. There is a wide variety of formats and an infinite number of designs that can be applied to a brochure. In thinking about putting together a brochure, it is useful to follow the diagram on this page. Those in charge of the production of the brochure need to decide first on the purpose it is to serve. They should ask, "Why is this brochure necessary? What problem will it solve? What audience is it directed to?"

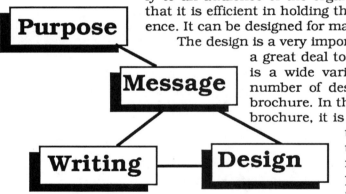

Figure 8-2
The producers of a brochure or pamphlet have to decide on the publication's purpose and message first. Writing and design decisions are then made — often simultaneously.

Following closely on these questions is the message that the brochure is to convey. Is the brochure supposed to describe the organization in general, or does it have a more specific message? Is it to persuade its audience to do something, or is it simply to inform? (The thinking that goes into a brochure is much like the thinking that goes into an advertisement. In fact, a brochure can be considered a kind of advertisement for an organization. For a more in-depth review of this process, see Chapter 7.)

Once the purpose and message of a brochure are decided, the design and writing decisions are made. These decisions may be simultaneous; that is, the writing and design may take place at more or less the same time. A PR practitioner who is proficient at both writing and design

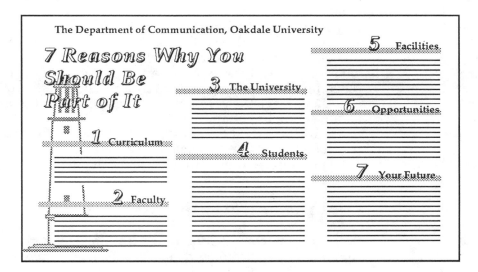

Figure 8-3
Here are two brochures about the same organization, but they use different approaches. The top one is informational; the bottom one is persuasive. The persuasive brochure is aimed at a narrower audience — potential students of the department. The informational brochure could be given to anyone interested in the department.

will often do this. Or one decision could follow the other. For instance, a designer may come up with a design for a brochure and then give it to a copywriter; or a writer may write the copy first and hand it over to the designer. In any case, the design and writing are closely linked.

Many people make the mistake of thinking that simply presenting information is a good persuasive method. While information is necessary for a persuasive argument, it usually needs to be crafted in a way that will emphasize its persuasive factors. Sometimes that can be done by the order in which the information is presented. Very often it is done by the graphic techniques in the brochure. If a PR practitioner is not good with design and layout, he or she needs to find someone who is and work closely with that person.

Annual reports and other types of reports. Companies that sell stock to the public are required by law to produce an annual report. Many other organizations that do not come under this requirement also produce annual reports. These reports give people inside and outside the company an idea of what the company is all about and how the company is doing financially. Many companies, particularly larger companies, consider the annual report one of the most important forms of communication they have. One legal requirement for annual reports is that they must be truthful. While a company may try to put on its "best face" in an annual report, the information the report contains must be factual.

The writer of an annual report—usually someone in the company's public relations department—is often required to translate a lot of complicated financial data and industry jargon into a simple, clear account of the company's activities and position. The writer must use understandable English and write for an audience that does not know the ins and outs of the company.

Other kinds of reports a company may require are quarterly or semi-annual reports or reports about an organization's activities that are directed to a special audience. Nonprofit organizations may compile these kinds of reports when they embark on fund-raising campaigns. Writing these kinds of reports takes a lot of intelligence and skill in using the language.

Annual reports must contain financial information about the organization and some descriptive information about the company's structure and activities for the year. Beyond that, companies have wide latitude in what they may include in an annual report. Large organizations sometimes put thousands of dollars into the production of an annual report, and they target these reports for specific audiences and purposes, such as attracting investors, holding onto stockholders, and creating a stable image within a field of competition; for non-profit organizations, the purpose of an annual report might be to attract members, increase visibility in community, and report on otherwise hidden activities.

Oral presentations

Speeches, statements, and other oral presentations are among the most common forms of public relations writing. The major difference between this kind of writing and the writing that we have discussed previously is that, like writing for broadcasting, oral presentations are written for the ear, not the eye. They are written to be spoken, not read silently.

Consequently, many of the principles of broadcast writing apply to this kind of writing. Oral presentations should be written in simple, clear, concise language. Sentences should be short. Modifiers and modifying phrases should be kept to a minimum. The content of the speech should be simple; the points made should be easy to follow.

In writing any oral presentation, the PR practitioner must take three major factors into consideration: the audience, the speaker, and the subject of the presentation.

The writer should know, as precisely as possible, who will be listening to the speech. For instance, a company president may be asked to speak at a high school graduation. The writer should understand that while the speech may be directed to the graduates, the audience will also contain their parents and other relatives. This may make a difference in how the speech is structured. The writer will also need to have some idea of what the audience is "expecting" to hear and how important it is to meet those expectations. For instance, if the local college football coach is asked to make a speech before the Lion's Club in early August, the audience will expect him to comment on the upcoming season. They are likely to be disappointed if most of his speech is devoted to the previous season.

The speaker is an important part of how the writer approaches a speech. His or her personality will have much to do with the content of the speech. For instance, the writer may need to know if the speaker is comfortable telling funny stories or if the speaker likes to quote certain people. The speaker may have some ideas he wishes to use in the speech, or he or she may even want to write a draft of the speech for the writer to polish.

The subject of the oral presentation, of course, is an all-important factor for the writer. The subject matter is usually connected with the position of the speaker, although that is not always the case. In the case of the high school graduation speech just mentioned, the company president is not expected to talk much (if at all) about his company. Too many comments about the organization might be inappropriate in this setting. In other cases, however, the audience will expect to hear about the organization that the speaker represents.

Three of the most common types of oral presentations that PR practitioners are asked to write are slide presentations, statements, and speeches.

The **slide presentation** (or presentation using transparencies) is very popular with many organizations, and its use is very likely to increase. Slide presentations are an effective means of presenting information, particularly to small groups of people. They are especially helpful in sales presentations. Slides can supplement the words of the speaker and can help focus the attention of the audience on the points that the speaker wants to make.

One of the reasons that slide presentations are growing in popularity is technology. With DTP equipment, it is much easier and less expensive than it was only a few years ago to produce quality graphics that can be made into slides. Producing such graphics, as well as writing the presentation, may become the duties of the PR person—yet another reason for the student wanting a public relations career to become knowledgeable about DTP technology.

The writer of a script for a slide presentation needs to understand the relationship between the script—that is, what the presenter will say —and the slides themselves. In almost all presentations, the slides are used to supplement and enhance what the speaker is saying, but the main information comes from the speaker. The slides themselves should be simple and uncluttered and should have a consistent format. The script contains the major part of the information in the presentation.

Another concept the writer of a slide script needs to understand is that of pacing. Pacing simply means how fast the slides appear to the audience. Some presentations need to be fast-paced; that is, the slides are shown rapidly throughout the presentation, possibly as many as 10 per minute. A fast-paced script means that the slides contain no detailed information that the audience must absorb. If the slides do contain such information—such as graphs that indicate something about an organization's progress—the presentation should be at a slower pace. Some presentations call for slides to be shown at a rate of only one or two per minute. For most presentations, a minute per slide is probably too slow; the audience will expect a faster pace than that.

A **statement** is a short oral presentation; its length depends on the forum in which it is presented. A statement that precedes a question-and-answer session at a press conference should be relatively short—one to two pages at most. A statement that is read to a legislative committee might be longer, depending on the subject and the time allotted to the speaker. A statement has few of the formalities of a full-blown speech. It is an attempt to summarize facts and make points as efficiently as possible. It often sets the stage for what is to come later, particularly if it precedes a news conference. A statement should be cleanly and efficiently written. It should present its facts and make its points and then stop.

Speeches come in a wide variety of forms. They may be informative, persuasive, entertaining, or a combination of all three. They may last only a few minutes or all day (although modern Western audiences are likely to think a speech is too long if it exceeds 30 minutes). Many of our most memorable sayings were delivered in speeches. For instance:

> And so, my fellow Americans, ask not what your country can do for you; ask what you can do for your country.
>
> John F. Kennedy
> Inaugural address, 1961

> The only thing we have to fear is fear itself.
>
> Franklin Roosevelt
> Inaugural address, 1933

> I never met a man I didn't like.
>
> Will Rogers
> Speech in Boston, 1930

> Four score and seven years ago, our fathers brought forth on this continent, a new nation, conceived in Liberty, and dedicated to the proposition that all men are created equal.
>
> Abraham Lincoln
> Gettysburg Address, 1863

> I have a dream.
>
> The Reverend Martin Luther King, Jr.
> Civil rights march in Washington, 1963

Writing a speech is not an easy task, but it is a common one for many PR practitioners. Writers may begin their work by thinking of a speech as consisting of three parts: an opening, a middle, and an ending.

The opening should do a number of things. It should allow the speaker to introduce himself or herself to the audience with some sort of personal reference. In most cases, an audience will already know something about a speaker; the speaker may have been formally introduced by someone else. The opening allows the speaker to say something about himself or herself and establish a relationship with the audience.

Many speakers also use the opening to "warm up" the audience with a humorous story. Such a device works best when the point of the story can be directly related to the points that the speaker is trying to make in the speech. A funny story for its own sake may help the speaker get going, but it is not as effective as the one that is part of the speaker's message.

Most important, the opening of a speech should establish the speaker's subject and should give the audience clues to the direction in which the speaker is headed. An audience should detect in a speech a logical progression of thought, and that progression should be evident from the very beginning of the speech.

The middle of the speech should take whatever points are made—or alluded to in the opening—and expand on them. A speaker may use a variety of techniques to do this. One of the most effective is telling a story. People of all ages like to hear stories; they enjoy following narratives. The stories, of course, should support the points that the speaker is trying to make in the speech, and they should do so in a fairly obvious way. A speaker who tells a story and then tries to explain what that has to do with the points in a speech has failed in using this device.

Another useful technique for a speech writer is the striking quotation. A speaker who can use quotations from other sources can add interest, strength, and credibility to his or her own remarks. Consider these remarks from a Vietnam combat veteran who was asked to speak to a local civic club about his war experiences:

> Occasionally, I am asked to describe what it was like to be in Vietnam. From the perspective of those who lived in America during that time, Vietnam was somehow a different kind of war. It has often been pointed out that it was the first war we saw on television. To the combat soldier, however, that made little difference. We knew that all wars are essentially the same. William Tecumseh Sherman, speaking more than a hundred years ago, summed up our feelings about war when he said, "I am tired and sick of war. Its glory is all moonshine. It is only those who neither fired a shot nor heard the shrieks and groans of the wounded who cry aloud for blood, more vengeance, more desolation. War is hell."

Adapting an ancient quote to a modern purpose is another useful way to add interest to speeches. A person speaking on the environment used a biblical quote in this way.

> The Book of Ecclesiastes says there is "a time to cast away stones, and a time to gather stones together." Generations before us in this century have been casting away the stones of our environmental systems. I firmly believe that it is the charge of our generation to gather those stones together. Now is the time.

Making a striking statement is another technique that speakers can use to make a point and gain the attention of their audience. Sometimes that statement can come in the form of challenging conventional wisdom, like the following:

> Most people believe that the Golden Rule—"do unto others as you would have them do unto you"—is the simplest and best formula for good human relations. I'm here to tell you that it isn't. In fact, that formula, despite the best intentions of some people, is a disaster.

Sometimes an obscure but striking fact can gain the attention of the audience in the same way. The following is from a speech about how people can rebound from failures early in life and go on to success later:

> Back in 1919, the New York Yankees were looking for an outfielder who was also a good hitter. They thought they had a promising young man, but he managed only two hits in 22 at bats. The Yankees then went out and purchased Babe Ruth from the Boston Red Sox. Everybody knows what Babe Ruth accomplished, of course. But what about that young man who only got the two hits? Whatever happened to him? He decided that baseball wasn't his game after all, so he gave football a try. That game was obviously better suited to his abilities, and he became a star. In fact, many consider him to be the father of professional football. His name was George Halas, the long-time owner of the Chicago Bears.

These are just a few of the techniques that a writer can use to expand the body of a speech. Whatever techniques are used, the speech should follow a logical line—one that the audience can follow, too. If the speech goes off on tangents and never returns, the points will be lost and the audience will be dissatisfied.

The closing of a speech can be used to make the final, major point of the speech or it can offer the audience a summary of what the speaker has already said. The same rhetorical devices that you can use in any other parts of the speech—telling stories, using quotes, making striking statements—can be used to close a speech. Speech writers should remember, however, that a good speech does not need a dramatic flourish at the end. It can simply end with a story that summarizes the subject of the speech, a listing of the points already made by the speaker, or a conclusion that can be logically drawn from what the speaker has said.

Conclusion

Public relations work is mostly writing. Employers will look for people who can write to fill their public relations jobs. Public relations writing requires a versatility on the part of the writer that is demanded of few other jobs. While it is exciting and rewarding, the field of public relations is one that demands intelligence, skill, and hard work.

Points for consideration and discussion

1. At the beginning of this chapter, the author describes the field of public relations and some of the things that public relations practitioners do. From this description and what you know about the field, what is the most attractive thing about public relations work to you? What is the part of the work that you would like the least?

2. Many people who work in journalism and elsewhere have a very negative opinion of the field of public relations. Why do you think they have such an opinion?

3. A public relations practitioner has to have a wide range of knowledge and understanding to do his or her job well. What other courses in the curriculum of your college or university would you think a person should take if he or she is interested in becoming a public relations practitioner?

4. What are the advantages and disadvantages of writing a letter as opposed to making a telephone call when you want to make personal contact with someone?

5. The author says that the design and the content of a brochure or pamphlet are closely related. Try to find some examples of brochures or pamphlets and see if you think the people who put these together did a good job of relating the design and content.

6. The author lists several techniques for writing speeches, such as adapting ancient quotes and telling personal anecdotes. Can you think of others?

Further reading

Allen H. Center and Scott M Cutlip, *Effective Public Relations, 5th Ed.,* Englewood Cliffs, NJ: Prentice-Hall, 1978.

George A. Douglas, *Writing for Public Relations,* Columbus, Ohio: Charles E. Merrill, 1980.

Richard Weiner, *Professional's Guide to Public Relations Services,* New York: Richard Weiner Inc.

James J. Welsh, *The Speech Writing Guide,* New York: Wiley, 1968.

EXERCISES

The following section contains a variety of public relations writing exercises. You should follow your instructor's directions in completing them.

News releases

Write news releases based on the following information. Follow the directions given to you by your instructor.

YMCA

You work for the YMCA in your city, and as part of your job you have to write news releases about the organization's many recreational and educational programs. One such program is an on-going series of swimming lessons for children, young people, and adults. You have to write a release including the following information about the fall series:

Children's classes begin August 25 and are held on Mondays, Wednesdays, and Fridays. One class is held for each of five different age groups: tiny tots (ages 1-3); kindergarten (ages 4-6); elementary (6-9); youth (ages 10-13); and teens (ages 14-17). All of these classes meet twice each week until November 30 on the following schedule:

Tiny tots meet on Mondays and Wednesdays from 1 p.m. until 2 p.m.

The kindergarten class meets on Mondays and Wednesdays from 2 p.m. until 3 p.m.

Elementary students meet from 3:30 p.m. until 4:30 p.m. on Mondays and Wednesdays.

The youth class runs from 4:30 p.m. until 5:30 p.m. on Mondays and Fridays

The teen class meets from 5:30 p.m. until 6:30 p.m. on Mondays and Wednesdays.

Two classes are held for adults (ages 18 and older). One meets on Monday and Tuesday nights from 7 p.m. until 8 p.m. The other meets on Saturday from 1 p.m. until 3 p.m.

Registration will be held at the YMCA office from August 15 until August 22. Classes are limited to 15 students each, and the registration cost is $20 per child or $25 per adult for YMCA members, $30 per child or $35 per adult for non-members.

Information: Mrs. Bertha E.L. Ifont, 774-4567.

Registration: See Mr. Bob N. Diver at the YMCA office.

No cash refunds for registration fees will be given. Those who register for classes but find it necessary to cancel should be sure to notify Mrs. Ifont immediately so that a credit memo may be issued for the amount of the registration fee. This memo can be applied to registration for other YMCA classes at some future date.

Department head leaves

You are public relations director for a local private hospital, Mountain East Medical Center. During the past few months, there has been considerable friction between the hospital's board of directors and the head of the purchasing department, Bob Wilkinson. Wilkinson's tight-fisted purchasing practices have been criticized by some of the medical staff in spite of the fact that the borad of directors had ordered him to cut costs by 15 percent.

Write a press release using whatever of the following information you feel is important.

Wilkinson's resignation is effective immediately. He will be replaced by the assistant head of the department, Johnny Toler, who has been with the hospital for 13 years.

Wilkinson was a 1972 graduate of the state university's school of hospital administration. He came to Mountain East Medical Center in 1975 after working for a small rural community hospital as purchasing chief. He will take a job as a purchasing agent with the City Memorial Hospital.

Toler's background is in pharmacy. He began as an assistant druggist in the hospital pharmacy 13 years ago and was moved to the purchasing department in 1978 as an assistant after the hospital pharmacy closed. Toler's wife, Carolyn, is head of the gynecology department at MEMC. They have two children.

Hospital administrator Harry Illscott had this comment: "Bob's abilities will be greatly missed at this hospital, but I know that Johnny Toler is a person we can all depend on to do whatever is necessary to keep his department going. I have great faith in him and in this hospital."

Toler gave the following statement: "This hospital means a great deal to me and my family, and I will give my best efforts to making our purchasing department the best. I learned from a fine man-Bob Wilkinson-and I hope I can continue to build on the foundation he established."

Honorary degrees

Each year, your university awards honorary degrees to people who have made outstanding contributions to the state or to society in some way. This year two honorary degrees will be awarded at the commencement exercises to be held at 11 a.m. on May 14 in Memorial Coliseum.

You work part-time at the university's public relations depatment, and your boss asks you to write a press release announcing that the following people will be receiving honorary doctorates at the Saturday morning ceremony:

George T. Hale, 63, a 1945 graduate of the university who established the state's first cable television system back in the early 1960s, will be cited for his "ability to envision the future and make it a reality for the state's telecommunications industry." When he retired from the presidency of Hale Communication, Inc., last year, the company had more than 40 percent of the cable market. Hale, a multimillionaire, has donated thousands of dollars to the development of educational television at both major universities in the state. In addition, he built a camp for physically handicapped adults on his mountain estate and sends more than 300 individuals there each spring and summer for an extensive recreation training program. Hale lives in Birmingham with his wife of 30 years, Elizabeth. Although they have no children of their own, they are parents to two Korean children: Lee, 21, and Ben, 18.

Rachel Cabanis, 44, an Alabama native and 1956 graduate of Goucher College, completed law school at Harvard after a 20-year career as a legal secretary with her husband's law firm in Montgomery. Her famous book about her decision to go to law school and her experiences there, *Breaking Through*, has been lauded as "the greatest statement of one woman's choices written in this decade." It won her a Pulitzer Prize (and at least a year's worth of speaking engagements). Mrs. Cabanis, now separated from her husband, Roy Cabanis, will return to Montgomery as a full partner in another law firm. She is being honored by the university for her "honesty and integrity in making difficult choices in a complex world and succeeding despite numerous obstacles."

New plant

You work for the Holesome Donut Company of Wilmington, Delaware. Your company wants to open as many plants as possible in the Sunbelt, and company officials have decided to establish a new doughnut factory in Repton, Alabama.

Write a press release announcing plans for the complex. Include as much of the following as you feel is significant.

Repton city officials had been bargaining for the new plant for two years. At least 12 small towns in Tennessee, Georgia, and Mississippi also wanted to be the site of the new plant. Repton was chosen because of its desirable location, the low interest rates local banks offered for development, and the willingness of city officials to help build roads and sidewalks, waste disposal facilities, and recreation areas near the plant.

Repton currently has a 14 percent unemployment rate, slightly below the state average. However, its main industry, a shoe factory, is reducing its payroll by half at the beginning of next year.

Construction on the $3 million doughnut factory is slated to begin on March 31. A tentative completion date of November 15 is set, and the factory should be in full operation by the beginning of next year.

The plant will provide 700 jobs for local people, and more than 100 families are expected to be brought in to work for the company.

The plant will make and package doughnuts for shipping to all parts of Alabama.

Company president Lonny Joe Underwood, an Alabama native who once owned a grocery store in Repton, made the following comment: "We believe that the future of America, like its past, lies in small towns like this. We want to be an integral part of this community and make it just as prosperous as it should be."

Tuition decrease

You are working in the public relations department of your university. The board of trustees is about to meet to consider tuition costs for next year. One of the proposals before the board is that tuition be lowerd by 10 percent for all students, in-state, out-of-state, graduate students, and undergraduates. The president of the university has already polled most of the board on this issue and has general agreement from the board on this action. Your first assignment is to prepare a news release on this action with an embago time of 11:45 a.m. Friday, which is when the board meeting will be finished.

You can use the following information to prepare your news release:

The president's statement: "I am extremely pleased that the board has seen fit to follow our recommendations on lowering tuition costs. During the past several years we have had to raise tuition a number of times for all of our students. Out-of-state students have been particularly hard hit. For some time we have been afraid that we have been pricing ourselves out of the market, even with in-state students. With more and more people attending junior colleges and other universities in the state, we have recognized that those who want to come to this university must have some relief.

"Unfortunately, of course, the board's actions will have some negative effects on some parts of the university. Cutting tuition means a reduction in our income, and that reduction will have to be made up in other areas. No faculty or staff member will lose his or her job because of these cuts, but we will not be able to offer as many of the programs as we have in the past. The faculty and staff members whose programs will be eliminated will be absorbed into other areas of the university. I am very pleased about that. The students attending these programs, of course, must find alternatives."

Programs to be cut: Women's Studies, Ornithology Department, Arts and Sciences Honors Program, Women's Golf Team, Men's Golf Team, Human Resources Management Institute, University Hosts and Hostesses Program, and Department of Eastern Languages; the Geology Department will be merged with the Geography Department.

Tuition costs during the last five years:
Tuition per semester

Undergrad (in-state)	$250	$275	$325	$400	$525
Undergrad (out-of-state)	$400	$400	$500	$600	$700
Graduates (in-state)	$275	$325	$375	$450	$600
Graduates (out-of-state)	$425	$500	$550	$600	$850

Each of the final figures in the table above will be reduced 10 percent for the next term.

Overall enrollment increased at the university in the last five years from 14,500 students five years ago to 16,275 this year; however, last year the total enrollment was 16,700. Applications for next semester are down, and if they continue at the current rate, a 10 percent drop in enrollment from this year's figure is anticipated.

After the news release, you are to prepare two advertisements to run in the state's major newspapers telling about the new tuition rates at the university.

Press Association

You are the public relations officer for your state's Press Association. This association counts as its members all of the state's daily and weekly newspapers, and it performs a number of services, such as a statewide advertising bureau (if an advertiser wants to advertise in all of the state's newspapers, he or she can come to the Press Association and place the ad rather than going to the individual newspapers), information about the state's newspapers, a professional training program with a local university for people who work with the state's newspapers, and a lobbying service in the state legislature on bills that affect the press.

Recently, the Press Association board of directors decided that your office should do some special promotion for National Newspaper Week. Also, the press association has recently hired some university professors to conduct a survey about newspaper leadership in your state. That survey has been completed, and the board has decided to release the results and have them serve as the basis for this promotion.

Consequently, the Press Association has called a press conference for next Monday, the first day of National Newspaper Week. The press conference is scheduled for 10 a.m. The executive director of the Press Association, Ken Billiard, and this year's president of the Press Association, Slade Luketon, editor of the Rogersville Register, will be there to announce the results of the survey and to talk about newspapers.

Here are some facts about the survey: The survey was conducted during a two-week period in the fall by a polling organization at the state university. The number of people surveyed was 500, randomly selected from all across the state. The margin of error for the results is plus or minus 4 percent. The survey showed the following things: newspaper readers are a "quality audience" (they tend to be married, more highly educated than the average person, have more annual income, own their own home, and vote regularly); newspaper readership is positively linked with income (only 43 percent of those with incomes of less than $30,000 read a newspaper regularly while 96 percent of those with incomes of more than $30,000 read newspaper regularly); and 80 percent of everyone in the state reads a newspaper regularly; on the average, two newspapers are read in each home; more than half the people in the state read a newspaper every day; newspapers were named by 70 percent of the people as the most "thorough" medium (that is, giving the most complete reports), by 65 percent as the "most trustworthy" media (as opposed to television, 25 percent, and radio, 10 percent); about 85 percent of the people in the survey said they regularly made decisions based on newspaper advertising.

Luketon's statement, to be released at the time of the press conference: "The results of this survey show that newspapers are a trusted and useful medium. We believe that a newspaper is the best buy that an advertiser or a consumer can make in today's market. Newspapers have been hiding their lights under a bushel for a long time. We haven't bothered to tell people how good we are and what we can do for them. We hope that our attention to National Newspaper Week will help us tell this story.

Billiard's statement: "These results clearly show that newspapers are here to stay. While a few have gone out of business elsewhere, the newspapers in this state have a strong following among many people. Those newspapers plan to continue to provide the excellent service to advertisers and readers that we have provided in the past."

You are to prepare a 200-word press release incorporating these statements and summarizing the results of the survey. The press release will be handed out to other media in the state.

You are also assigned to prepare two advertisements based on the survey results. At least one should be for print and will run in the state's newspapers. The other may be for print, radio, or television.

Speeches and statements

The following situations require that you draft speeches or statements. Follow the instructions below or those given to you by your instructor.

Commencement speech

You are writing in the public relations department of a local company which manufactures computers, computer parts, and computer-related equipment. The president of your company has been asked to be the commencement speaker for this year's high school graduation ceremony. The president asks you to draft a speech for him which should be about 5 to 10 minutes long. He says he wants to bring a hopeful message—one that says that despite a period of locally high unemployment, the future looks bright for today's high school graduates.

Kiwanis speech

Look at the press release on page 230. The president of American Southern has been invited to make a short speech to the Midville Kiwanis Club after this announcement has been made. He wants to tell them a little more about why his company chose Midville for the location of the plant. Here are some of the reasons:

    -- the educational system; Midville has one of the best in the state; a high percentage of students graduate from high school and go on to college (85% and 62%, respectively; the company feels that this is the kind of community that it can ask its managers and their families to live in.

    --the waterways; the manufacturing process used in the new plant will require abundant sources of water; it will also require rivers that can be navigated to major shipping areas; the Blount River in Midville is such a river.

    --a generally favorable business climate; the state has some of the lowest business taxes in the region and that's what prompted American Southern to look at the state for a location here in the first place.

    You may also use information found in the press release.

The Kiwanis Club is a service organization. The members get involved in a lot of community projects. They will want to know about American Southern's planned involvement in the community. The president wants to tell them that community involvement is important to the company; they offer to contribute money and people to worthy causes such as the United Way; they generally sponsor YMCA soccer, basketball, and baseball teams in the youth leagues. He wants to tell them that once American Southern is located there, they will see what the needs of the community are and try to help out.

    The speech should be 750 to 1,000 words long.

College day

The Chamber of Commerce in your hometown is sponsoring "College Day," and the president has asked you to come back and tell them about your experiences in college. You'll be one of three people who have been asked to speak at the meeting that day on this subject. The president tells you that he wants you to talk purely from your own experiences. Try to give the listeners a flavor of what it was like to go to the college you attend; how you felt about going to your first class; when and how you made friends; how much money it costs; what some of the things are that they could tell their high school-age children about college.

    The speech should be 500 to 750 words long.

Letters

Write letters based on the following information. Follow the directions given by your instructor.

Letter of apology

Just after Christmas, a large department store receives a letter from a woman complaining about the rudeness of the sales people in the women's ready-to-wear department. The wo-man is not specific about her complaints but says that she was in the store twice before Christmas and she was ignored completely once and spoken to rudely by a young sales girl the other. The department head, on seeing the letter, says that Christmas was a very busy season, the store always seemed to be crowded, and the department had to hire some temporary and untrained people to work during that time. She says she doubts that the woman would feel slighted by the regular employees. Draft a letter of at least 150 words for the store manager's signature responding to the woman's complaint.

Employee dinner

You are working in the public relations department of the home office of an insurance company. The company is planning an employee appreciation dinner for home office employees. This is the fifth year the company has had such a dinner. One of them will be named Outstanding Home Office Employee for the year. Another will receive the Community Service Award, which is given to the home office employee who has contributed the most to the community. A string quartet from the local university will provide the entertainment for the dinner, and Paul Harvey, the radio commentator and newspaper columnist, will give a speech. You should draft a letter to all the employees to encourage them to attend. The dinner will begin at 6:00 p.m. at the Hilton Hotel on April 5. Employees who plan to attend should inform their supervisors by April 1.

Fund-raising letter: United Way

The president of your university wants to send out a letter to all employees encouraging them to support the annual United Way fund drive. As a member of the PR department, you have been assigned to draft the letter. The letter should make the following points (but not necessarily in this order):

— contributing to the United Way fund is easy and convenient; employees can sign up for a monthly payroll deduction; the

card to do this with will accompany the letter;

— the university has always been a major contributor to the community's United Way; last year, more than $200,000 was raised from university employees also; this year's goal is $250,000;

— United Way supports more than 50 community projects; more than 95 percent of the contributions will stay within the community;

— each department within the university has been given a goal; so it is important for every individual employee to respond.

The letter should be between 150 and 200 words.

Fund-raising letter: Public radio

The manager of the local public radio station (for which you are a volunteer) has asked you to draft a letter announcing an on-air fund-raising campaign for the station. The campaign is to begin in two weeks and will run for five days. The goal is $50,000 from the listeners. The letter that you are drafting will go to people who contributed last year. These people already have supported public radio, and they know the kind of programming that public radio has: the news shows "Morning Edition" and "All Things Considered" from National Public Radio; the classical music during the weekdays and the jazz and bluegrass on the weekends; the special broadcasts of musical events in the community.

This year's fund-raising campaign is particularly important, and it's important that the station get off to a good start with early contributions from previous supporters. It's important for the following reasons:

— the station needs a new emergency generator; bad weather had knocked the station off the air a number of times;

— the station needs to purchase a new compact disk player so it can play many of the new releases, some of which are available only on compact disks;

— the cost of many of the programs that the station has to buy has gone up during the past year-some by as much as

25 to 30 percent; some of these programs may have to be dropped if the station doesn't get more money.

The letter should be between 150 and 200 words.

Pamphlets and brochures

Swimming

Below is the design for a pamphlet that the local YMCA wants to publish and distribute about the benefits of a regular swimming program. The purpose of the pamphlet is to get people to join the Y and begin swimming or doing some form of exercise. The pamphlet will be distributed to local businesses, especially those close to the Y.

The pool at the YMCA is open during the following hours: 7-9 a.m., 11 a.m.-1:30 p.m., and 4:30-7:30 p.m. on Mondays through Fridays; 3-6 p.m. on Saturdays. People who want to join the Y should come by or call, 876-0987. A year's membership costs $35.

Here are some of the benefits of swimming:

— it's aerobic exercise, meaning that it conditions the heart and lungs; this exercise can help prevent heart disease, the nation's number-one killer;

— it can help control body weight;

— it can help to build up stamina in a person;

— it can relieve tension; many doctors believe that exercise is a good antidote for depression and other emotional stress;

— swimming is a particularly good exercise because it is not hard on your joints; this is important especially for elderly people who are more likely to suffer from arthritis; swimming often offers a lot of relief for arthritis;

— swimming exercises almost all the major muscles of the body;

— regular exercise is good for the self-image; you just feel better about yourself.

YMCA officials also caution that people may need to consult their doctors or physicians before beginning an exercise program.

You need to write about 300 words of copy for this brochure.

Travel brochure

The Chamber of Commerce for the county next to the one you live in wants your public relations agency to design and write a short travel pamphlet about the sights in the county. This pamphlet will be distributed by the State Department of Tourism and will be found in hotels, travel bureaus and agencies and interstate rest stops.

Using the design below, write about 300 words that would persuade a traveler to visit that county. Here are some facts that you can use:

Probably the major scenic attraction of the county is the four covered bridges; all have been well preserved and date back to the 1800s; they are (1) the Morton Mill Bridge, the highest covered bridge above water (about 75 feet), located five miles east of Smithville on Highway 6; it's 220 feet long; built in 1877 and restored in 1976; located next to the bridge was Morton Mill, where farmers brought their corn and wheat to be ground from about the time the bridge was built until the 1930s; (2) the Ensley Bridge, the oldest one in the county, built in 1821; legend has it that there was a skirmish between companies of Confederate and Union soldiers during the Civil War; several were killed, and locals say you can hear them rustling through the grass and trees at dusk; it's located on Highway 42 west of Springtown; (3) the Swann Bridge, built in 1921, is the newest of the four bridges; it is on the Old Barterville Highway, just south of Masontown; there was also a mill located next to it, and part of that mill building has been restored and is open to tourists; (4) the Nactor Bridge was built in 1900 and is to be found in the western part of the county on Highway 69 west of Smithville; the reason it was built is unclear, although some say a mill was located next to it for a while; if that's the case, it wasn't there very long because there are no records of it. Just why covered bridges were built is not exactly clear, although the ones that were located next to mills were probably built so that farmers would have some protection from the weather while waiting to get their wheat and corn ground. Since this is a small and still mostly rural county, the covered bridges are a big part of the heritage of the people.

The county offers some other attractions. It has several lakes and recreation areas, plus Rickwill Caverns, a 280-acre state park that is open all year around. The Caverns features a restaurant that is actually located inside the cavern; you can also explore the caverns for a small admissions fee.

Finally, every October, there is the "Old Times Festival," a week-long fair that features everything from a tennis tournament to a quilt show; special tours of the covered bridges are conducted then.

APPENDIX A

Copy editing symbols

The following is a standard listing of editing symbols that you should learn as quickly as possible.

Indent paragraph	⌐The president said
Take out letter	occas**s**ionally
Take out word	the ~~red~~ hat
Close up words	week‿end
Insert word	take it⁀run (and)
Insert letter	encyclop(e)dia
Capitalize	president washington
Lowercase letter	the President's cabinet
Insert hyphen	up⤬to⤬date
Insert period	end of the sentence⊙
Insert comma	He said⸜ "I'll stop
Insert quotation marks	the "orphan quote
Abbreviate	the (United States)
Spell out	(Gov.) Sam Smith
Use figure	(one hundred fifty-seven)
Spell out figure	the ③ horses
Transpose letters	pejo⤸tive
Transpose words	many |problems|difficult|
Circle any typesetting commands	(bfc)(clc)
Connect lines	the car wreck ~~xxxxxx~~ ⌐injured two people

APPENDIX B — Grammar Exam

A Note to Instructors: This exam has been designed to test a student's ability to recognize correct grammatical formations. Students should be given about 50 minutes to complete the exam.

1. There_____many possible candidates. (a) is (b) are (c) was (d) none of the above

2. None_____ so blind as he who will not see. (a) is (b) are (c) either of the above (d) none of the above

3. Both of your excuses_____ plausible. (a) sound (b) sounds (c) either of the above (d) none of the above

4. Several of the members_____ absent. (a) was (b) were (c) either of the above (d) none of the above

5. Few of my family really_____ me. (a) understand (b) understands (c) either of the above (d) none of the above

6. Many_____ surprised at the final score. (a) was (b) were (c) either of the above (d) none of the above

7. Some of the money_____ missing. (a) is (b) are (c) either of the above (d) none of the above

8. All of the cherries_____ ripe. (a) look (b) looks (c) either of the above (d) none of the above

9. _____ any of this evidence been presented? (a) Has (b) Have (c) either of the above (d) none of the above

10. Mary Sloan, one of the brightest girls, _____to represent the school in the contest. (a) were chosen (b) was chosen (c) have been chosen (d) none of the above

11. Baker took the handoff,_____ his way within one foot of the goal line. (a) bulldozes (b) bulldozing (c) bulldozed (d) none of the above

12. I will_____ you to swim. (a) learn (b) teach (c) either of the above (d) none of the above

13. Fans cheered as the touchdown _____(a) had been made (b) was made (c) either of the above (d) none of the above

14. The team plans_____ tomorrow. (a) to celebrate (b) to have celebrated (c) either of the above (d) none of the above

15. _____ the tickets, Mr. Selby took the children to the circus. (a) buying (b) having bought (c) either of the above (d) none of the above

16. It is customary for ranchers_____ their cattle. (a) to have branded (b) to brand (c) either of the above (d) none of the above

17. The pond has begun freezing because the temperature_____ (a) has dropped (b) dropped (c) either of the above (d) none of the above

18. They_____ Mary from the invitation. (a) accepted (b) excepted (c) either of the above (d) none of the above

19. The citizens_____ many reforms. (a) affected (b) effected (c) either of the above (d) none of the above

20. A large_____ of disgruntled men barred the entrance. (a) amount (b) number (c) either of the above (d) none of the above

21. What honor is there_____ the forty thieves? (a) among (b) between (c) either of the above (d) none of the above

22. You have_____ friends than she. (a) fewer (b) less (c) either of the above (d) none of the above

23. Is an author to blame for what the public_____ from his work? (a) infers (b) implies (c) either of the above (d) none of the above

24. My house is_____ his. (a) different from (b) different than (c) either of the above (d) none of the above

25. It is handy for everyone to know how to cook for _____. (a) hisself (b) himself (c) theirselves (d) themselves

26. The old man fascinated_____ children with stories of his adventures. (a) them (b) us (c) we (d) none of the above

27. Between you and_____, the food could have been much better than it was. (a) I (b) me (c) she (d) none of the above

28. Why don't you get_____ some lunch? (a) your selves (b) yourselves (c) yourselfs (d) none of the above

29. Judy has just as much time to wash the dishes as_____.(a) I (b) me (c) them (d) none of the above

30. _____ and_____ dad have the same hobbies. (a) She, her (b) Him, his (c) Them, their (d) none of the above

31. The reforms_____ many citizens. (a) affected (b) effected (c) either of the above (d) none of the above

32. The construction of fallout shelters_____ being considered. (a) was (b) were (c) are (d) were not

33. Your contribution, in addition to other funds,_____ the success of our campaign. (a) have been assuring (b) assures (c) assure (d) were assuring

34. A combination of these methods_____ sure to succeed. (a) were (b) are (c) is (d) none of the above

35. Each of their children_____ a different instrument. (a) have (b) play (c) plays (d) either a or b

36. Val_____ me the very record I would have _____. (a) give, choosed (b) gave, choosed (c) give, chosen (d) gave, chosen

37. By the time the sun_____, we had_____ nearly a hundred miles. (a) rised, drove (b) raised, driven (c) rose, driven (d) had raised, driven

38. As I_____ there, my hat was_____ into the river. (a) sit, blowed (b) sit, blown (c) sat, blown

39. Mr. Greenfield's lost eyeglasses_____ the object of everyone's search at the church picnic. (a) were (b) was (c) is (d) be

40. He is one_____ broke it. (a) who (b) that (c) either of the above (d) none of the above

41. _____ of class standing, everyone will take the test. (a) Regardless (b) Irregardless (c) either of the above (d) none of the above

42. I must_____ find a job. (a) try and (b) try to (c) either of the above (d) none of the above

43. The theater was_____ full by seven o'clock. (a) already (b) all ready (c) either of the above (d) none of the above

44. The cast was_____ for the curtain call. (a) already (b) all ready (c) either of the above (d) none of the above

45. Everything will be_____.(a) alright (b) all right (c) either of the above (d) none of the above

46. Don't pay the bill_____ you received the goods. (a) unless (b) without (c) but (d) whether

47. Both the doctor and his nurse_____to work on foot. (a) come (b) comes (c) has come (d) has came

48. If you_____, you would have passed easily. (a) would have took my advice (b) had taken my advice (c) had taken my advise (d) would have took my advise

49. If you will_____ me your radio, I'll fix it for you. (a) bring (b) take (c) either of the above (d) none of the above

50. Why don't you_____ someone else have a turn? (a) let b) leave (c) either of the above (d) none of the above

51. Phil_____ and waited for his turn. (a) sit (b) set (c) sat (d) none of the above

52. Will they let_____ fellows use the pool? (a) us (b) we (c) either of the above (d) none of the above

53. Andy shot two more baskets than_____ .(a) he (b) him (c) her (d) either b or c

54. I_____ back in my chair and relaxed. (a) lie (b) laid (c) layed (d) lay

55. Dick_____ his books on a vacant seat. (a) layed (b) laid (c) lay (d) lie

56. I_____ down and waited for the dentist to call me in. (a) set (b) sat (c) sit (d) sitted

57. I lay awake, wondering where I had_____ the receipt. (a) lay (b) laid (c) lain (d) layed

58. The meat was still frozen, though I had_____ it on the stove to thaw. (a) set (b) sat (c) sit (d) layed

59. Glen_____ me the pictures he had taken at the game. (a) brung (b) bringed (c) bring (d) brought

60. I_____ past a house on which a tree had fallen. (a) drived (b) drive (c) driven (d) drove

61. The new teacher,_____ I met today, came from the South. (a) who (b) whom (c) whose (d) who's

62. The new teacher,_____ has taken Mr. Breen's position, came from the South. (a) who (b) whom (c) in formal usage, either would be correct (d) none of the above

63. Leroy feels quite_____ about getting a scholarship. (a) hopeful (b) hopefully c) either of the above (d) none of the above

64. The detective's solution to the crime was_____ right. (a) altogether (b) all together (c) all to gather (d) all too gather

65. Henry is the_____ of the two. (a) more strong (b) strongest (c) stronger (d) most strong

66. You cannot vote_____ you are eighteen. (a) unless (b) without (c) unless being (d) without being

67. Ann_____ three lessons. (a) taking (b) taken (c) has taken (d) has took

68. Cross the streets_____.(a) careful (b) carefully (c) most careful (d) carefuller

69. There is no use feeling sorry_____ the vase is shattered on the floor. (a) for (b) as (c) besides (d) because

70. The weather looks_____ it is about to change for the better. (a) like (b) as (d) like as

71. The girl waved goodbye,_____ her mother did not see her. (a) because (b) whether (c) but (d) since

72. It was_____ paid the bill. (a) her who (b) she who (c) her whom (d) her who

73. The two students assigned to this project are you and me. (a) Correct as is (b) you and I (c) I and you (d) me and you

74. Will you please tell me_____ I can solve this problem? (a) in as much as (b) whenever (c) with that which (d) so that

75. He walked right_____ the trap we set for him. (a) up on (b) in (c) into (d) in upon

76. She gets a larger allowance_____ she is older. (a) being that (b) because (c) being because of (d) none of the above

77. Too much food and rest_____ circus animals lazy. (a) make (b) makes (c) either of the above (d) none of the above

78. The footprints under the window_____ burglary. (a) suggests (b) suggest (c) either of the above (d) none of the above

79. Tracy Avenue is the only one of our streets that_____ from one end of the city to the other.   (a) run (b) runs (c) either of the above (d) none of the above

80. The man acts as though he_____ the owner. (a) is (b) was (c) were (d) none of the above.

81. If he_____ registered later, he would have had the right classes. (a) would have (b) had (c) either of the above (d) none of the above

82. Each one of the ladies_____ splashed by the passing car. (a) was (b) were (c) are (d) a and c above are correct

83. The natives believe that noise, smoke, and dancing_____ away the evil spirits. (a) drives (b) drive (c) drived (d) none of the above

84. Please tell me_____ you_____ during the winter. (a) at where, live (b) where, live at (c) where, live (d) where at, live

85. _____ he_____yet? (a) Have, ate (b) Has, ate (c) Have, eaten (d) Has, eaten

86. *The New York Times* still_____ a wide circulation. (a) has (b) have (c) either of the above (d) none of the above

87. Athletics_____ required of every student. (a) are (b) is (c) either of the above (d) none of the above

88. On the wall_____several posters. (a) was (b) were (c) is (d) either a or b

89. I_____ back in my chair and relaxed. (a) lie (b) laid (c) layed (d) lay

90. Dick_____ his books on a vacant seat. (a) layed (b) laid (c) lay (d) lie

91. He misspelled _____ words on this exam. (a) less (b) fewer (c) lesser (d) more fewer

92. Sue had_____ the cake on a kitchen chair. (a) sat (b) set (c) sitted (d) sit

93. The police will not_____ you park there. (a) leave (b) let (c) either of the above (d) none of the above

94. The gift from_____ and Bert came on Christmas Eve. (a) she (b) her (c) either of the above (d) none of the above

95. Norm and_____ share the same locker. (a) he (b) him (c) either of the above (d) none of the above

96. Ron doesn't live as far from the school as_____.(a) us (b) we (c) they (d) either b or c

97. The children amused_____ by asking riddles. (a) theirselves (b) themselves (c) either of the above (d) none of the above

98. I was sitting all by_____ in that last row. (a) my self (b) myself (c) either of the above (d) none of the above

99. Four of the committee members_____ married. (a) were (b) is (c) are (d) either a or c

100._____ and_____are good friends. (a) Her, me (b) He, she (c) She, I (d) either b or c

APPENDIX C — Diagnostic Exam

Note to Instructors: This test has been designed to help you determine levels of understanding about knowledge and use of the language. The final 10 questions on copyreading and editing symbols may or may not be relevant to your instruction.

1. Robert_____ from his bike.
(a) had fell (b) had fallen (c) fallen (d) falling

2. The plane with its crew_____ trying to take off now.
(a) is (b) be (c) are (d) been

3. Is the atmosphere on the moon_____ the atmosphere here on earth?
(a) different from (b) liken to (c) different than (d) as different as

4. Why is the referee so_____ the players?
(a) angry at (b) angry with (c) angry in (d) angry over

5. Why_____ allowed to join?
(a) was Ann and he (b) was Ann and him (c) were Ann and he (d) were Ann and him

6. Someone_____ turned on the automatic sprinkler.
(a) must of (b) might of (c) must to (d) must have

7. I noticed the dog as he_____ on the porch.
(a) laid (b) lay (c) lain (d) lied

8. Share the work_____ all the workers.
(a) between (b) amongst (c) betweens (d) among

9. The trunk was_____ heavy_____carry.
(a) to, to (b) too, too (c) too, to (d) to, too

10. Will you_____ come?
(a) try and (b) try to (c) be trying and (d) trying to

11. It was Ann who_____ the book on the table.
(a) layed (b) laid (c) lain (d) lay

12. The committee_____ holding an open meeting on Thursday.
(a) are (b) is (c) been (d) be

13. The new suit is_____.
(a) alright (b) al right (c) allright (d) all right

14. I am happy to_____ your offer to go to the games.
(a) accept (b) except (c) have excepted (d) having accepted

15. He spoke very_____.
(a) strange (b) stranger (c) strangest (d) strangely

16. He speaks_____.
(a) good (b) goodly (c) well (d) more better

17. She_____ finished the job in half the time.
(a) could of (b) can't of (c) could have (d) could had

18. Please_____ here.
(a) set (b) sit (c) to be set (d) to be sitted

19. He_____ a pint of milk.
(a) has drank (b) have drank (c) has drunk (d) have drunk

20. Either you or your friends_____ to blame for the accident.
(a) is (b) are (c) been (d) was

21. Neither Barbara nor Sara_____ homework on Saturdays.
(a) do (b) does (c) are doing (d) were doing

22. None of the programs_____ free from station breaks.
(a) is (b) are (c) be (d) being

23. Why are you still angry_____ me?
(a) at (b) with (c) by (d) against

24. If everyone does_____ share, we shall certainly finish on time.
(a) their (b) his or her (c) there (d) they're

25. _____, the majority of the board members promises to support him.
(a) Regardless of who is chosen (b) Regardless of whom is chosen
(c) Irregardless of who is chosen (d) Irregardless of whom is chosen

Choose the correct style in exercise 26 through 35:
26. (a) in a baptist church
    (b) in a Baptist Church
    (c) in a baptist Church
    (d) in a Baptist church

27. (a) a Mother's Day gift
    (b) a Mother's day gift
    (c) a mother's day gift
    (d) a Mother's Day Gift

28. (a) the new Fall colors
    (b) the new fall colors
    (c) the New Fall Colors
    (d) the New fall colors

29. (a) the Brother of mayor Bates
    (b) the brother of Mayor Bates
    (c) the Brother of Mayor Bates
    (d) the brother of mayor Bates

30. (a) a brazilian pianist
    (b) a Brazilian Pianist
    (c) a Brazilian pianist
    (d) a brazilian Pianist

31. (a) at Eaton High School
    (b) at Eaton high school
    (c) at Eaton high School
    (d) at eaton high school

32. (a) on the North Side of Pine Lake
    (b) on the north Side of Pine Lake
    (c) on the North side of Pine lake
    (d) on the north side of Pine Lake

33. (a) Dodd tool company
    (b) Dodd Tool company
    (c) Dodd tool Company
    (d) Dodd Tool Company

34. (a) any Sunday in July
    (b) any sunday in july
    (c) any Sunday in july
    (d) any sunday in July

35. (a) a College Football star
    (b) a college football star
    (c) a college Football star
    (d) a College Football Star

36. Mabel asked, "To which colleges has Joan_____
    (a) applied."
    (b) applied"?
    (c) applied".
    (d) applied?"

37. _____ should be free of loose dirt and paint.
    (a) Before you paint the surface, of course,
    (b) Before you paint the surface of course,
    (c) Before you paint, the surface, of course,
    (d) Before you paint, the surface, of course

38. All the _____
    (a) students, whose reports were not handed in, failed.
    (b) students, who's reports were not handed in, failed.
    (c) students who's reports were not handed in failed.
    (d) students whose reports were not handed in failed.

39. "Before starting to write your _____ Miss Wright advised.
    (a) composition plan what you are going to say,"
    (b) composition plan what you are going to say"
    (c) composition, plan what you are going to say,"
    (d) composition, plan what you are going to say",

40. Choose the correct possessive case:
    (a) everyones friend
    (b) childrens' toys
    (c) the school's reputation
    (d) Is this your's?

41. Built in 1832,_____ is now a museum of early American life.
    (a) Dunham Tavern at 6709 Euclid Avenue in Cleveland, Ohio,
    (b) Dunham Tavern, at 6709 Euclid Avenue in Cleveland, Ohio,
    (c) Dunham Tavern, at 6709 Euclid Avenue in Cleveland Ohio
    (d) Dunahm Tavern, at 6709 Euclid Avenue in Cleveland, Ohio

42. "When you come to the stop_____"make a full stop."
    (a) sign", Dad repeated,
    (b) sign: Dad repeated,
    (c) sign," Dad repeated
    (d) sign," Dad repeated,

43. Every_____ lose his license.
    (a) motorist, who is caught speeding, should
    (b) motorist who is caught speeding should
    (c) motorist who is caught speeding; should
    (d) motorist, who is caught speeding should

44. _____ stimulates the heart and raises blood pressure.
    (a) Caffeine which is present, in both tea and coffee,
    (b) Caffeine, which is present in both tea and coffee,
    (c) Caffeine, which is present in both tea, and coffee
    (d) Caffeine, which is present in both tea and coffee

45. Choose the correct possessive case:
    (a) Barton's and McLean's store
    (b) Jack and Tom's responsibility
    (c) moons rays
    (d) editor-in-chiefs' opinion

Choose the correct spelling in exercises 46 through 65.

46. (a) fullfil (b) fulfil (c) fullfill (d) fulfill

47. (a) seperate (b) sepurate (c) separate (d) saperate

48. (a) defenitley (b) defientely (c) definitely (d) definitly

49. (a) calander (b) calandar (c) calendar (d) calender

50. (a) acomodat (b) accomadate (c) accommodate (d) accomodate

51. (a) amatur (b) ameteur (c) amateur (d) amater

52. (a) defisite (b) deficit (c) deficite (d) defecite

53. (a) auxelary (b) auxilary (c) auxiliary (d) auxilairy

54. (a) conceintous (b) consientius (c) conscientious (d) consentious

55. (a) presedent (b) presedant (c) precedent (d) precedant

56. (a) superentendent (b) superintindent (c) superintendint (d) superintendent

57. (a) recieve (b) riceive (c) ricieve (d) receive

58. (a) adaptability (b) adaptabilaty (c) adaptibility (d) adaptibilaty

59. (a) alegance (b) allegance (c) alegiance (d) allegiance

60. (a) privilege (b) priviledge (c) previledge (d) preveledge

61. (a) concede (b) conceed (c) consede (d) conceede

62. (a) elegible (b) eligible (c) elegeble (d) eligeble

63. (a) camoflauge (b) camouglauge (c) camouflage (d) camalage

64. (a) athleet (b) athlete (c) athelete (d) athilete

65. (a) genarosity (b) generosity (c) genatousity (d) generousity

66. Copyreading symbol for new paragraph: (a) The (b) The (c) The (d) The

67. Copyreading symbol for deletion: (a) paineted (b) paineted (c) paineted (d) paineted

68. Copyreading symbol for spell out a number: (a) 6 (b) 6 (c) 6 (d) 6

69. Copyreading symbol for use numerals: (a) forty (b) forty (c) forty (d) forty

70. Copyreading symbol for eliminate space:

(a) ques tion (b) ques tion (c) ques tion (d) ques tion

71. Copyreading symbol for insert comma:

(a) however (b) however (c) however (d) however

72. Copyreading symbol for retain copy:

(a) never (b) never (c) never (d) never

73. Copyreading symbol for center copy:

(a) John Doe (b) John Doe (c) John Doe (d) John Doe

74. Proper mark to indicate that the story does not end on this page:

(a) More, (b) add, (c) continued, (d) ——

75. Proper mark to indicate the end of the story:

(a) end, (b) —— (c) —30— (d) —-

APPENDIX D

Advertising Copy Sheets

Copy platform sheets
Copy sheets
Radio script sheets
Television script sheets
Television storyboard sheets

COPY PLATFORM

Ad subject:

Ad problem:

Product characteristics:

Advertising objective:

Target Market:

Competition:

Statement of benefit and appeal:

Creative theme:

Supportive selling points:

COPY SHEET

Product:
Medium:
Client:
Writer:

_____

Headline:

Subhead:

Body copy:

Subhead or slogan:

Signature:

COPY SHEET

Product:
Medium:
Client:
Writer:

Headline:

Subhead:

Body copy:

Subhead or slogan:

Signature:

COPY SHEET

Product:
Medium:
Client:
Writer:

Headline:

Subhead:

Body copy:

Subhead or slogan:

Signature:

RADIO SCRIPT SHEET

Product:
Client:
Title:
Writer:
Length:

Source	Audio

RADIO SCRIPT SHEET

Product:
Client:
Title:
Writer:
Length:

Source   **Audio**

RADIO SCRIPT SHEET

Product:
Client:
Title:
Writer:
Length:

Source   **Audio**

TELEVISION SCRIPT SHEET

Product:
Client:
Title:
Writer:
Length:

Video   **Audio**

TELEVISION SCRIPT SHEET

Product:
Client:
Title:
Writer:
Length:

Video   **Audio**

TELEVISION SCRIPT SHEET

Product:
Client:
Title:
Writer:
Length:

Video   **Audio**

TELEVISION STORYBOARD

Product:
Client:
Title:
Writer:
Length:

Video   **Audio**

Frame time

Frame time

Frame time

Frame time

Frame time

Frame time

Frame time

TELEVISION STORYBOARD

Product:
Client:
Title:
Writer:
Length:

Video   **Audio**

Frame time

Frame time

Frame time

Frame time

Frame time

Frame time

Frame time

TELEVISION STORYBOARD

Product:
Client:
Title:
Writer:
Length:

Video   **Audio**

Frame time

Frame time

Frame time

Frame time

Frame time

Frame time

Frame time

Index